D1491161

# The I-55 Series:
# CUBS VS. CARDINALS

**George Castle**
**Jim Rygelski**

SportsPublishing Inc.
www.SportsPublishingInc.com

Director of Production, book design, layout: Susan M. McKinney
Cover design: Terry N. Hayden
Insert design: Scot Muncaster


ISBN:1-58261-032-0
Library of Congress Number: 99-62979


Printed in the United States.


SPORTS PUBLISHING INC.
804 N. NEIL
CHAMPAIGN, IL 61820
www.SportsPublishingInc.com

*To my wife, Nina Castle, with love for shouldering a tremendous personal burden so I could help finish this book, and to my late mother, Vera Castle, for always believing in me through the upheavals of growing up.*

*— George Castle*

*To the real Cardinals and Cubs fans, and to their continued rivalry. May it always remain fun for both.*

*— Jim Rygelski*

# ACKNOWLEDGEMENTS

The authors pestered a lot of folks to help complete this book.

Leading off is sports director Luis Hernandez of WJNO-Radio in West Palm Beach, Florida, for assisting in interviews of Cardinals personalities in spring training. Next up is Jay Rand of the Cubs' publications department for digging out his master file of newspapers and magazines to glean historical information. The Cubs and Cardinals media relations departments also deserve credit for putting up with us, particularly the Cardinals' Steve Zesch.

Also coming out of the bullpen to help with some hard-to-find historical facts was Don Zminda, the publications maven of STATS, Inc. and one of the sharper analysts of baseball trends anywhere.

Cubs manager Jim Riggleman, with his Chicago-St. Louis resume, was gracious with his time in writing the foreword. So was a host of present and past Cubs and Cardinals players and executives to share views of the rivalry. We'll never forget Bob Tiemann, the pre-eminent baseball historian in St. Louis, whose familiarity with the box score of every major league game ever played was invaluable. And there's the helpful staffs at the University of Missouri-St. Louis library, the Harold Washington downtown library in Chicago, and the Skokie (Illinois) Public Library.

Much welcomed was the prose of the many sports writers for newspapers in both St. Louis and Chicago over the last century. Their work, produced under deadline pressure and preserved on microfilm, brought back to life many great Cardinals-Cubs games.

As usual, the folks at The Dreaming Dog Group in Indianapolis should get kudos for their work.

Finally, there's Laura Elizabeth Castle, high school freshman, who was always available to conduct classes in Computers 101 when the old man showed his technological obsolescence.

# CONTENTS

Foreword ........................................................ vi

1 The Rivalry:
Views From Players, Execs and Fans ........................ 1

2 The Best and Worst of Both Worlds:
Dual Identity Players ........................ 21

3 Harry Caray: Pied Piper of Two Cities ..................... 31

4 Roots of the Cubs-Cardinals Rivalry ..................... 39

5 Great Cubs Games vs. the Cardinals ..................... 47

6 Great Cardinals Games vs. the Cubs ..................... 63

7 Great Cubs Player Performances vs. the Cardinals ........ 89

8 Great Cardinals Player Performances vs. the Cubs ........ 107

9 A Dual Great Player Performance ..................... 135

10 Jenkins vs. Gibson ..................................... 139

11 McGwire vs. Sosa:
A Year-After Viewpoint ........................ 151

12 Brock for Broglio ..................................... 157

13 The Trading Market ..................................... 177

14 Mr. Holland's Opus, 1956-1975 ..................... 189

15 The Kennedy Administration 1976-1981 ..................... 203

16 Foibles, Fumbles and Fracases ..................... 209

17 The Mason-Dixon Line of Illinois ..................... 233

Appendices ..................................... 244

# FOREWORD

I can bring an insider's perspective to the Cubs-Cardinals rivalry; so much of my professional life has been tied up with both franchises. You know me best now as the Cubs' manager since 1995, but I also worked for the Cardinals from 1976 to 1990 as a minor league player, minor league coach, minor league manager, director of player development, and first-base coach for the big-league club under Whitey Herzog. So I believe I have seen both ballclubs from almost all angles possible.

The Cubs and Cardinals are much more alike than not. During my tenure in each city, the two teams had corporate ownership that was first-class and respected, Anheuser Busch for St. Louis and the Tribune Co. for Chicago. Each parent company had brilliant people in high management positions, and both companies had developed strong, distinctive identities away from baseball ownership. That helps with perception. You'll have the advertising with Budweiser, the Clydesdales, WGN. It's all first-class.

There's also great similarity in the fan bases of both teams. Both are extremely loyal. Some of that comes from the fact Chicago and St. Louis used to be the furthest west of all the major league teams. The loyalties used to be passed from generation to generation. If you were in Missouri, Arkansas, Tennessee—all through that area—you were a Cardinals fan. Further north, you were a Cubs fan. Those regional loyalties stayed firm even as more teams were added to the majors. Cubs and Cardinals fans were like the Hatfields and the McCoys for decades on end.

The loyalties were helped by a great tradition of broadcasting with each club. The Cardinals had that huge radio network all over the area with Harry Caray and Jack Buck. The Cubs televised the most games of any team, with Jack Brickhouse, succeeded by Caray, the mainstays at the microphone over a 50-year span. These were all Hall of Fame announcers bringing the news about each team to the listeners and viewers.

Even the uniforms are traditional. The designs of the Cubs' and the Cardinals' uniforms have stayed the same for many decades. St. Louis' bat with the two cardinals perching on each end on the shirt is one of the longest-appearing logos anywhere. The Cubs have had the blue pinstripes with the red Cubs "C" since 1957.

But then there are differences between the two clubs. The Cardinals had a long tradition of player development dating to when Branch Rickey set up the first true farm system in the 1930s. St. Louis almost always has been able to produce many of its players through the decades. The Cubs didn't put as much emphasis in the farm system through much of that same time. However, in recent years, a lot of positive steps have been taken for Chicago to become a more consistently productive player-development operation. In spite of the Cardinals' advantage in developing players, the Cubs haven't done too badly in head-to-head matchups with a 1,003-959 all-time record against St. Louis going into the 1999 season.

The nature of the two teams' ballparks also provides a stark contrast. Different Cubs management regimes over the years may have looked toward the quick fix, importing various power hitters at the expense of developing young players, because of cozy Wrigley Field. The power alley may be labeled "368 feet" in left-center field, but the dimensions are probably shorter. Meanwhile, the Cardinals knew they had to emphasize speed with the spacious dimensions of Busch Stadium power alleys about 20 feet deeper than Wrigley Field—prior to the re-doing of the field and seats in the last few years, making it more conducive to power hitters.

Both the similarities and differences are on display when the two teams play each other. Personally, as a manager, I don't get up any more for a game against the Cardinals compared to other opponents. But the fans get more energized, and that energy seems to filter into our clubhouse and dugout—and it's probably the same with the Cardinals. Ten minutes prior to the game, you look around the stands, and you see 10,000 or 15,000 more people than usual. You'll see a lot of red in the stands in Chicago; in St. Louis, it's full of Cubs blue. Then you see it's big, and you start feeling that excitement. It doesn't change how you manage the game, but it does send a message to you about how much this means to all these people. You feel, Let's go, let's get after it.

I think an ideal Cubs-Cardinals situation would be one winning the National League Central and the other club winning the wild card. Both teams in the playoffs at the same time, possibly playing each other to get to the World Series, would really excite the fans of each club and the world of baseball in general. The presence of the wild card makes that a realistic possibility. No longer do both teams have only a first-place finish as an entrée to the post-season. So that provides additional hope to players and fans.

But even short of such a dream matchup, the tradition and drama involving the Cubs-Cardinals rivalry will keep your interest. This captures the flavor of the rivalry. It will be a good read for the fan; it is an even better show in person at either Wrigley Field or Busch Stadium.

— Jim Riggleman, April 1999

# THE RIVALRY:
# A PERSONAL VIEW FROM CHICAGO

My subterfuge was complete. I had observed my mother's note-writing for several years, and I could do a decent imitation. The note excusing my absence from Mather High School on Chicago's North Side on Tuesday, April 6, 1971, had to look authentic. I certainly didn't want school disciplinarians Abe Fink and Carl Myrent to believe anything was askew.

But maybe in this rebellious era, Fink and Myrent didn't have too many sophomores cutting classes to go to the Cubs' season opener at Wrigley Field. What was passion for the Cubs in 1967-69 by many of the then teen-age Boomers had probably evolved into devotion for the Rolling Stones, The Who and Led Zeppelin, and sneaking marijuana on some remote part of the school grounds. Perhaps I was some kind of geeky throwback at 15, carrying the torch for something as old-fashioned as baseball.

Around 9 a.m., I climbed aboard a Devon No. 155 bus at Western Avenue, rode to the Loyola L station two miles east, and hopped aboard a southbound "B" Howard train. Half an hour later, I was at the northeast ticket window of Wrigley Field. The bleachers looked too crowded already; they had been a trendy choice—to a fault, anyway—over the past four seasons. So I opted for a $1.75 grandstand seat in right field. The crowd already had filled much of the unreserved area, so I had to take a seat near the back row.

Bad mistake. The wind chills of an early Chicago spring had made the shaded area of the grandstand ice cold. The temperature would not break 40 degrees during the afternoon. Foolish me, I forgot to bring gloves, tricked by the sun in which that the luckier bleacher fans basked.

The visiting Cardinals took the field for batting practice. I worked my way down to the front row for a closer look. Matty Alou, a St. Louis newcomer after tormenting the Cubs and this day's starter, Fergie Jenkins, for so many years in Pittsburgh, began limbering up. A leather-lunged fan tried to get Alou's attention. "Hey, Mateo, how's your brother JEEE-SSSUS!," cried the wise-ass bloke. Soon I returned to my seat.

Again, bad idea. Sitting still in the chill numbed my hands. I tried to fill out my scorecard with the lineups, but I got only as far as a scraggly "Brock, LF" on the St. Louis side before I had to stuff my hands in my pockets to keep them warm, waiting for the game to begin at 1:30 p.m.

But at least Jenkins and mound opponent Bob Gibson cooperated. They kept the pace as brisk as the winds. The Cubs scored one, the Cardinals scored one, and the two great aces could have pitched forever in their seemingly effortless rhythm.

Both the Cubs and the Cardinals had their familiar faces besides Jenkins and Gibson—Billy Williams, Ron Santo, Don Kessinger and Glenn Beckert for the Cubs; Lou Brock, Joe Torre and Ted Simmons for the Cardinals. I was particularly interested in how a Cubs rookie handled himself in center field. Jose Ortiz, acquired from the White Sox recently, led off the latest three platoons of center fielders Cubs manager Leo Durocher employed in that era. Some 15 different faces played center for the Cubs in 1969 and 1970. Ortiz would eventually give way to Brock Davis, who would give way to Cleo James, who would ...

By 3:30 p.m., 9 1/2 innings had been played. Jenkins and Gibson showed no signs of weakening. Then Billy Williams came to bat in the bottom of the 10th. He took one of his sweet swings. The ball was lofted toward the right-field bleachers. I never saw it land, but from the scramble in the bleachers and the screaming of the overflow crowd it was a game-winner. Cubs 2, Cardinals 1, typical of the games of this era.

Such a grandstand, bleachers or TV vantage point is how I viewed the Cubs-Cardinals rivalry in those days. For me, though, the blood-boiling point was provided not by the Cardinals, but by the Mets and White Sox.

The New Yorkers' 1969 miracle run was self-explanatory. How could the Mets leap from 73 to 100 wins in one year, not taking intermediate steps of development like the Durocher-era Cubs teams? And why did New York deserve yet another championship? Weren't they already drunk on titles with the Yankees, a team that could barely draw 1.5 million fans for a winning team amid a metro area of 14 million or so? Why couldn't the timing had been oh-so-slightly different so the Cubs could have sneaked in just one precious World Series appearance?

You could foam at the mouth at the thought of Mets' somewhat fluky successes and the televised sight of another squeaky-clean Tom and

Nancy Seaver commercial endorsement. But the real pressure-raisers were the verbal duels with fans of a team the Cubs never played except in exhibition games.

Far more than the Cardinals, the White Sox and their backers put a burr under the average Cubs fan. Even when the Sox lost a team record 106 games in 1970, their fans didn't crawl under rocks to hide. I had many a sparring match with Sox stalwarts Steve Ruby and Ron Eisenstein on the long morning walks to Mather. The Sox supporters practically became insufferable when their heroes leaped into the pennant race against the Oakland Athletics in 1972. Meanwhile, the Cubs lagged as second-place also-rans, just out of contention against the powerful Pirates, a team of free swingers that enjoyed a merry time against Chicago pitching in this era.

I could never figure out exactly why Sox fans hated the Cubs so much. After all, the Cubs, playing in the other league, never deprived some of their fine Paul Richards- and Al Lopez-managed teams of pennants in the manner of the Yankees. The only logical explanation was jealousy at all the publicity the Cubs received. Bill Veeck later picked up the media-coverage imbalance issue. Little did anyone realize at the time that the Cubs' schedule of all-day baseball at home gave them an advantage enjoyed by no other franchise in a two-team market. Of course newspapers and broadcast outlets were going to give more space and airtime to the Cubs; they played a lot better to their deadlines than the prime-time Sox did.

At one point, I even believed Sox fans rooted for the Cardinals because they were the Cubs' chief rival. If that was the case a generation ago, it has to change now with interleague play and Cardinals-Sox matchups.

Even after you got past your feelings toward the Mets and Sox, you still had the Cardinals. They were always nibbling and nicking the Cubs, who often found their long fly balls falling short of the fences in then-spacious Busch Stadium. Lou Brock, Garry Templeton, Bake McBride, Tony Scott and other speedsters would chop high bounders off the Astroturf or slash triples into the faraway gaps. The intermediate game was handled by the pesky duo of Mike Tyson and Ted Sizemore, who dribbled 20-bouncers through the infield. Always, always, to the backdrop of the Busch Stadium siren and Budweiser theme.

The Cardinals would hurt the Cubs; the Cubs would hurt the Cardinals. One overriding aspect was Brock's determination against his old team, whether at the plate or on the basepaths. Surprisingly, a man with a mediocre outfielding reputation applied the heartbreaker more than once against Chicago. I recall one bases-loaded rally in 1973 when a Cub crushed the ball toward the left-field wall. Up leaped Brock, Jordan-esque. Down he came with the rally, thwarting the Cubs once again.

There were comical moments, too. One late September day in 1972 at Busch Stadium, Cubs pitcher Joe Decker laid down a bunt with a man on second base. But the Cardinals' pitcher heaved the ball into left field trying for the force at third base. The ball rolled down the line, where Brock bobbled it in the corner. By the time the ball was relayed back to the infield, Decker had circled the bases.

On another night in 1975 in St. Louis, a Cardinals hitter rocketed the ball back to Cubs reliever Darold Knowles. The ball hit Knowles in his supporter cup so loudly the noise was heard up in the pressbox. Knowles fell to the ground, then somehow recovered—via instinct or competitive spirit or whatever—to throw the man out at first base before crumpling to the ground again. "He's a real pro; he didn't think of himself and got his man at first," Jack Brickhouse intoned on WGN-TV.

That broadcast booth in Busch Stadium was the site of several other interesting sidelights. Brickhouse tried to do a "Tenth Inning" post-game interview with Billy Williams in 1970 while a fleet of moths buzzed around the light reflecting off Brick's balding pate. Five years later, Brick and partner Jim West handled the introduction to the game on a blazing hot day. West was sweating a river, turning redder and redder live on the air, confined in his tie and WGN blazer as Brick happily went on and on about the upcoming game.

But the Cubs-Cardinals series never was personalized until I met Jim Rygelski.

Attending Northern Illinois University in DeKalb in 1976, I hooked on as a sportswriter on the *Northern Star*, the campus daily. I made the acquaintance of Rygelski, who had moved to Chicago a few years previously from his native St. Louis. Again, it was great to find a fellow baseball fan and someone who transcended the prevailing cliques on the *Star*, which appeared to be an extension of high school social life for many of its staffers.

Rygelski and I found the commonality of baseball as a reference point. We'd repair to the Twin Taps tavern on the south side of town to discuss the world. When we weren't analyzing his relationship with one particularly fiery redhead or the lack of a significant other for myself, we'd talk Cubs and Cardinals. Poor Jim, who I soon nicknamed "Harry," after Cardinals pitchers Harry Rasmussen and Harry Parker and, of course,

Harry Caray. All the guff he had to take about his St. Louis origins. Fellow Chicagoans gave him jibes not only about the Cardinals, but also the Mark Twain and Daniel Boone expressways, funny-sounding names of interstate highways in St. Louis that Jim, or Harry, protested that the natives didn't use.

In the summer of 1977, I finally found out first-hand about Rygelski's baseball experience. As a reporter intern on the Decatur Herald, I had the chance to drive down for a number of Cardinals games at Busch Stadium. The first contest featured John "The Count" Montefusco, then of the Giants, homering to beat the Cardinals. Next up were several Cubs-Cardinals games in which the visitors got thrashed. Then, during July 4 weekend, I met Jim's parents, John and Jessie, a wonderful couple as gracious as possible to the visitor from big, smug Chicago. I also learned about his fan background, going to games at the old Busch Stadium, and life in their former north St. Louis neighborhood as Cardinals fans were just like Cubs fans, wronged almost as much as exulting in success. One 1960 Rygelski scorecard featured Willie Mays doing a number on his beloved Redbirds. The kid had scrawled, "I hate Willie Mays!" across the lineup.

Jim and I saw some really strange baseball that holiday weekend, including five Cubs errors in the first inning of one game and Bill Buckner slugging a game-winning, three-run homer off Al "The Mad Hungarian" Hrabosky in the ninth inning of the next contest. In the miscue-strewn first game, amid an overflow, partying crowd, Cubs and Cardinals fans really got into it verbally in the left-field bleachers and brawls were narrowly averted.

Rygelski got a job on the *Galesburg Register-Mail* and returned the favor the next year in 1978, coming up one morning on the train to attend a Cubs-Cardinals game at Wrigley Field, then going back that night the same way. In 1979, I made my first Chicago-St. Louis trip via car with a whole bunch of right-field bleacher chums. In those days of the 55 mph limit, there was no more boring, endless drive than I-55 through the cornfields of central Illinois. Six hours on the road seemed like 12.

In the five-game Friday-through-Monday Cubs-Cardinals series that climaxed with Lou Brock's 3,000th hit off Dennis Lamp in the finale, I experienced one of the freakiest mid-August spells of weather in St. Louis history. I wore a light jacket to the Saturday night game in Busch Stadium in the 60-degree weather. When was the last time that happened? The next afternoon, in box seats down the left-field line, I witnessed how hot the Astroturf-covered ballpark could become. Although the air temperature was a relatively comfortable 85 degrees with low humidity for St. Louis, the sun beating down on the below-ground field and heating up the turf made it feel 10 degrees warmer. I can't imagine how fans handle watching games from those seats when it's in the high 90s with heavy humidity.

By 1982, I had married. My wife, Nina, and I accepted another invitation to visit Jim, or Harry, over another Fourth of July weekend. This time, living in the north St. Louis neighborhood of Baden, he volunteered to play tour guide when we weren't attending games. Rygelski also offered the use of his apartment for our lodging, gratis, while he stayed with his parents. There was one caveat: He lived Spartan, without air conditioning.

We watched the Cubs and starting pitcher Tom Filer (fodder for trivia buffs) dodge numerous bullets to win 2-1 on a Saturday night, then enjoyed a nice Italian meal in south St. Louis. But then we perspired continually and couldn't sleep as storms battered the area during the night. I tried to cool off by sitting in Jim's bathtub. Guess this was a sample of normal life in St. Louis 40-some years previously. How did they survive the summers? The next day, the three of us attended a 1 p.m. game in Busch Stadium's right-field bleachers. I can never remember experiencing more stifling humidity, not even when Chicago was hit by a deadly 105-degree heat wave in 1995. The St. Louis-area mercury climbed into the mid-90s and an exhausted Nina actually fell asleep on a bleacher bench. She didn't miss anything; the Cubs got pounded.

Rygelski made it up to Chicago for games other than the Cardinals' visits. He was indicative of many Cardinals fans; he truly enjoyed watching baseball at Wrigley Field. And through the more than two decades I have known Jim, or Harry, I discovered that Cubs and Cardinals fans were more alike than not. St. Louis fans have just been a little luckier, their farm system having been more productive, their trades having been more astute and their pitchers having not gotten hurt as often as their Chicago counterparts. But both sets of rooters had undying loyalty for their respective teams that was hardly matched elsewhere in baseball.

Cubs' fans loyalty and belief in a universal fairness was tested even further when strikeout wunderkind Kerry Wood's precious ulnar collateral ligament snapped in spring training 1999, costing his services for at least the following season. Cardinals fans never suffered through 40 years of promising pitchers being injured, of which Wood was the worst case.

Start with the quartet of Dick Drott, Moe Drabowsky, Glen Hobbie and Bob Anderson, ready for delivery just when Lou Brock, Billy Williams, Ron Santo and Kenny Hubbs came up through the farm system, yet all breaking down before a contender could be crafted. Move ahead to Ernie Broglio, traded for Lou Brock, and breaking down with the same injury as Wood, making the deal the worst in Cubs history. How about the entire starting rotation of Rick Sutcliffe, Steve Trout, Dennis Eckersley and Scott Sanderson, re-signed at great expense, going on the disabled list together in 1985, costing the Cubs a repeat first-place finish? And don't forget Mike Harkey, rated almost as highly as Wood in the late 1980s, eventually going lame after shoulder miseries.

It's enough to believe a black cloud follows the Cubs around, decade after decade, relentlessly never letting up, keeping the Chicagoans wandering in the baseball wilderness far longer than Moses' flock. Not even Sam Sianis' hex-busting billy goat, trotted out onto Wrigley Field every few years, seems to have much of an effect.

But, perhaps there's a lesson. Maybe you don't have to win a pennant to derive enjoyment at a baseball game. That's what happens when there's a special relationship between fans and franchise. Baseball, like life, isn't fair; that's why pennants often are won in cities whose residents hardly appreciate them. Pennants aren't plentiful in St. Louis, and much less so in Chicago. But it hardly matters in the end, because both cities have something that is duplicated in very few other big-league outposts: real fans, real tradition and a real rivalry that has stood the test of time.

—George Castle, April 1999

# THE RIVALRY:
# A PERSONAL VIEW FROM ST. LOUIS

I've seen the Cardinals-Cubs rivalry from both sides and prefer to bleed Cardinal red. But because of some pleasant experiences in Wrigley Field a quarter century ago, I'll always have a soft spot for the Cubs — except when they play the Cardinals.

Growing up in north St. Louis in the late 1950s, a short bus ride or a long walk from the Busch Stadium once known as Sportsman's Park, I didn't consider the Cubs a rival for my Cardinals.

The Cardinals were usually contenders and the Cubs weren't. The Cardinals' rivals in those days were the teams St. Louis had to beat for the pennant, which never included Chicago.

Still, the Cubs were an irritant, especially in Wrigley Field.

I recall dashing up the stairs to our family flat on May 15, 1960, to turn on the radio and hear what the Cardinals had done in the second game of a Sunday doubleheader in Chicago. (I'd been out with my parents, and since we took the bus to and from a visit to a relative, I hadn't been able to listen to the second game.) Harry Caray was shouting that it was a no-hitter, and, as the Cardinals had won the opener, I presumed whoever had pitched for them had turned in the gem.

What a shock to find out that the Cardinals had been held hitless by Don Cardwell.

I don't even recall wanting to go to a Cardinals game against the Cubs in the late '50s and early '60s. They had Ernie Banks, but who else?

The only Cards-Cubs game at Busch I can remember attending in my early days was in 1962, when some young Cub outfielder named Lou Brock hit a home run off Ernie Broglio onto the pavilion roof near our seats in the right-field upper deck. It didn't matter as the Cardinals came back to win that one.

That's not to say I wouldn't watch a televised game from Wrigley. Since televised games were rare in St. Louis, and never shown from Busch except for Stan Musial's farewell in 1963, it was a treat to see one from Wrigley. There was something fascinating about that brick wall behind the plate, so different from any other park. The TV cameras always focused on it during the announcers' pregame comments.

We St. Louisans looked upon the Cubs in those days like poor cousins who we could kind of pull for (except when they played the Cardinals) mainly because we felt so sorry for them.

From my reading of baseball history I learned that once upon a time the Cardinals and Cubs had been rivals, and that my youth was the end of a 20-year dormant period.

So when the Cardinals and Cubs had a real pennant race during the summer of 1967, I welcomed it as did many others from both cities. I was at Busch Stadium the night in late July when Ray Culp beat the Cardinals and allowed the Cubs to tie them for first place. It was one of the longest rides home ever.

But, two nights later I was back, keeping score, rejoicing as the Cardinals whipped the Cubs and moved two games ahead of them, never to be topped again that year.

After the 1968 season, I went into the Army and, with an assignment in Europe for two of my three years, didn't see much Cardinals baseball for the next three seasons. But through the Stars and Stripes newspaper and a gift subscription to *The Sporting News* from a boyhood friend, I kept abreast of baseball.

I rejoiced, as did most everyone in the nation except the North Side of Chicago, when the 1969 Mets won the pennant and World Series.

And I laughed aloud at breakfast one June morning of 1970 in Vicenza, Italy, where I was stationed, when I read that the Cardinals had extended the Cubs' losing streak to 11 games. (They'd make it 12.) If the Cardinals couldn't contend that year at least they could prevent the Cubs from doing so.

The 1973 season was an apex of sorts. A Cardinals team that lost 20 of its first 25 suddenly played like world-beaters for the next three months. They got by the slumping Cubs and into first place at the All-Star break, then picked right up from they left by beating the Cubs the first two games after the break.

But both the Cardinals and Cubs collapsed the second half and in 1974 I made a break with the past. Transferred to Chicago through my job, I immediately took to the city and thought I might make my permanent home there. I figured it would be easier to root for a baseball team I could see on a regular basis.

It seemed logical to root for the White Sox because Harry Caray was then the team's announcer and Dick Allen, a former Cardinal I hadn't been able to see because of my overseas assignment in 1970, was also there.

But the American League then believed in controlled excitement, and since I was living on the North Side (Edgewater Beach neighborhood) and a National League fan I thought it only right to root for the Cubs. I was already familiar with Vince Lloyd and Lou Boudreau since in my teens I'd often picked up WGN broadcasts on a shortwave radio.

So in 1974 I changed allegiance and rooted for the Cubs, even when they played the Cardinals. That 1974 Chicago bunch was the most miserable team I've ever pulled for, much worse than any Cardinals team I'd seen. But I still rooted for them every game and believed in them like I once had in the Cardinals.

I even immersed myself in Cubs history, poring over accounts of seasons past. One thing I could never figure, though, was why the most popular Cubs team among the people I spoke with was the 1969 one, which in the space of six days in September had blown a 5 1/2-game first-place lead and eventually finished eight games behind the Mets.

Another disturbing curiosity was the *Chicago* magazine article in the spring of 1975 that listed 13 reasons why the Cubs wouldn't win the pennant. I'd never seen anything like that in St. Louis.

The 1975 Cubs got off to a 20-10 start. But then they folded. By then I had already made plans to go back to college to finish a journalism degree. I was also breaking up with my fiance, a wonderful Chicago girl who'd gone with me to a few games even though she was a lukewarm fan. So, one day, with the three most important things in my world—baseball team, love life and job (and in that order of importance)—in flux, I went to the newsstand at State and Lake streets that sold out-of-town newspapers. I bought a *St. Louis Post-Dispatch*, saw a color photo of the Cardinals' Lynn McGlothen beating the Braves, and stood there trembling. I wanted to drop to my knees and beg every Cardinals fan—both living and dead—to forgive me and take me back. Then I went out and bought a red Cardinals cap.

I've never strayed since. But I'm glad I had that 1 1/3 seasons in Cubbie blue. It was like being a foreign exchange student. Boy, what I learned.

As a Cardinal fan I hate to see them lose to any team, but especially the Cubs. Just as important as Mark McGwire's edging Sammy Sosa in the Great Home Run Race of 1998 was the Cardinals taking the season series 7-4 from the Cubs that year. Yet when the regular season was over, and as much as I dislike the wild card concept, I rooted for the Cubs against both the Giants and Braves.

If the Cubs were fighting for a title and playing a Cardinals team that had already been eliminated, I'd still pull for my Redbirds. But if the Cubs won it fair and square, I think from a distance I could appreciate the joy they're due.

I still think from time to time about the Cubs fans I regularly saw in the right-field bleachers in 1974. (One of them was my co-writer on this book, though we weren't to meet until two years later while in journalism school at Northern Illinois University.) The fans who regularly went to Wrigley Field in that kind of season are the real Cubs fans and the ones who deserve to see a pennant.

That's, of course, after the real Cardinals fans, who went to games at Busch in seasons such as 1986, 1988 and 1990, and long before Mark McGwire arrived, to see their team in the World Series.

My friendship with George Castle has produced its share of arguments about who's really America's team. He once stated that the 1984 Cubs had achieved that distinction, while I countered that long before WGN became a TV superstation the Cardinals had achieved that distinction through KMOX radio—and had kept it over the years.

It's sometimes surprising that the Cardinals-Cubs rivalry has retained its intensity for more than 30 years. Pennant races involving both teams have been rare. Yet every year their games draw well.

I'm not going to try to understand why. I'm just glad it's there, and hope that every year rekindles it. It really has been a healthy rivalry, something that for the most part has brought much more of the best than the worst in both players and fans.

As I write this my hope is that the three-game series between the Cardinals and Cubs that concludes the 1999 season decides which of the two teams claims the Central Division title while the other one goes home for the winter.

That would baseball like it oughta be.

—Jim Rygelski, April, 1999

# 1

# The Rivalry: Views From Players, Execs and Fans

**NOBODY who has ever been involved** in the Cubs-Cardinals rivalry—as a player, manager, front-office executive, broadcaster or fan—is neutral about it.

The games each team has played against each other have left a lasting impact on both participants and witnesses. Even latecomers to the Chicago-St. Louis games get quickly caught up in the emotion and fun of one of sports' top geographic rivalries.

"From what I understand before I moved over here from Oakland, they've had the best rivalries in the game," home-run king Mark McGwire said. "Every time we go into Wrigley (Field), every time people come into Busch (Stadium), when we play each other, it's great games. People really get up for it. I don't know if it had anything to do with myself and Sammy (Sosa)."

The rivalry was so entrenched that it didn't require any enhancement from the McGwire-Sosa race to the home-run record.

"I don't believe so," McGwire said. "The history goes too far back. It's a Cubs-Cardinals game, and it's the biggest thing in the Midwest."

Such a newsworthy event generates more memories than can be shared here. Following is a compilation of the some of the best remembrances of the Cubs-Cardinals rivalry.

# Ernie Banks, Cubs Hall of Famer

"Mr. Cub" knows the subject matter of the conversation ahead of the time. He's not in the shower, but he sings anyway, to an audience of one.

"Meet me in St. Louie, Louie, meet me at the fair..."

Somehow, St. Louis became Ernie Banks' second favorite city...

"Most of my friends married St. Louis women," he said.

Let's steer the subject back to baseball. Why were the Cardinals so hospitable to Banks? He slugged his first two career homers against St. Louis, No. 1 being off Gerry Staley in 1953. He belted his fifth grand-slam homer of the 1955 season against Lindy McDaniel at old Busch Stadium. Homer No. 400 came against the Cardinals in 1965. His final career two-homer game came against Steve Carlton in new Busch Stadium in 1970—and Banks left the Cubs lineup as a regular, for good, the following night due to knee problems.

The greatest Cub of all-time befuddled the best minds the Cardinals put up against him. One day in the late 1950s, according to McDaniel, St. Louis manager Fred Hutchinson called a team meeting. The subject was not the upcoming opponent, the Cubs, but one-man-gang Banks.

The meeting sure did a lot of good—Banks drove in all the runs in the Cubs' 6-2 victory.

"I can't explain why St. Louis was always there in my life," Banks said. "Maybe because Stan Musial was my idol, and I tried harder in the games I played against him."

Perhaps stories have been embellished through the decades. But Banks believes that Gussie Busch figured if he couldn't beat Mr. Cub, then he should join the Cardinals.

"Busch once offered P.K. Wrigley $500,000 to buy me," he claimed. "That was pretty inspiring to me. I figured, 'Wow, I have some value.'"

Banks appreciated the professionalism and friendliness of Cardinals foes, starting with Musial.

"Stan taught me how to play the harmonica with 'Mary Had a Little Lamb,'" he said. "I got him to visit the Better Boys Foundation with me in Chicago.

"All the Cardinals I played against played hard themselves: Bob Gibson, Lou Brock, Kenny Boyer, Wally Moon, Larry Jackson, Curt Flood, Bill White. Right after I broke in, Red Schoendienst had an all-star game after the season, and I remember taking the train from Dallas to St. Louis to play in it."

Banks recalled the hospitality he received from St. Louis' African-American community when he and Gene Baker broke in as rookies. The city was still largely segregated, but the locals made the young players feel comfortable in a potentially tense situation.

"We'd go to a restaurant, people knew we were there," he said. "They made sure we didn't stay out too late or drink too much.

"I remember playing all those games in the old ballpark. Most of the people were very sportsmanlike, very hospitable."

Guess they appreciated quality, even though Ernie Banks always had St. Louis pitchers squarely in his sights.

## Whitey Herzog, former Cardinals manager

You'd figure that Whitey Herzog would be steeped in the Cubs-Cardinals rivalry growing up in Cardinals country east of St. Louis in Illinois.

Surprisingly, not. But he got into it when he became the White Rat of the St. Louis dugout.

"Growing up down here I listened to the games and followed the Cardinals when they played the Cubs," he said, "but I didn't know about it being such a great rivalry until I took over managing the Cardinals.

"When I took over the club in 1980 we were in Atlanta and later that week we went to Chicago. We were in last place but there were 40,000 people in the stands for every game. I said to Red (Schoendienst), 'What the hell's goin' on?' He said, 'It's the Cubs and Cardinals.'

"Every game you don't know who the team is (because of the large number of visiting team fans)."

Oddly enough, Herzog once was the Cubs fans' choice to manage their team. In a Windy City newspaper poll in the 1979-80 off-season, Herzog, then between jobs after his departure from the Kansas City Royals, was picked as the fans' favorite. Cubs general manager Bob Kennedy instead chose old managerial war horse Preston Gomez, who lasted half a season. Herzog was hired on to the Cardinals later in 1980, and the rest was history.

Herzog might not have liked the Cubs job, anyway. He joked that he'd have been the world's biggest alcoholic, waiting out the evening rush hour at Wrigley Field-area bars following day games. On other times, frustrated by the capricious winds that promoted football-like scores, he suggested that Wrigley Field ought to be blown up.

"I never really did like managing in Wrigley," Herzog said. "With that wind, you could have a 2-1 game in the early innings and then the wind would change and it would end up 10-8. Wrigley Field was the only park where I made my lineup up out after checking the flags to see which way the wind was blowing."

## Billy Williams, Cubs Hall of Famer

Back in 1990, Bob Gibson was asked if he remembered serving up Billy Williams' game-winning homer in the bottom of the 10th on Opening Day, April 6, 1971 at Wrigley Field.

Gibby professed to not remember Billy's blast. He must have an awfully poor memory. Williams practically owned Gibson, slugging 11 homers off the fireballer in his career. The sweet swinger perhaps is the top Cards Killer among the ranks of all-time Cubs.

Williams, now the Cubs' bench coach, has no ready explanation of why he hit Gibson and his teammates so well. Maybe it was just the juices flowing in a storied rivalry.

"The rivalry between the Cubs and Cardinals was a big part of my career," Williams said. "It made you reach a little higher when you played the Cardinals. The games almost always were exciting. They'd score three in the first, you'd score one, but somehow the game ended up tied in the eighth."

Busch Stadium also ranked as the only locale where Leo Durocher ever got on Williams. One day, Williams went from first to third on a single to center. Curt Flood, who players normally didn't run on, had a sore arm that Williams had learned about through the players' grapevine. Durocher thought Williams was foolhardy and got on him as only The Lip could. Williams jawed back about the Flood sore arm. Leo never again got on his classic hitter.

## Willie McGee, Cardinals outfielder

The Cardinals' most senior player has seen the rivalry with the Cubs from every possible angle since he made his big-league debut in 1982. Willie McGee likes what he sees.

"It's just a great rivalry, not a blood-type rivalry," McGee said. "It's a fierce rivalry. Each team wants to win badly. But there's respect. You go into Chicago, the fans are great. They're on you, but on you in good nature. You do something good, they respect it. You do something bad, they boo you. But it's not like being in some of the cities where it's real personal.

"It's a fun series, an energetic time. Sometimes it rejuvenates you for the remainder of the next month or the next week. It's something that's just special."

## Ryne Sandberg, former Cubs second baseman

Cardinals fans need no introduction to Ryne Sandberg.

He authored one of the most sensational one-man clutch slugging exhibitions in recent history at St. Louis' expense, slugging two consecutive homers off Bruce Sutter on June 23, 1984 at Wrigley Field. That was truly the jumping-off point for Sandberg's Hall of Fame-bound career, but not the end of his fond memories of games against the Cardinals.

"You know that as soon as you get into town, it's the Cardinals and St. Louis, a big turnout and a lot of enthusiasm among the fans. It definitely rubs off on the players," said Sandberg, now back in the game part-time as a Cubs spring-training instructor.

Sandberg had to navigate "some secret ways" to get to and from Busch Stadium from the Marriott Pavilion Hotel, across the street. "There would be a lot of fans waiting between the hotel and stadium, where the players usually walk. But I found out that if I walked out this different door, there wasn't a crowd. It probably took me about 15 minutes longer to get into the stadium. It was just tough crossing the street."

## Red Schoendienst, former Cardinals second baseman and manager

Red Schoendienst got his big-league baptism in the midst of the Cubs-Cardinals rivalry. His first game as a rookie was on Opening Day 1945 at Wrigley Field. He started in left field for the Redbirds as the Cubs won 3-2, only one of six victories in 22 games the pennant-winning Chicagoans managed against St. Louis that season.

"Missouri and Illinois are connected to one another," Schoendienst said. "In the winter, the Cardinals do their caravans through Illinois, as far as Peoria and Decatur, where there are a lot of Cubs fans and Cardinals fans. You see a lot of interest in both clubs.

"I know the Cardinals fans just love to go into Chicago, and it's just about the same way going into St. Louis. They bet on this and bet on that. I know there are families where half are Cardinals fans and half are Cubbie fans. It's good for baseball."

Schoendienst said there wasn't a particularly special feeling for a Cardinal player performing against the Cubs.

"You go to Wrigley Field, that's a tough park to manage in," he said. "You never know what's going to happen there, especially when the wind's blowing out. You have your bleacher bums; they're going to do their thing in left field and right field. They're good fans in St. Louis and good fans in Chicago. They just root hard for their team."

## Mark Grace, Cubs first baseman

Next to Willie McGee and Shawon Dunston, Mark Grace has experienced the Cubs-Cardinals rivalry longer than any other active player.

"I think it's extremely intense for the fans," 12-year veteran Grace said. "The fans make that rivalry. When we take the field for batting practice in St. Louis, we're getting booed—and cheered. Same goes for the Cardinals in Chicago. You get that kind of electricity in the air, and the McGwire-Sosa duel added more of that in 1998.

"Cardinals fans really hate the Cubs, and vice versa. But I don't hate anybody on the Cardinals. I don't think anybody hates us from the Cardinals. I'll guarantee it, though, with those big crowds, you really want to win that game probably more so than any other. Both teams really want to do what it takes, at all costs, to win it."

The Cubs victories over the Cardinals that Grace would especially covet would be in a pennant race involving both teams. But ever since the 1940s, the Cubs and Cardinals have only battled once—in 1989—into September for first place. The Cubs were mathematically involved in a five-team NL East race in 1973, but were in all honesty limping along under .500 going into September.

"That would be like Dodgers-Giants going down to the wire," Grace said. "It would be unbelievable if that were the case. It was electric in 1989 (a three-game showdown in Wrigley Field September 8-10). The only thing more electric was the one-game playoff against the Giants (in 1998)."

The Cubs fans get a charge trying to meet their heroes at the Cubs' hotel, the Marriott Pavilion, across the street from Busch Stadium. They have deluged the players so much that Grace has had to stay in another hotel in St. Louis for the past five years.

"One time, I came back late at night and there were three people in sleeping bags, sleeping outside my door," he said. "It was a father, a daughter and a son. That scared me. Ask Monica Seles about fanatical fans. I just decided it might be in my best interests to stay at another hotel. The odds of someone holding a knife or a gun in their sleeping bag are very small. But I don't want to take that chance."

## Tony La Russa, Cardinals manager

Tony La Russa spent so little time as a Cubs player in 1973—one pinch-running appearance, carrying home the winning run on Opening Day against the Expos—that he never got a chance to experience the Cubs-Cardinals rivalry up close and personal.

But since 1996, La Russa has been learning via osmosis.

"Both fans have a lot of similarities," he said. "They're very loyal to their club. It's a healthy rivalry in the sense that fans come to the ballpark to have a good time, cheering for their ballclub and cheering against the other one. It's not something that's a negative. There's a lot of passion on both sides in a healthy way."

La Russa, who spent 17 seasons as an American League manager, said the rivalry is second to none in the game.

"I think it's tied for first with the best you can find," he said.

## Fergie Jenkins, Cubs Hall of Famer

The Cardinals never liked to see Fergie Jenkins throwing strikes in machine-like fashion to them. The control artist, greatest Cubs pitcher of the last half of the 20th Century, often dominated the Cardinals lineup.

Jenkins was a major reason the Cubs-Cardinals rivalry revived so well in 1967, first of his six consecutive 20-victory seasons in a Chicago uniform. But just prior to his arrival in Chicago in a great trade early in the 1966 season, the big Canadian did not hear encouraging words about Cubs-Cardinals matchups.

"I was on the Phillies, and Bill White had just come over from St. Louis," Jenkins recalled. "He said the Cubs were losers, a team the Cardinals used to clean up on. He said they'd go into Chicago expecting to win three in a row.

"But when I went over there in a trade, I thought we could beat those guys. As we got stronger in 1967-68, we didn't fear them. The team we feared was Pittsburgh. I believe our starting staff was just as strong as the Cardinals. If he had a stronger bullpen, no telling where we could have gone."

Jenkins was one of the big-name Cubs who socialized with the gaggle of Bleacher Bums who camped out at the Chase Park Plaza Hotel, the Cubs' team hotel in St. Louis prior to the 1970s.

"I knew about half a dozen guys who were Bleacher Bums," he said. "We'd have drinks at the hotel bar. But I don't know about the real wild parties they were supposed to throw. I do know some of the Bleacher Bums threw water balloons off ledges onto the people in the parking lot next to the hotel."

Jenkins discovered St. Louis-area nightlife. "I used to go to East St. Louis to clubs there," he said. "They had some good bands in St. Louis. I'd also go over to Ted Savage's house when he played for us. St. Louis was pretty good for entertainment. The sleepy towns in my career supposedly were Cleveland and Pittsburgh. LA and New York and Montreal were the big club towns. In Montreal, you'd see European acts, French girls, table dancers..."

There was some control over the players' late hours in St. Louis. Due to its proximity from Chicago, Cubs wives came down for the series. Kathy Jenkins, Fergie's then-wife, and Shirley Williams would visit.

On duty on the mound at Busch Stadium, Jenkins was an amazing sight in the 120-degree field temperatures. He only changed his blue long-sleeved undershirt, but never his outer flannel jersey. He was one cool customer who seemingly didn't perspire in the ultimate baseball sweatbox.

"The biggest thing in St. Louis was to have an ice bucket in the tunnel next to the dugout," Jenkins said.

Did Ernie Banks ever say, "Let's play two," in the sauna bath of a St. Louis Sunday afternoon?

"No," laughed Jenkins.

## Jack Buck, Cardinals broadcaster

After some 45 years as a Cardinals announcer, Jack Buck knows when a rivalry ebbs and flows. He believes the Cubs-Cardinals rivalry was not always No. 1.

"When I began broadcasting the Cardinals' rivalry with the Dodgers prevailed more than with the Cubs," Buck said. He said he wasn't sure when the Cards-Cubs rivalry began but that it was probably in the '60s.

"But the Cardinals-Cubs rivalry is a good rivalry, wholesome," he said. "There's none of the animosity that you see with the Mets and the Phillies, nothing like the fights you see at Shea Stadium or Veterans Stadium."

He's seen that rivalry become a consistent thing from year to year. "Some years, when we were both out of the running, playing the Cubs was the only fun we had," he said.

Buck got an early introduction to the windy ways of Wrigley Field. During his first season broadcasting in St. Louis, he saw the Cardinals lose a 23-13 game. "It's always interesting up there in Wrigley Field. You can hit a pop fly and it'll fly out of the ballpark," he said.

Buck will always remember the great pitcher-hitter matchups. "It seemed like every time the ninth inning rolled around, no matter what the score was, Billy Williams came to bat against Bob Gibson."

He acknowledged that Cardinals and Cubs fans traveling to each other's ballparks was rare when he started broadcasting but has become commonplace because of a good economy and a more mobile lifestyle. He doesn't see that, or the Cardinals-Cubs rivalry diminishing.

"It'll go on forever and ever," Buck said.

## Steve Trachsel, Cubs starting pitcher

Steve Trachsel has more Cubs-Cardinals history in his blood than just serving up Mark McGwire's 62nd homer in 1998. He had a winning record (8-6) against St. Louis going into the 1999 season.

When he's not on the mound and just soaking in the red and blue colors of the rivalry, Trachsel can sit back and enjoy it.

"Obviously, the fans love it and the cities love it," he said. "When I'm pitching, I don't hear anything, no matter where I am and who I'm playing against. But when I'm not pitching, it's outstanding, a lot of fun.

"It's amazing. It's fun to hear the fans trash-talking each other. You see the signs out there, both places. It's a big rivalry, a lot of bragging rights between the cities."

Like Mark Grace, Trachsel can't wait until the blessed day when the Cubs and Cardinals could battle it out for first place right down to the wire.

"You saw the city last year (when the Cubs and Giants were tied for the wild card at the end of the regular season)," he said. "If it were to be for first place against the Cardinals, in Busch Stadium, it would be awesome. We get a lot of fans in St. Louis anyway, and there'd be even more."

## Garry Templeton, former Cardinals shortstop

In his prime in the late 1970s, Garry Templeton spent some quality work time motoring around the bases against the Cubs. But he didn't need to slash a double or triple as one of his era's best switch hitters to get on the move against the Cubs.

"You always got fired up for a Cubs-Cardinals game," said Templeton, now a minor league manager with the Anaheim Angels organization. "I didn't know how big a rivalry it was until I played in a game. It was amazing. The fans are going crazy, they're fighting in the stands. In Chicago or St. Louis, it didn't matter. You see a sea of blue, a sea of red. It was wild. Those were really exciting times."

Templeton remembers "quite a few" Cardinals fans staying at the Chicago hotel. "For the most part, with our rivalries, I don't think fans are as wild as they are now about the athletes because of the amount of money they have and the exposure. The rivalry gets more exposure now through the media. Back then, we knew it was just a great rivalry. We just had a lot of fun with it, now it's just exposed more."

What was Templeton's stick-out moment?

"I hit a home run to straightaway center field off Ray Burris, a game winner, the first home run I ever hit in Wrigley Field," he grinned.

## Rod Beck, Cubs relief pitcher

Throughout 1998, Rod Beck got a quick education in the Cubs-Cardinals rivalry. He had grown up in Los Angeles, and then played for the Giants, so he didn't really know of its impact.

"If anything, with the Brewers moving to the National League, I thought they'd be rivals with the Cubs," Beck said. "I really knew nothing about the Cubs and the Cardinals being rivals. I grew up in the LA area, and I thought the Dodgers and Giants were the baddest rivalry it was.

"The biggest thing that amazed me was around the ballpark and the hotel when we were in St. Louis, it was like the winter Cubs Convention. You could go down and sit in the hotel lobby like in other cities. You'd have to go down and go directly to the ballpark. Otherwise you'd get mobbed by Cubs fans in St. Louis.

"As a Giants player going into St. Louis, you'd see red everywhere. But as a Cub, you saw as much blue as red in the stadium. The volume of the place was much more than in the past. To see your fans in a visiting city, it makes you feel good not only about your ballclub and your chances, but it also takes your game to another level."

Beck, the common man's relief pitcher, has a lot of respect for St. Louis baseball rooters.

"I've always thought very highly of Cardinals fans," he said. "They always came to the ballpark. They knew their baseball. A lot like Cubs fans. They have football there, but more so than anything, it's the Cardinals. It's a baseball town. It's a rivalry between towns that love baseball."

## Todd Worrell, former Cardinals relief pitcher

Todd Worrell could power his 100 mph fastball toward Cubs hitters as the Cardinals ace closer in the late 1980s. But sometimes that still wasn't enough to master the Chicago hitters. Everyone was psyched up for the duels.

"It's a classic rivalry," said Worrell, who continued to make his home in the St. Louis area even after playing for his hometown Los Angeles Dodgers after his Cardinals days ebbed.

"The players enjoy it as much as the fans. But it's a clean rivalry. The Giants and Dodgers—that is pretty ugly. The fans get out of perspective with it.

Worrell believed it was a challenge to warm up in bullpens in both Wrigley Field and Busch Stadium, where the fans could get on players or even reach out and touch them.

"The fans in both ballparks do all they can to distract the opposing team's players and get you out of the game," he said. "For the most part, I think it brought out the best in me as a player."

The rivalry meant a lot to the players, even if both teams were out of contention.

"That's what brings people to the ballpark," Worrell said. "They remember a play by Ozzie (Smith) or a home run or a great pitching performance. These types of games had something more than a game in Cincinnati."

"Wrigley Field was good to me. I had a lot of success there. There were just some great nail-biters."

## Ken Hill, former Cardinals pitcher

Ever since he left St. Louis, Ken Hill has made virtually a grand tour of the majors, including a tenure in the American League. So he can compare the Cubs-Cardinals rivalry with others in the game.

"The Boston-New York rivalry is different," said Hill, now an Angels pitcher. "The fans are different than Midwest fans. The fans are more laid-back, but still into it. In Boston or New York, you go down the street, the fans are fighting.

"The Cubs-Cardinals rivalry was great. It was intense. A lot of the guys really got into it."

## Ed Lynch, Cubs general manager

Ed Lynch got to hurl himself into the Cubs-Cardinals rivalry as a Chicago pitcher in 1986 and 1987. But as emotional and stirring as the duels could be, the Cubs-Cardinals face-offs never carried the bitterness of the Cardinals' rivalry with the New York Mets, the team for whom Lynch pitched for six seasons prior to his arrival with the Cubs.

The Cardinals and Mets engaged in bench-clearing brawls-in spring training, no less.

"The main reason was we were both good clubs in the 1980s—'84 through '88, both teams battling it out for the divisional title every year," Lynch said. "Both clubs were evenly matched with very competitive people.

"The added thing with us was we shared the same stadium (Al Lang Field) in spring training. It was our feeling that we were treated like second citizens there. They got to use the home clubhouse and keep their things in there all the time. We had to bus in from a local workout facility for the game and then leave right afterward. Familiarity breeds contempt when you play each other every day."

The presence of Keith Hernandez on the Mets added more fuel to the fire.

"Their best player had been traded to our club," Lynch said. "There was some bad blood between Keith and some of the people in St. Louis. He and Whitey Herzog weren't the greatest of friends. Keith wanted to beat the Cardinals. He made all of us that much more intense."

Lynch said the Cubs-Cardinals is a more congenial rivalry.

"I haven't seen the hatred among the players that existed in the 1980s," he said. "It's intensely competitive, but it didn't have that personal side to hit, not that real animosity among the personalities involved."

## Walt Jocketty, Cardinals general manager

When Walt Jocketty served as assistant general manager of the Oakland Athletics in the early 1990s, he didn't see a hot rivalry with the San Francisco Giants, across the bay.

The two teams didn't play each other, in different leagues. And even with interleague play, the cross-bay interest is a lot more tepid than the Cubs-Cardinals rivalry. Football, in the form of the 49ers, is king in the area.

"It may not be as important to fans as the Cubs-Cardinals rivalry is in the Midwest," Jocketty said.

After half a decade as Cardinals GM, Jocketty rates the duels with Chicago as a pace-setter in the game,

"If it's not the best rivalry in the game, then it's certainly one of the best," he said. "The only possible rivalry that could challenge this is Red Sox-Yankees, going back to Babe Ruth being sold to the Yankees. It is clearly the best rivalry in the National League.

"I was surprised in 1995, when I started with the Cardinals, how many people were there. We were coming off the work stoppage. We weren't drawing that well, but we drew well for the Cubs series. That what makes it fun, having the stadium with different pockets of Cubs fans sitting with the Cardinals fans."

## Ned Colletti, assistant general manager, San Francisco Giants

In his present job, Ned Colletti is the only ex-Wrigley Field Left Field Bleacher Bum with the ability to make trades. What a youthful dream-come-true.

Colletti now is Giants GM Brian Sabean's right-hand man. He got his first dose of talent-judging watching Cubs games from the bleachers, growing up in the Chicago suburb of Franklin Park. Colletti witnessed a lot of the key Cubs-Cardinals games of the 1960s and early 1970s from that perch.

In between Bleacher Bums and inner-sanctum flesh-trading days, Colletti also saw the best Cubs-Cardinals action in the 1980s in the Cubs' media relations department, first as assistant director, then director.

"The games were both cities' World Series, no matter what place they were in the standings," he recalled. "The ballparks were packed, half the fans in red, half in blue.

"The Marriott Pavilion hotel in St. Louis was a nightmare. I'd get a room on the lowest floor I could, because taking an elevator with all those Cubs fans was tough. A lot of players took the stairwell down, behind the elevators, to avoid the crush of fans. You really couldn't get into a car to go around the block to get into the ballpark.

"But everyone looked forward to it. Good things happened in those games. We once pulled off a triple steal. And that last weekend in 1984, it was turned up a few notches, when the Cubs were closing in on clinching the NL East. It was the most exciting of any weekend that I've been down there. People came down who didn't have tickets, but just wanted to be near the place."

Colletti also loved the January Cub Caravans through central Illinois.

"They were neat," he said. "You'd go to Springfield with the Cardinals' farm team there. Or Peoria. You'd have people showing up at the caravan dinners to razz Cubs fans or players."

## Pete Cooper, congressional aide, Busch Stadium scoreboard operator

Pete Cooper gets to work in two of our favorite sports: baseball and politics. He's an aide to U.S. Rep. Jim Talent of Missouri by day, a scoreboard operator at Busch Stadium at night and weekends. And he's made pilgrimages to Wrigley Field in 1985 through 1990, and 1993 and 1998.

"It doesn't matter if the clubs are in first or last place," Cooper said. "When the Cardinals and Cubs meet it draws out the best in fans, sometimes the worst."

While he has a begrudging respect for the Cubs fans, "I could never root for the Cubs."

At least Cooper's not in a split-loyalties family.

"I remember once we were sitting behind a family where the dad was a Cubs fan and the mom a Cardinals fan," he said. "The Cubs got off to a big lead early and you can see dad playing up to the kids, trying to get them on his side. Late in the game Mitch Webster goes in for the Cubs and makes an error, and the floodgates opened. Well, the Cardinals came back and won, and that dad just sunk in his chair."

# Mike Murphy, radio talk-show host and ex-Bleacher Bum bugler

Maybe Mike Murphy has never really stopped tooting his bugle. He used to dance atop the left-field wall at Wrigley Field as bugler of the Left Field Bleacher Bums. Now he sounds a different kind of charge as a sports-talk show host on WSCR-Radio ("The Score"), one of three all-sports stations in Chicago.

Every so often, Murphy can work his travels as a fan into his show. One story he can conjure up is how the Bleacher Bums adopted their trademark yellow construction helmets. They were obtained after the Bums chartered a bus to St. Louis in 1967, when the Cubs engaged in their revival under Leo Durocher and briefly challenged the Cardinals for first place.

"There was always a misconception of Cubs-Cardinals crowds in St. Louis being split down the middle," Murphy said. "People in central Illinois did not hop in car and stay in hotel to view favorite team like they did later on. At the time, there weren't any good hotels in downtown St. Louis to stay in. It was an empty wasteland downtown; the ballpark was only the start of the revival. Many times out of 45,000, there were only a few hundred blue hats. Now it's 20,000 of each.

"We got the helmets when the Cardinals fan threw anything at us they could get their hands on three-game series: wadded-up fruit, sandwiches. We had to be protected the next time we went to Busch Stadium."

In 1969, the Bleacher Bums stayed at the then-team hotel: the Chase Park Plaza, a few miles west of downtown, not far from the St. Louis Zoo. But the Animal House conditions were in the hotel, not in the zoo cages.

"The Bleacher Bums stayed 20 to a room in Chase Park Plaza," Murphy said. "We were college students, Vietnam vets, and we didn't have any money. It was a high-priced hotel, so everybody chipped in a buck or two to stay. In the evening, we'd go down to the Steeplechase Lounge, and with only a couple of bucks to our name, we'd nurse a 25-cent beer. One night Leo Durocher threw down a $20 bill and said the drinks were on him that night.

"The Cubs players would come down and party with us. Players in same age bracket as us: Ron Santo, Glenn Beckert, Fergie Jenkins, they'd find us. We'd also go with them to the local race track."

Murphy believes that in Chicago, the Cubs-White Sox rivalry is more heated than the Cubs-Cardinals duels.

"Growing up in Chicago, that was the only rivalry in Chicago that Chicago fans looked at," he said. "St. Louis always been a great rivalry, but I can't imagine anything bigger than the Cubs fans hating the White Sox and vice versa."

## Kevin Carbery, Cardinals fan

Kevin Carbery, a designer for the Suburban Journals, a big weekly St. Louis-area newspaper chain, has traveled with friends to Wrigley Field with fellow St. Louis Cardinals fans since the mid-1980s.

"My friends Jeff and Dave and I have generally gotten along well with the Cubbie fans, except for sometimes when we sit in the bleachers," he said.

Carbery told of a May, 1998 Wrigley Field incident that showed the worst of fans.

"We went to the park early to watch batting practice and got good seats down low," he said. "We were wearing our St. Louis hats and shirts, of course. Once the game started and everyone was crowded in, people started throwing half-drunk cups of beer at us. We got ticked off after a while and told a large usher nearby about the beer bombs, but he brushed us off.

"Well, not 10 seconds after he'd ignored us, another cup of beer came flying down, buzzed by Dave's head and proceeded to explode all over the usher when it hit his thigh. You better believe he became more attentive to the beer throwers from that point on. As it happened, he caught a few of them and escorted them out of the park. We felt vindicated. I've seen plenty of Cubs fans at Busch Stadium over the years, and I've never thrown anything at them. You can yell anything you want, but throwing beer bombs can hurt someone."

Carbery said he plays the rivalry with Cubs fans for fun.

"At times it has been fun for my friends and me to talk to Cubbie fans at games, during which both sides would badmouth their own teams," he said. "A few years ago, a Cub supporter sitting near us was bemoaning the fact that one of the Cubs' crummy hitters was coming to the plate. We replied that he shouldn't worry, the Cards had Todd 'Third Degree' Burns pitching.

"You have these kinds conversations all the time. In the first few years that we went to Cards-Cubs games at Wrigley in the mid-1980s, the Chicago fans were harder on their players than we were. I can still remember guys screaming at how horrible they thought Ron Cey and Larry Bowa were. It was a hoot listening to their venom for their own team. We did that to some of our guys, too.

"A knowledgeable fan is aware that more games are lost through incompetence than are won through skill.

## Frank Maloney, Cubs ticket director

When Cubs single-game tickets go on sale in late winter, Frank Maloney always knows he can expect a lot of cash flow from purchasers in the 314, 217 and 618 area codes. He doesn't mind taking Cardinals fans' money; it's eminently legal tender.

"The Cubs-Cardinals weekend series in the spring or summer is always our No. 1 series," Maloney said. "The first day of sales, we're always jammed with calls from Cardinals fans. They're calling from the end of the previous season to find out when the tickets go on sale.

"A lot of people ask, 'Why do you sell all those tickets to St. Louis people?' Well, we say it's hard to discriminate against someone by where they live. We don't know whether they're Cubs fans or Cardinals fans."

So how does that sea of red suddenly show up in prime Wrigley Field box seats for the best dates?

"They must get them from scalpers or brokers, who in turn get them from season-ticket holders," Maloney said. "Or they get them from corporate accounts. When we go on sale (with individual-game tickets), there are no box seats on sale."

Bleacher seats for the weekend Cardinals series sell out within a half-hour of the start of sales. Maloney has heard of the bleacher seats, normally $15, being scalped for as high as $75.

"The Saturday game always goes first, then Sunday and Friday," he said. "After a day or two of sales, it's a hard-to-come-by seat."

Wrigley Field can cram in about 40,000 fans, using all standing-room tickets. For the mid-summer Cardinals series, Maloney wishes he had a much bigger stadium.

"Unquestionably," he said when asked if he could sell 50,000 seats for many Cardinals games. "We could easily do 60,000, especially on a summer weekend.

"One of the ironies is that I hate to see the Cardinals come in a prime weekend in June, July or August. They would fill the place anyway. I'd rather play them in May or September, when maybe it's a little more iffy about what we'll draw. Or I'd love to have them Tuesday-Wednesday-Thursday to boost the attendance."

That's the bottom-line aspect. But what's more symbolic of the good in the game than wrangling a tough ticket and fighting the crowds for a Cubs-Cardinals showdown on a summer Saturday or Sunday?

## John McDonough, Cubs vice president of marketing and broadcasting

Don't expect a Beanie Baby promotion during a weekend Cubs-Cardinals series at Wrigley Field.

"When you play the Cardinals on a Memorial Day weekend (as in 1999), those three games sell out on their own," said John McDonough, the Cubs' marketing chief. "You try to schedule promotions against teams like Montreal and Philadelphia. The Cubs-Cardinals rivalry sells itself."

McDonough was thrilled that the Cubs added a natural geographic rival when the Milwaukee Brewers joined the National League Central in 1998. But nothing can quite equal the Cubs-Cardinals.

"I think it's better than the Yankees and Red Sox, better than the Dodgers and Angels," McDonough said. "The Cubs and Cardinals go so deep, so far back, all the way to the foundation of baseball. Regardless of where the teams are playing, it's great for the fans. It's not an acrimonious relationship at all."

## Jerry Vickery, Missouri Sports Hall of Fame curator

Jerry Vickery of Belleville, Ill., curator of the Missouri Sports Hall of Fame in St. Louis, grew up in nearby East St. Louis, Illinois. His earliest memories are of Cards-Cubs matchups in the early 1960s.

"Our neighbors had grandkids in Chicago and when they would visit we'd have the Cardinals vs. the Cubs Indian ball in the backyard," he said. "The kid that was my age stayed a Cub fan, but his younger brother became a Cardinals fan because he wanted to be on my team."

"I had an uncle who every year on Easter would ask me how the Cardinals were going to do and then would say the Cubs would beat them. But I think he secretly was a Cardinals fan."

Vickery learned early that it took ammunition to fight off the Cubs fans, but he had it. "I learned about 1908 when I was 7 years old," he said, referring to the taunt that Cardinals fans often throw at Cubs fans about the last time their team won a World Series.

"I've been up to Wrigley Field on a few bus trips with the people who live next to us. One year they swept us and coming back on the bus we had to listen to them touting their team. One guy had a microphone and went on about it. The next year, we won the series and coming back all the guy with the microphone could talk about was how Wrigley Field is the most beautiful ballpark in the country. I finally hollered out, 'Where did they hide all those World Series banners?' They didn't have a comeback on that."

## Jerry Pritikin, "The Bleacher Preacher"

Omnipresent Cubs fan Jerry Pritikin, *aka* "The Bleacher Preacher," didn't just want to stick it to the Cardinals with his trademark voodoo doll. He actually performed a "conversion" of a Cardinals fan to a Cubs fan.

But don't think life has been easy for the pith-helmeted Pritikin when he deals with Redbird rooters at Wrigley Field.

"One of my pith helmets was smashed by Cardinals fan," Pritikin said. "A security guy saw it and kicked the guy out. About a year later, I was sitting in a grandstand seat because I couldn't get bleachers tickets that day. A guy sitting behind me, wearing this hat with beer cans on each side, said I had him kicked out twice. It was the same guy. Well, he was kicked out only once.

"He was drinking and getting so belligerent that by the seventh inning, guards came and did eject him. So he counted right—he was kicked out twice."

In addition to Pritikin's voodoo ritual of sticking it to the opposition, he walked around with bird seed in his pockets to pass out to shower on Cardinals fans. He also had red feathers to give to Cubs fans to "pluck the Cardinals."

Long before he went into business as "The Bleacher Preacher," Pritikin was just a plain ol' fan in the cheap seats, then 60 cents. His memory time-trips him to the late 1940s.

"One time Harry Brecheen pitching no-hitter for the Cardinals in the fourth inning, but rains came and delayed the game," Pritikin said. Peanuts Lowery had been batting with a 1-and-1 count when the delay started. I was one of few fans out in right field when game resumed. Lowery homered on the first pitch, and I caught the ball in the bleachers.

"It was about 40 years before I caught another homer, by Keith Hernandez of the Mets, in 1987."

## Tom Meyer, Cardinals fan

Tom Meyer of South St. Louis County works for a brick company in St. Louis. As a 19-year-old college student sitting in the left field bleachers of Busch Stadium in 1973, he had an unforgettable encounter with a group of Cubs fans.

"These Cubs fans were shooting off their mouths, only God knows why," he said, "considering their team's track record, going on and on about their Cubs. Hoping to silence them, I said to one who I thought was a few years older than me, 'The Cubs haven't won a pennant in your lifetime.' He just looked at me and said, 'Well, they haven't won one in yours, either.'"

Meyer shook his head, looking for the logic in that statement. Every year he predicts the Cubs will not win the pennant, and said he will hold to that prediction.

# 2

# The Best and Worst of Both Worlds: Dual Identity Players

**BLUE and red can be matching colors.** But Cubbie blue and Cardinals red seem diametrically opposite.

Surprisingly, these colors fit a gaggle of prominent players who wore the uniforms of both teams.

Some of the most prominent players of modern baseball times were both Cubs and Cardinals, as upcoming chapters on trades between the two teams indicate. And when these players finished their migration between the two cities, they could compare the contrasts: night ball in St. Louis, day games in Chicago; sauna-like heat and humidity in Busch Stadium, bees-in-the-bat wind-chill in Wrigley Field; bon vivant beer baron Gussie Busch in St. Louis, introverted gum magnate Cubs chieftain Phil Wrigley in Chicago. And on and on.

Yet the most lasting impression left on many of the dual-identity Cubs/Cardinals players is the atmosphere surrounding both teams. Here are some of the surest clues as to why the Cardinals have appeared in their fair share of World Series through the decades, while the Cubs entered 1999 defying at least 100-1 odds on not making a Fall Classic since 1945.

Former outfielder George Altman picked up on the perceptible difference between the two clubs based on just his one year in St. Louis-1963-after two seasons as one of the NL's best left-handed hitters while a Cub.

"I thought the Cardinals were a lot more professional," said Altman, now a Jefferson City, Mo., Resident. "They had a lot of class players. Little things didn't come up. With the Cubs, it was how you wore your socks."

Former Cardinals "bonus baby" pitcher Lindy McDaniel, traded from St. Louis for Altman after the 1962 season, picked up on the same attitude contrasts.

"St. Louis was a very competitive organization," McDaniel said. "There was a lot of pressure to win. They had a strong organization. And when we played the Cubs, we figured we could beat them.

"When I was with the Cubs, they were laid back. It was more of a country club atmosphere. If they won two, three games in a row, they'd celebrate. But if they lost, it didn't seem to matter much. On the bus, if they lost two or three games in a row, they were cutting each other up. They'd be singing in the shower after a loss."

Perhaps the all-day baseball schedule prior to 1988 contributed to the less intense atmosphere with the Cubs, compared to St. Louis. Former catcher Steve Lake, who played with a rare Cubs winner in 1984, three years prior to backing up Tony Pena on the Cardinals' 1987 World Series team, believes there was a correlation.

"I did notice a difference," Lake said. "Especially for the fans, it was a more casual atmosphere without lights. Wrigley Field was more of a neighborhood park. St. Louis was more of an atmosphere where you dress up, go out for evening. People who are Cubs fans are still oriented for daytime."

Wrigley actually promoted the concept of having a picnic at Wrigley Field in the sun while, incidentally, watching a baseball game. The basic concept of falling back on the ballpark's appeal when the team goes sour even applies today. In contrast, according to former pitcher Jim Brosnan, a Cub in 1954 and 1956-58, then a Cardinal in 1958-59, Anheuser-Busch seemed to actively promote the ballclub as baseball.

The Cardinals apparently were more advanced in human relations a generation ago despite the fact they operated in a city where legalized segregation was still common in the 1950s. McDaniel said Ernie Banks wanted to room with him on the road in 1963 after the pitcher came to the Cubs. McDaniel, who hailed from Oklahoma, said fine. But management, still objecting to interracial roommates, nixed the idea.

Over the years, the Cubs' losing tradition was never really purged despite two NL East divisional titles and the 1998 NL wild-card playoff berth. But Dallas Green's tenure as GM in the 1980s did make the Cubs far more attractive to opposing players while developing more home-grown products of the farm system. That comfort zone was cited by two present-day players who possess dual identities of both the Cubs and Cardinals.

Third baseman Gary Gaetti was most happy getting a longtime wish to play in Wrigley Field late in the 1998 season, a career dream fulfilled even though he grew up a Cardinals fan in downstate Centralia, Illinois. Gaetti killed the Cubs as a visiting St. Louis player. He didn't miss a beat, hitting so well in the Friendly Confines immediately after being released by the Cardinals, who replaced him at third base with Fernando Tatis.

"It's a baseball Mecca-type atmosphere," he said. "Everyone talks about Wrigley Field, everyone talks about the atmosphere. It was a great place to play. I still can't explain it other than I like playing there. I just feel a certain (good) way when I take the field there."

Gaetti said he tried to sign with the Cubs after the 1991 season, when then-Cubs general manager Jim Frey had a hole at third. He tried to fill it with Gary Scott, with disastrous results for the very-green rookie.

But if you wind the clock back a generation, Busch Stadium would have been the preferred destination for Gaetti. He grew up a Cardinals fan in Centralia, Illinois almost directly east of St. Louis.

"I liked Mike Shannon and Joe Torre a lot when he won the MVP with the Cardinals (1971)," Gaetti said. "Ken Reitz, too. Whoever was playing for the Cardinals."

Torre wasn't the only Italian-American third baseman to whom Gaetti paid attention. "I like Sal Bando with the Athletics. He was great," he said. "And I always followed Ron Santo, even though he beat the Cardinals when he was a Cub. We had Ron Santo's pizza in Centralia.

"I thought St. Louis was a pretty great baseball town. It's pretty comparable with Chicago. You can go around the country and see how popular the Cubs are."

Gaetti and wife Donna would have had to field an unbelievable offer from elsewhere to not have returned to the Cubs.

"It was never easy to leave something familiar, all your friends," Donna Gaetti said of departing St. Louis. "But after a few games, the girls (Cubs wives) were so pleasant and made it easy to make the transition. Gary played so well, and that helped our decision. Our first choice was to come back here."

"It was nice to be able to have an opportunity to say, 'This was one of my choices,'" Gaetti said.

Meanwhile, the Cubs identity was so strong with longtime Chicago shortstop Shawon Dunston that he misspoke royally—upsetting many Cardinals fans—when he arrived at St. Louis' 1999 spring training camp in Jupiter, Florida. Nearing the end of his career after moving around to the Giants, Pirates and Indians, Dunston had been signed up as a utility infielder by the Cardinals.

"It's funny, but it's life. I'm a Cub now . . . I mean I'm a Cardinal now and I'm going to try my best to beat them every time we play the Cubs."

Even after stating all his *mea culpas*, Dunston admitted all the Cubbie blue probably could never be purged out of him. He still keeps his Cubs jersey at his San Francisco-area home, and his three-year-old wears it.

"I can't get it out of my mind," he said. "Do you know my son is six now and he's playing baseball. Guess who he's playing for? The Cubs. No kidding, that's his team. And he is going to wear No. 12."

The comfort zone cut the other way, too. Players traded away from St. Louis to Chicago missed the Cardinals' atmosphere while learning how to play hardest against the Cubs. One was Ken Reitz, the Cardinals' popular third baseman from 1972 to 1975 and 1977 to 1980.

Reitz's first memory was arriving on the Cardinals bus at Wrigley late in the 1972 season. "Some fan came up and pounded on the bus. 'Redbirds is deadbirds,' he was hollering," he said.

"You learned early not to like the Cubs. Even if you had friends on the Cubs you slid into them hard on a double play."

"In Wrigley Field you were so close to the fans. You'd take a swing in the on-deck circle and you'd knock somebody's beer of the railing in the box seats." He said the back-and-forth bantering between fans and players and fans was ongoing.

Reitz had a special reason for wanting to beat the Cardinals after he came over to the Cubs in 1981. He resented having been traded, having been part of the package that brought Bruce Sutter to St. Louis the previous off-season. "Whitey (Herzog) was an outsider, not part of the family, and he got rid of us all," Reitz said of the housecleaning Herzog did after taking over in 1980. But Reitz couldn't argue with the end results. Under Herzog, the Cardinals had the best record in the National League in the fractured, strike-torn 1981 season and won the 1982 World Series, after the club had gone 14 years without reaching the Fall Classic.

Strong player loyalties mark the rivalry. But the Cubs will only catch up in winning tradition when they build up the same kind of efficiency of player development as the Redbirds.

Only for a short period of time immediately before and after 1960, and later under Dallas Green in the 1980s, did the Cubs consistently produce quality big leaguers out of their farm system. Improvements in player development and scouting have been implemented under the Andy MacPhail regime, but the talent pipeline isn't flowing freely quite yet.

To St. Louis, funneling players up the big club is old hat. Branch Rickey truly was the Mahatma of the farm system, developing the first widespread player-development operation for the Cardinals in the 1930s.

"Rickey was ahead of his time," said baseball storyteller Joe Garagiola, Yogi Berra's neighbor on St. Louis' south side as a youth, who went on to catch for the Cardinals from 1946 to 1951, then did a stint for the Cubs in 1953-54 before broadcasting came a callin.' "He established the farm system in St. Louis, then did it again in Brooklyn. He went to Pittsburgh, and he did it a third time, but it took longer due to injuries."

Meanwhile, Phil Wrigley starved his farm system and scouting staff for capital, creative ideas and a sense of direction. Both longtime Cubs stalwart Phil Cavarretta and broadcaster Lou Boudreau noticed the problem as far back as the late 1930s. Around 1962, Wrigley even ordered his scouts not to sign new players out of high schools and colleges, apparently upset by signing-bonus money that went for naught when the players did not pan out. That cutoff of the talent spigot made a shaky farm system even worse. Braves manager Bobby Cox, who played for the Cubs' Triple-A team in Salt Lake City in 1965, said the team was trying to cull warm bodies from all over baseball just to stock the roster with the dearth of young players rising through the system.

"P.K. might have been right-on principle," said Jim Brosnan. "You don't spend money on an unproven product unless it's proven he can come through. He was against the 'bonus baby' rule."

But baseball is a different business than, well, business. Wrigley, who according to Brosnan, "didn't give a damn about baseball," followed the advice of lesser-light functionaries he put in charge of the Cubs. In contrast, Gussie Busch put men in charge of running his team "who were as enthusiastic about baseball as P.K. was about the gum business."

The end result? "The Cardinals farm system was much more disciplined and regimented," Brosnan said. "The players knew what they had to do to improve and reach the majors. I remember how Bruce Edwards, a former home-grown Dodger under Rickey, was managing Springfield. He sat in front of a hotel one day, and bitched and moaned about how fundamentally unsound the Cubs prospects were. I was invited to spring training after a 4-17 season in Triple-A. With the Cardinals, Dodgers and Yankees, no way would I have been invited to spring training."

"The Cards simply had better players," Garagiola said. "We finished higher. Tradition? Tradition is winning."

Apparently, the spirit is willing everywhere. But the flesh is weaker in some places compared to others.

"All pro baseball players love to win and hate to lose," Garagiola said. "At Pittsburgh in 1952, we lost 112 games, and our desire was not any less than Cardinals. But our ability was less. I don't buy the country club atmosphere that was pinned on the Cubs and Red Sox. When we played the Cubs in the mid-1940s, there weren't any tougher competitors than Phil Cavarretta and Stan Hack. And look at last year with Sammy Sosa and Mark Grace. Wasn't that a winning atmosphere?"

Even if the Cubs often were beaten and bedraggled in the years after their 1945 pennant, they got up to play the Cardinals. Garagiola found that out not only as a St. Louis player, but also on the two lousy Cubs teams he played.

"Cubs-Cardinals games always were intense," he said. "The Cubs knocked us out of a pennant, beating us two out of three games at the end of the 1949 season. Bob Chipman beat us. In 1946, when Cubs beat us at the end of the season, I never saw better play in left side of the infield from the Cubs. They played the living daylights out."

The 65-89 Cubs team of 1953 held their own against the superior Cardinals at 11-11 in the season series. The following year, the Cubs were only 64-90, but were 14-8 against the Cardinals.

Now, in the free-agent era, both teams can operate on a more even playing field. The 1998 wild-card season elevated the Cubs' expectations to the level the Cardinals traditionally have demanded.

"Winning was inbred in you," Cubs center fielder Lance Johnson said of his days in the Cardinals farm system that culminated in a promotion just in time to play in the 1987 World Series against the Twins.

"And now we expect to win here, too."

That could only help the rivalry, one day producing a long-awaited, down-to-the-wire pennant race between the two teams.

But despite the heightened intensity of Cubs-Cardinals games, the properly-concentrating player should not get too caught up in the hoopla.

"Players don't go into a ballpark and say, 'Wow, look what I'm around,'" Steve Lake said. "If I'm doing my job as a catcher, I'll be concentrating on the hitters. I only notice fans when I'm hit in back of head by a hot dog, like I was at Shea Stadium. Players enjoy playing in front of a lot of people no matter where. But you don't see faces, you don't hear anybody. You hear a mumbled roar."

That's what makes the rivalry go—the people who pay for it.

Even with the hoopla of the McGwire-Sosa home-run race, some of the old-time appeals of the rivalry actually have been dissipated in the free-agent era, according to Ken Reitz. He doesn't think the Cardinals-Cubs rivalry is the same for the players as it once was.

"For the fans, yes, but not the players," he said, adding that the nucleus of the Cubs and Cardinals during his day seemed to remain from year to year, unlike today's frequent changes through free agency. "We when we went to play the Cubs, they had the same players: Williams, Hundley, Kessinger, Beckert. We had Brock, Gibson, Simmons."

The fans keep the rivalry strong through all the personnel shuffles.

"Cubs fans are some of the best fans in the world," George Altman said. "Cardinals fans are good, too. They're knowledgeable. But the Cubs fans are a little more long-suffering."

And even happier when the blessed event of a World Series ever arrives.

## "Big Lee" strides in slowly-but efficiently—for both teams

If there was one record-breaker who linked the Cubs and Cardinals in the modern era, it was the slow-gaited "Big Lee" Smith, whose 100 mph fastball of his early Cubs years was augmented by a tricky forkball a decade later with the Cardinals. All of which helped him amass a record 478 saves in a career that finally petered out after the 1997 season, 22 years after he signed his first Cubs minor league contract.

Smith, a man of ribald humor, got soured on his 1980-87 Cubs tenure toward the end. Top management didn't want him to throw a slider because he hung one to Candy Maldonado for a game-winning homer. Although his fastball was one of the game's best, he became a little predictable and hittable.

The 6-foot-6 man-mountain from rural Louisiana believed that he was regarded as the bad guy by Cubs fans, in contrast with knight-in-shining-armor Ryne Sandberg. St. Louis was more to his liking and pacing. He said he could eat dinner with his family in an area restaurant and not be bothered too much by fans.

Smith was taught the forkball by former Cubs teammate Frank DiPino in 1990 when the former came over to St. Louis from the Boston Red Sox. That helped prolong his career after the old edge was being taken off his fastball. Smith saved 160 games for the Cardinals through 1993, including a high of 47 in 1991.

Now he's mellowed about the imagined or real wrongs of the past. All old Cubs come home again, or at least it seems that way. Smith appeared at the January 1999 Cubs Convention, happily signing hundreds of autographs and posing for photos with the same fans who he once believed dissed him.

"I can't say I have any regrets about anywhere I played," said Smith, who literally has gone fishing back home in retirement. "I never thought I'd get over 400 saves or pitch that many games. I was just be happy to be a part of baseball."

Actually, both the Cardinals and Cubs can thank the ol' Rebel, Randy Hundley, for Smith's contributions. Hundley, managing the Cubs' Double-A Midland (Texas) club in the late 1970s, converted Smith to short relief.

"This man was out of his mind," Smith said of Hundley with a big chuckle. "I had more walks than any other pitcher the year before. Something just clicked. I began throwing strikes."

While Smith fought to find his control under Hundley, a brave 10-year-old kid went into the bullpen to try to catch the wild pitcher. Boy's name was Todd Hundley, Randy's son and future star catcher. He certainly got over his fear of the baseball catching Big Lee. Eventually, in the early 1990s, the two squared off as batter and pitcher.

"Todd was always a tough kid," said Smith. "The first thing he said to me when he got to the big leagues was, 'I remember when you used to pick me up by my head in Midland.' He used to drive me nuts about paying pepper with him. Todd was one of those guys who I thought would be a good catcher because he was in the dirt all the time, playing ball with us."

Two Smith traits marked both his Cubs and Cardinals tenures: that snail's pace walk in to the mound from the bullpen and mid-game naps in the trainer's room. Explain, please.

"I think the Cubbies, Cardinals and Expos still owe me money for the concessions that they made (during the slow walks)," he said. "I never claimed to be a rocket scientist or anything like that. I wanted to make sure I took the time to figure out what to do with the hitter when I got out there. I didn't want to run out to the mound and be, like, stunned, now what I am going to do? When I pitched, I took my time because I knew I wasn't going to get a second opportunity. I wanted to make sure I got it right the first time."

As for the naps, Smith said the shut-eye depended on if he had seen his opponents previously.

"If I knew what I was going to do in certain situations, I'd relax," he said. "All the pressures of the game, to get it off your mind, and then wake up, refreshed and your mind is clear about what I want to do. Not see the guy hit a home run in the third inning and say, 'Oh, God, he hit a bullet in the third inning, what am I going to do in the ninth inning?'"

Rubbing the sleep from his eyes, Big Lee knew exactly what he was going to do. More often than not with both the Cubs and Cardinals, it was say good-night for the hitters.

# 3

# Harry Caray: Pied Piper of Two Cities

**WITH coke-bottle glasses and a roundish figure,** Harry Caray was no classic matinee idol.

Didn't need to be. He was something better—a pied piper for baseball in two Midwestern cities over a span of 53 seasons. Harry Caray, formerly a poor orphan from St. Louis, was the best salesman both the Cardinals and the Cubs ever had.

Caray obviously represented the little devil in all of us. He said what he wanted about whoever he wanted, stayed up late and got up early, imbibed without paying the price in his liver, and above all, got to hold down his dream job for 53 seasons, going out "with his boots on," as he had long desired.

We would all love to be on our feet, loving what we've always loved, at age 83. That was Caray's fate. He'll never be forgotten as he towers over all other modern baseball announcers in stature and appeal.

He was first and foremost a personality in the Cubs' TV and radio booths, a man who had paid so many dues and seen so much baseball that he earned the privilege of playing himself. Near the end of his life, Caray had long since ceased to be a technically competent baseball announcer.

But anything close to perfection wasn't necessary. His personality and Arne Harris' expert direction of the telecasts carried the day. So what if he mangled names? Caray was virtually the host of a satellite-borne daily summer drama that more often than not had a downbeat ending for the heroes.

Caray's Cubs days were actually his third career incarnation as an announcer. He had made his reputation in his hometown. There may never have been a more exciting, riveting baseball announcer than Caray in his prime on KMOX-Radio and the far-flung Cardinals network.

Cardinals fans loved Caray, not only for the word pictures he painted, but also for his status as a St. Louis native who grew up a Cardinals fan long before he got behind the mike. And he wanted to announce Cardinals games because he thought the people he'd grown up listening to were boring.

One other significant fact about Harry Caray in St. Louis is that he was primarily a radio announcer for most of his 25 years (1945-1969) in St. Louis.

Regular-season Cardinals home games were never televised through most of Gussie Busch's stewardship, the exceptions during Caray's tenure being Stan Musial's farewell in 1963 and the opener at the downtown Busch Stadium in 1966. Even during the some-40 televised Cardinals road games, Caray was primarily a radio man.

He made the St. Louis baseball-announcers' job one of the biggest, if not the biggest, in the country.

"Remember, at the time my grandfather started, St. Louis was the westernmost and southernmost team," Cubs announcer Chip Caray said. "And baseball was a radio game anyway. The KMOX clear-channel signal was so strong. Even now, I can hear KMOX in Orlando (his off-season home) better than WSB in Atlanta."

Cardinals fans liked it that way, Caray being presented mostly on radio deep into the TV era. They knew what Harry looked like and didn't have to see him. But when they couldn't see the game they had to hear him.

He brought Cardinals baseball inside their homes, onto their back porches, inside their cars. And he was there every Cardinals game. He did college sports and some professional basketball games, but only after or before the baseball season. (To his great credit, he never deserted the White Sox or Cubs during the season for side ventures.)

"He was summer in St. Louis," said Terry Edelmann of St. Louis, public information director for the city's Catholic school system. Edelmann grew up listening to Caray in the 1950s. "You could walk down the street and hear him on the radio in every house," she said, describing a time before most people had air-conditioning.

"Harry painted more of a picture of a ball game on radio than any announcer I've heard," said John Ring of Galesburg, Illinois. A salesman who also hosts a sports-talk show on a local radio station, Ring grew up listening to White Sox and Cubs announcers, and chose the Cardinals as his team partly because of Harry Caray.

Harry exaggerated his calls occasionally. But when he did, it didn't take away from the truth of his reporting. If a ball hit only halfway up the pavilion screen in right field and Harry said it hit the top of the screen, well, maybe it should have hit that high.

In St. Louis, Harry invented such phrases as "It might be outta here, it could be . . . It is! A home run." On radio it worked; on TV it never did.

And then there was his signature phrase: "Holy Cow!"

His "Cubs win, Cubs win!" has often been voiced by young Chicagoans. But it pales next to "the Cardinals win, the Cardinals win, the Cardinals win!" that Caray often belted out when the Redbirds had pulled off a last-inning victory.

St. Louis fans who remember Harry have to be at least in their late 30s to have done so, and most are much older. Those memories never leave.

Pete Cooper, now one of the operators of the large manual scoreboard installed at Busch Stadium in 1997, was only 10 years old when listening in his bedroom to Harry Caray's play-by-play of a crucial Cardinals-Cubs game in July 1967. The Cubs had the tying run on first with two out and, and Cooper remembers 29 years later not just the big play that followed but also what Harry said before it.

"Harry had a prescience about it," said Cooper, also an aide to a St. Louis-area congressman. "He mentioned that (Ted) Savage was a fast guy who could come all the way around if (Al) Spangler got a hit."

Spangler did, into center field and Savage tried to score from first, only to be thrown out.

When WGN broadcast a 1994 tribute to Harry to mark his 50th anniversary in the booth, it played the entire 3 1/2-minute sequence of Musial walking up to the plate and getting his 3,000th hit against the Cubs in 1958. That segment displayed Harry doing the following:

•Never going much longer than a minute without giving the score and the inning, two immensely important pieces of information that fans who are constantly tuning in want to know right away.

•Following the ball from the moment the pitcher began his delivery until the play was over, giving the count after each pitch.

•Providing useful information about the pitcher-batter matchup, not just stats for stats' sake.

•Keeping the accomplishment of the 3,000th hit within the context of the game—Musial's double drove in a run and put the tying one in scoring position.

•Working in the fans at the right moment ("Listen to the crowd").

•Doing all of the above with enthusiasm.

Harry was a fan who always put his fellow fans first. He questioned the motives of management and players that he knew the fans were wondering about back home.

"I don't know how we lose some of these ballgames, but we do," he lamented after the Redbirds had lost a game in 1964 they should have won.

Cardinal fans still chuckle about his admonishment of Mike Shannon, then a Cardinals right fielder and now a Cardinals broadcaster, when Shannon let a pop fly fall in front of him in the final game of the 1964 season with the pennant on the line.

"C'mon, Mike, take those kind," Caray had said.

It was that kind of riding a player to bring out his best that Caray took with him to Chicago.

And for some fans, seeing him as anything but a Cardinals announcer was difficult.

"I remember the first time I saw him doing 'Take Me Out to the Ballgame' in Wrigley Field," said Cardinals fan Mary Lou Geary, a secretary for the St. Louis Catholic schools system. She had grown up listening to Caray's broadcasts from a farm in rural Missouri. "It was so emotional. I felt betrayed. I wanted to say, 'He's really still our announcer.'"

Ah, but you perhaps couldn't hold Caray back. One theory holds that maybe it was his time to move to an even bigger market at the time of his shocking firing from the Cardinals in 1969. He was a true entertainer and needed a bigger stage. Being caught up in rumors of an affair with Gussie Busch's then-daughter-in-law damaged his reputation not one iota —and actually served as the catalyst for Caray's greatest fame.

After one year in the remote baseball outpost of Oakland in 1970, Caray was hired by a struggling White Sox franchise. Given a $30,000 attendance bonus, he was charged with rekindling interest via a jerry-built network of small AM and FM stations, mostly on the fringe of the Chicago market, after the Sox had lost their 50,000-watt outlet, WMAQ-

Radio. Darned that Caray didn't pull it off. Sox attendance increased so much that management had to cancel the attendance bonus, Caray having fulfilled it and then some.

Caray truly became a wild man in the booth, firing at Sox players and manager Chuck Tanner while reveling in a growing image as the "Mayor of Rush Street." Always a night owl, Caray could extend his waking hours much better in Chicago with the active nightspots and 4 a.m. bar closings. No Chicago baseball announcer had even been so unabashed, outspoken and colorful, and he soon became bigger than the team for whom he announced. When Caray was eventually paired with Jimmy Piersall in the booth in 1977, the two conducted a nightly guerrilla theater of the air for the next five years.

The same era saw Bill Veeck take over the Sox, running the franchise on a lot of promotional momentum and very little money. Veeck and Caray were made for each other. Veeck came up with the idea of singing "Take Me Out to the Ballgame" for the seventh-inning stretch. Only Caray's voice was bad enough and his personality powerful enough to make it an institution that has survived his death.

As in St. Louis in 1969, it was Caray's time to move on to even greater fame when the Jerry Reinsdorf group took over the Sox in 1981. Caray and Reinsdorf were like oil and water, a rift that was never patched up the rest of Caray's life. But timing is everything in life. Tribune Co. had just taken over the Cubs and committed to beefing up the team's long-lagging farm system and marketing pizzazz. Caray was part of a new on-air image as the successor to longtime friend Jack Brickhouse.

The concept of Caray, announcer for the Cubs' two arch-rivals over the previous 37 years, working the North Siders' booth at first hit many Cubs fans wrong. But he made the transition seamlessly, his seventh-inning warbling immediately becoming a Wrigley Field tradition. The only caveat was Caray had to tone down his act a bit. Nervous Tribune Co. suits were concerned about his Sox image, and Cubs general manager Dallas Green laid down the ground rules to Caray: no personal stuff, but on-field failings were fair game. Caray accepted the management dictum, but didn't miss a beat in crafting an even greater profile.

Two factors boosted Caray to true superstardom.

WGN-TV became a superstation at the same time he signed on. The all-daytime home schedule made it the only game on through much of a country just at the same time millions of viewers were first signing up for cable TV. The Cubs' TV announcer was always bigger than his radio counterpart, simply because the team televised all home games starting in 1947—in contrast with the strict video ration in St. Louis—and added

60 or more road games starting in 1968. Watching the Cubs on TV was a tradition within range of the WGN signal, and now that signal could be received anywhere in the world.

Then, in 1984, the Cubs finished in first place for only the first time since 1945. Caray's frequent "Cubs win! Cubs win!" post-game cries set well with a captivated audience. The Cubs fielded a powerful, crowd-pleasing team with six players amassing 80 or more RBI each. Even though Chicago pulled a terrific *el foldo* to the San Diego Padres in the 1984 NL Championship Series, there was a huge afterglow. Interest in the Cubs was raised even higher than the level originally achieved by the Leo Durocher-era clubs of the late 1960s. That level has been virtually sustained ever since, win or lose. Wrigley Field now was established as one of Chicago's top tourist attractions, with Caray the off-key tour guide.

By now shaving at least six years off his real age in biographies, Caray didn't quite become bigger than life, but he became bigger than the players. One day in Houston Ryne Sandberg, Andre Dawson and Mark Grace all posed for a group photo with a gaggle of autograph seekers waiting. Caray suddenly poked his head out from behind the batting cage. The fans made a mad dash away from the great players to snare a Caray signature. Grace would late note that was the definitive signal of how the players ranked on the pecking order with Caray.

His 1987 stroke and several subsequent illnesses shook the city, but he always came back. The effects of the maladies and the inevitable effects of age slowed him down and contributed to a long string of on-air misidentifications and malaprops. Ryne Sandberg became Ryne Sanderson, Rafael Palmeiro became Rafael Palermo, Andre Dawson became Andre Rodgers and Sammy Sosa became Sammy Cepeda. But the only folks that seemingly were bothered were media pundits. Some suspected Caray got names wrong to generate headlines. Whatever the reason, he plowed on.

Caray obviously had a driving motivation to continue working long past retirement age. He loved baseball and hated the idea of being put out to pasture, thus the fudging on his age. When he was told by doctors to cut out traveling, he struggled for activities to fill his day when the Cubs were out of town. And, no doubt, remembering his hardscrabble boyhood, if work was offered, he would gladly take it.

Caray ended up as the ultimate dual-identity Cubs-Cardinals figure, bigger than Lou Brock, Dizzy Dean and all the others. But there's a creeping suspicion, here and among more than a few fans, that even as the fun-loving "Cubs fan, Bud man," he still had a big spot in his heart for the

Redbirds, that he never purged himself completely of his loyalty to St. Louis.

Wouldn't that have been something? A fellow rooting for both the Cubs and Cardinals? Only the likes of Harry Caray could have pulled that one off.

# 4

# Roots of the Cubs-Cardinals Rivalry

THE National League teams in Chicago and St. Louis adopted the nicknames Cubs and Cardinals shortly after the turn of the 20th century. But the rivalry between baseball teams representing those two cities has its roots in the 19th-century origins of the professional game.

Those late-1800s duels between the Chicago White Stockings and St. Louis Brown Stockings produced their share of drama as well as comedy—and featured a game that drew the most fans to any major league contest in that era. St. Louis and Chicago also battled for the championship of the baseball world in October of both 1885 and 1886.

Competition between the White Stockings and Browns (not to be confused with the later American League team) began in 1875 when both played in the National Association of Professional Baseball Players (NA), the country's first major league.

A baseball rivalry between Chicago and St. Louis was a natural complement to the geographical and economic competition they'd started after the Civil War. They were two "western" cities in a league largely based on the East Coast. And civic leaders in both towns jockeyed for bragging rights. Just five years before, the U.S. Census had shown St.

Louis with 310,864 residents, about 12,000 more than Chicago; by 1880 Chicago, rebuilding mightily after the great fire nine years before, had a half-million citizens, 150,000 more than St. Louis.

Shortly before the 1875 season opened, the *New York Times* carried this observation:

"The new St. Louis club, judging from the players engaged by the managers and the amount of capital invested, is going to make a good fight for the supremacy with its rival, the White Stockings of Chicago. The St. Louis club was not organized for the purpose of contending for the pennant so much as for becoming a permanent and formidable rival of the Chicago club."

Baseball then was played on rough-surfaced fields by men who caught the ball bare-handed. Rules prohibited a pitcher, 45 feet from the plate in a ground-level boxed area, from lifting his pitching arm above his waist, making everyone a submarine-style hurler. Batters could call for either a high or low delivery.

The NA's 1875 campaign was its fifth and final one. Its loose organizational structure was a reason many clubs had come and gone, often running out of money before they could complete their schedules. The association's inability to keep gamblers out of the ballparks often led to public skepticism that games hadn't been "on the square."

The first-ever professional baseball meeting between St. Louis and Chicago, in St. Louis's Grand Avenue Park May 6, 1875, helped ensure that both clubs could pay their expenses. It also gave gamblers plenty of business: a St. Louis newspaper listed the times that bets could be made at a local establishment which was to receive inning-by-inning results via telegraph.

A much larger than expected crowd filled all 3,000 seats in the wooden grandstand while more than twice as many other fans were allowed to stand behind roped-off areas along the field. All told, 8,251 patrons watched the Browns thrash the White Stockings 10-0.

Shutouts were rare then and labeled "Chicago games," from the whitewashing a Chicago team had suffered in 1870. St. Louis papers gleefully used the term "Chicagoed" in describing the result; the *Chicago Tribune* lamented, "Chicago is sorry she was ever rebuilt."

St. Louis edged Chicago 4-3 two days later before 8,728 spectators in St. Louis, the largest crowd for any NA game that season. The Browns and White Stockings split their 10 contests that year, each winning its home games. Both the fourth-place Browns and sixth-place White Stockings finished far behind perennial champion Boston.

Chicago, however, did have an easy time with a second team St. Louis entered in the NA that year. Known as the Red Stockings, it survived only 18 games, and lost all four it played against the White Stockings. Included in that was a 1-0 shutout Chicago gained over the Reds just five days after it had been humiliated by the Browns.

In the off-season, the presidents of the Chicago and St. Louis clubs put their competitiveness briefly aside to devise a reorganization plan for the NA that led to its rebirth as the National League the following year. "You and I can carry the day for everything we want," Chicago's William Hulbert wrote to St. Louis' Charles Fowle. St. Louis lawyer Orrick Bishop, under Hulbert's direction, wrote the NL's first constitution.

That constitution sanctified Hulbert's raiding of the champion Boston team and signing its four best players, including ace pitcher Albert Spalding, as well as versatile slugger Adrian Anson from Philadephia. That fab five transformed the White Stockings into champions of the NL's inaugural season. The third-place Browns, however, held the season series edge, 6-4, mostly because of the pitching of George Washington Bradley. He hurled all but four of the team's 577 innings, compiling a 45-19 mark (same as the Browns' record) with an earned run average of 1.23, right up there with Spalding's 47-13, 1.75.

Modern Cubs fans have been dismayed to see pitching greats Bruce Sutter and Lee Smith go to the Cardinals. A century before, St. Louis fans saw their pitching workhorse, Bradley, jump ship and don the White Stockings uniform for 1877. Since there was no reserve clause in contracts until 1879, the best players in the early days of the NL could go where they wanted, and Bradley simply took Chicago's better offer. A newspaper noted that he received "a rather hearty round of applause" when he beat his former teammates in St. Louis near the beginning of the season. But both he and his new team fared poorly in 1877. Chicago tumbled to fifth, 1 1/2 games behind fourth-place St. Louis, though the White Stockings won the season series 8-4.

For reasons never fully understood, the St. Louis club went out of business after that season while Chicago went on to win NL pennants in 1880, '81 and '82. It wouldn't be until the mid-1880s that baseball teams from Chicago and St. Louis would face each other again. A new St. Louis NL team, called the Maroons, lasted only two seasons, 1885-86, and served as batting practice for the powerful White Stockings as Chicago won the pennant in both years.

Those White Stockings, however, met a more formidable opponent from St. Louis each October in what newspapers called the "World's Championship Series." This one was a new St. Louis Browns, the perennial powerhouse of the American Association (AA), a major league that successfully challenged the NL's major league monopoly from 1882 through 1891.

Chicago's *Tribune* scoffed at the AA, calling St. Louis and its other members "a few . . . villages."

The two leagues—and their premier teams, Chicago and St. Louis —offered a complete contrast to each other. The NL didn't play on Sundays, charged 50 cents admission (about a half-day's pay for a working-man, who toiled six days and wasn't welcomed in NL parks for fear he would contaminate the higher society types the league appealed to). The NL also banned the sale of booze in the park. The AA played on Sundays, charged only 25 cents admission and sold liquor (its critics called it the "beer and whiskey league") so that workingmen could enjoy it all.

Al Spalding, the former star pitcher for the White Stockings, was now its president. An American blueblood, he'd also built a successful sporting goods business that supplied the official NL ball. Adrian "Cap" Anson, the only player still around from the White Stockings' first championship season, was the club's first baseman and manager.

The Browns' president was flamboyant German immigrant Chris von der Ahe, who'd owned a grocery-saloon just down the street from the Grand Avenue Park. He renamed the baseball grounds Sportsman's Park after declaring himself "boss president" of the Browns.

Von der Ahe often interfered with his club's performance, to the dismay of his players. Yet manager-first baseman Charley Comiskey (later owner of the American League's Chicago White Sox) still molded the Browns into four-time pennant winners, 1885-1888.

The Chicago and St. Louis clubs which met in the 1885-1886 world series also differed in style. Heavy-hitting Chicago—in its white caps and jerseys, blue pants and high white hose—often bludgeoned its opponents into submission; St. Louis—with its high brown stockings and brown-striped caps—relied more on pitching and defense. The two clubs even differed on base-running styles, the White Stockings often sliding in feet-first while the Browns went head first.

Chicago's heroes had nicknames such as "King" (slugger Mike Kelly), "Silver" (catcher Frank Flint) and "Unser Fritz" (second baseman Fred Pfeffer, who sported the league's longest handlebar mustache). St. Louis' stars were nicknamed "Tip" (outfielder Jim O'Neill), "Yank" (second baseman Billy Robinson) and "the Flying Dude" (third baseman and la-dies' man Arlie Latham). Overhand pitching by then had been allowed and some players, notably catchers, had begun wearing thin gloves, mostly to protect their palms.

The 1885 series was to be a best-of-17 affair, touring several cities besides Chicago and St. Louis. But when after five games it looked as if both clubs were going to lose money (fans in the neutral cities didn't care to attend), the clubs agreed to make Game Six the finale. They first agreed to forget about a forfeit win Chicago had gotten when Comiskey had pulled the Browns off the field to protest an umpire's call, making it two games apiece. But after St. Louis thrashed Chicago 13-4 to claim the crown, Spalding decided to count the forfeit win and declared the 1885 series a 3-3 tie, a decision most history books have accepted.

Both St. Louis and Chicago again won the pennants of their leagues in 1886. This time, von der Ahe and Spalding agreed to a best-of-seven series, the winner to take every penny of the gate receipts. The first three games were scheduled for Chicago, the next three in St. Louis and a seventh game, if needed, would be in the neutral city of Cincinnati.

Chicago blanked St. Louis 6-0 in the opener, and St. Louis won the second contest 12-0. That led some skeptics to call the games a "hippodrome," the 19th-century term for a fix. "These games are on the square," a Chicago player said in denying the charge. Chicago took the rubber game and looked forward to putting the Browns away in their home town.

However, because of injuries, Chicago had only one good starting pitcher left (the team had relied primarily on two during the season). Von der Ahe wouldn't let Spalding use a hurler he'd signed for the next season, and St. Louis used that advantage to take a three-games-to-two lead.

But going into the bottom of the eighth of Game Six, it looked as if the two teams would be Cincinnati bound for the finale. The White Stockings held a 3-0 lead. Thanks to a misjudging of a fly ball by Chicago left fielder Abner Dalrymple, the NL's best outfielder that year, the Browns rallied to tie the score. They won 4-3 in extra innings as center fielder Curt Welch danced across the plate following a wild pitch.

For six days' play that October, each of the Browns earned about $580, equal to about a full year's wages of the workingmen who'd supported the team.

Von der Ahe challenged Spalding to play the seventh game in Cincinnati anyway. Spalding responded: "Friend von der Ahe, . . . we know when we have had enough."

A deeply disappointed Spalding sold Dalyrmple and some other stars to other NL clubs and not see his team win another pennant for 20 years. The Browns would win two more AA pennants but no postseason series.

After the AA folded following the 1891 season, von der Ahe was allowed to move his Browns to the NL—without his star players, who were allowed to jump ship and happy to do so to get away from him. The Chicago-St. Louis rivalry in the 1890s, however, was a mere shadow of its former self: neither team seriously contended for the pennant and the White Stockings usually, and easily, won the season series.

"Rivalries had a tendency to disintegrate when one team becomes as bad as the Browns became," said baseball historian J. Thomas Hetrick of Pocol, Virginia, who's just published *Chris von der Ahe and His St. Louis Browns* (Scarecrow Press).

Von der Ahe sold his best players for cash to make ends meet, rarely buying or developing good athletes. The only real deal between the clubs in the 1890s was when St. Louis purchased the contract of outfielder-first baseman George Decker in 1898. He'd been a solid hitter for Chicago for six seasons but fizzled in his three months with the Browns.

Change was in the works as the century neared its end. Anson was fired as Chicago's manager after the 1897 campaign, causing the club to be referred to in print as the "Orphans," since they now were without their longtime leader. The Browns, meanwhile, almost became orphans of a different sort on Saturday, April 16, 1898. A match dropped by a fan started a fire that destroyed the grandstand of new Sportsman's Park.

Von der Ahe ordered his players to help rebuild the grandstand the next morning so that the Browns would not miss their scheduled game against Chicago. They joined tradesmen in putting up temporary seats but found themselves too pooped after the chore to play very well. Rested Chicago took advantage and pummeled St. Louis 14-1.

After yet another disastrous year, von der Ahe was forced out through a lawsuit filed by disgruntled stockholders. New St. Louis owners brought in new players for 1899, including legendary pitcher Cy Young. The Perfectos, as the St. Louis NL team of 1899 was often called in an attempt to break a losing tradition, got off to a 9-1 start and went to Chicago for an April 30 game.

It was perhaps that great beginning that prompted a record 27,489 fans to overflow the stands at Chicago's West Side Park that day. That, according to attendance stats compiled by baseball historian Robert L. Tiemann of St. Louis, was the largest crowd to ever see a major league game in the 19th Century.

"It was also the first good-weather Sunday in Chicago, which as sure to bring out a big crowd," Tiemann said.

Whatever reason, Chicago shut out St. Louis 4-0 (the term "Chicagoed" long having been discarded in newspapers). Both teams, however, were far from the top as the year ended.

As the 20th Century dawned, the NL discarded four of its 12 teams, settling on a league membership that would last for the next five decades. A St. Louis fan, remarking, "Oh what a lovely shade of Cardinal," at the sight of the team's new socks, led to the club's being renamed the Cardinals. Shortly before the Chicago club set the major league record for wins with 116 in 1906, newspapers and fans started calling it the Cubs and the little bear emblem began to appear on the uniform.

The nicknames stuck. And so has the tradition between the two teams, lasting through some lean times and blossoming into one of the best rivalries in sports history.

# 5

---

# Great Cubs Games vs. the Cardinals

## Cubs 1, Cardinals 0
### September 25, 1935, Sportsman's Park, St. Louis

**THE Cubs ensured they'd overhaul** the previously favored Gashouse Gang defending National League champions with their fabulous 21-game winning streak down the stretch in 1935.

But no win was tighter or more dramatic than the 1-0 thriller in which the slim edge in a classic pitching duel between the Cubs' Lon Warneke and the Cardinals' Paul Dean was broken up by the youngest man on the field—19-year-old Cub hometown hero Phil Cavarretta.

Gaining revenge for the taunts about his youth from the Redbird bench jockeys, Cavarretta lofted a homer onto the roof of the right-field pavilion in the second inning. That clinched at least a tie for the NL pennant and provided the winning margin for No. 19 in a row.

"We were all hepped up," Cavarretta recalled. "We were young and feisty, guys like myself, Augie Galan and Stan Hack. We felt we could do the job and made up our minds to concentrate on these games."

Paul Dean had beaten the Cubs three out of his previous four starts going into the game. "Paul beat us pretty regularly, and he was tougher on us than his brother," Cavarretta said. The younger Dean probably would have done it again had not Cavarretta performed well beyond his years.

An uncommonly large weekday mid-Depression crowd of 19,989 showed up on a dark, gray, misty day. Many attendees were Legionnaires from Illinois, Iowa, Indiana and Wisconsin—and made up a large pro-Cubs vocal rooting group. They saw Dean, the younger version of the famed Cardinals brother mound act, outdo himself against his favorite foes by setting a strikeout record starting out. Daffy fanned Galan and Billy Herman before Fred Lindstrom doubled over third. Gabby Hartnett left Lindstrom stranded by fanning, too.

Dean whiffed Frank Demaree leading off the second, just before Cavarretta came up. The pitcher specialized in high fastballs, while Cavarretta was a low-ball hitting left-hander.

"One of his fastballs must have gotten away," Cavarretta said. "I got underneath it. The Good Lord must have been on my side. I just wanted to get on base, and here I hit it out. I was on Cloud Nine going around the bases. It was the biggest hit I ever got."

Billy Jurges struck out to end the inning. Dean felt confident that by limiting the damage early, he'd give his hitters plenty of time to overcome the one-run lead. But Warneke simply stifled the Cardinals.

"Before he hurt his arm, Warneke had one of the greatest curveballs I've ever seen," Cavarretta said. "He had great location on all his pitches. He reminded me of Tom Glavine."

Nicknamed the "Arkansas Hummingbird," Warneke, who would find his way into a St. Louis uniform after another full season, mowed down his opponents until minor league callup Lynn King singled in the fourth. No other Cardinal reached until Jimmy Collins doubled with one out in the eighth. Leo Durocher, normally a popgun hitter, gave Warneke his only real scare one batter later when Galan crashed into the left field wall to flag down his long drive.

Both pitchers continued to hold firm. Warneke nailed down the victory by getting Charlie Gelbert to ground out, pinch hitter Virgil Davis to pop up, and Pepper Martin to ground out to end the game. His teammates swarmed Warneke with what the *Chicago Tribune*'s Irving Vaughan described the "die-for-dear-old-Rutgers spirit."

Cubs manager Charlie Grimm suggested his team would sweep the remaining four games of the series. The Cardinals bravely put up a front, ranging from braggadocio to hope-against-hope.

"It's hard to beat a team playing perfect baseball," Dizzy Dean, the September 26 pitcher, said. Dizzy then remembered he had won five of his previous six 1935 starts against the Cubs: "But I'm going out tomorrow and beat 'em anyway. I'm going to pitch a more than perfect game."

"They're a good, young hustling outfit and only a superhuman effort by the Cardinals will beat them," Cardinals manager Frankie Frisch said. "I'm hopeful my team, which plays best in a tight spot, will do it."

But the Cubs and right-hander Bill Lee went on to beat Dizzy Dean to clinch the pennant, and won the next day to complete the 21-game streak.

"That's still a record, especially in the month of September, when games are tough to win," said a proud Cavarretta.

The Cardinals won the final two games of the series and of the season. It was too little, too late. The veteran, confident Gashouse Gang had razzed Cavarretta's youth from the bench all year. But youth got some sweet revenge at just the right time.

## Cubs 8, Cardinals 1; Cubs 4, Cardinals 2 (doubleheader)
## September 23, 1984, Busch Stadium

A loss and a late-summer rainout spoiled a real pleasure for the Cubs: clinching their first first-place finish in 39 years against the Cardinals.

Jack Brickhouse, retired from Cubs' play-by-play for three years, was brought in for the occasion to supplement Harry Caray's "Holy Cow!" with his own trademark "Hey Hey!" for a potential clincher. But Brickhouse had to save it for September 24, 1984 in Pittsburgh as the Cubs had to settle for merely nailing down a tie for the NL East crown.

"They wouldn't let us play three today or maybe we could drink the stuff right now," Cubs manager Jim Frey said.

Limited to playing two on a hot, sun-splashed Sunday afternoon, the Cubs dropped their magic number to one by sweeping the Cardinals 8-1 and 4-2 as Steve Trout and Dennis Eckersley stymied the Cardinals. The Cubs felt a huge sense of relief after going into a week-long slump and delaying the inevitable clinching/celebration.

Southpaw Trout, putting it all together for one blessed season, mowed down St. Louis on an amazing 22 ground-ball outs in a complete game in the opener while driving in the first Cubs fun with a sacrifice fly. Trout's sacrifice and Gary "Sarge" Matthews' bases-loaded double keyed a six-run fourth.

Then Eckersley out-dueled Joaquin Andujar in Game 2 as Matthews, continuing his late-season clutch hitting in '84, slugged a two-run homer in the first inning. The Cubs turned it over to Big Lee Smith in the eighth, who nailed down the victory with a tidy save.

Trout was so effective he had just 55 pitches going into the seventh. He had the Cardinals beating the ball into the ground so expertly that the Cubs outfield recorded just one putout—a seventh-inning fly to Keith Moreland by Lonnie Smith.

"I came in here between innings," Trout said of the Cubs' clubhouse," and he (pitching coach Billy Connors, tossed out of the game in the first inning) said, 'Don't go for strikeouts. Just get the ball to sink and let Ryne (Sandberg) and (Larry) Bowa play their defense.'

"I didn't feel like I had my really good fastball, but evidently it was sinking. I can only tell by the catcher. I asked a few times if it was moving and he said, yeah, it was moving well."

Trout thus completed a fine 13-7 season that was never duplicated due to injuries and his somewhat eccentric personality. A good season by a Cubs lefty starter was a rarity indeed. Since St. Louis-area native Ken Holtzman's heyday from 1966 to 1971, Trout and Greg Hibbard (15-11 in 1993) remain the only Cubs southpaws to win as many as 10 games in a season.

Eckersley and Smith continued the fine pitching in the nightcap. Although Rick Sutcliffe was the 1984 Cubs sensation with a 16-1 record after being acquired in June, Eckersley was a tough pitcher down the stretch in his own right with an 8-3 second-half record.

Ensuring against a celebration from the thousands of Cubs fans in Busch Stadium, St. Louis police ringed the field after the sweep to protect the ballpark's new $2 million artificial surface carpet.

"We were going to jump out on the field," said Cubs fans Art Wann of Palos Hills, Illinois. Peoria resident Barb Branan suggested that Matthews should catch her if she did a swan dive from the upper deck into left field.

"I'm glad they didn't do it here," said St. Louisan Bob Hughes, wearing the 1984 AL champion Detroit Tigers' hat. "The games didn't matter to me. I just didn't want to see them tear up our AstroTurf."

The Cardinals didn't like the previous day's rainout with all the Cubs fans in town. Team officials estimated they lost $300,000 due to ticket refunds and lost concession sales.

But the Redbirds and their fans had a last laugh of sorts exactly two weeks later. Former Cardinal Leon "Bull" Durham's error on a seventh-inning ground ball enabled the Padres rally from behind and upset the Cubs in the deciding Game 5 of the National League Championship Series. The promised-land World Series berth for the Cubs would be delayed again...

## Cubs 3, Cardinals 2 (10 innings)
## September 9, 1989, Wrigley Field

The Cardinals were hard-charging and the Cubs were back on their heels. The previous day, St. Louis overcame a 7-1 deficit to beat the Cubs and cut the latter's first-place lead down to 1/2 game. And on this drizzly Saturday afternoon, the Cubs were in trouble again, trailing 2-1 going in the bottom of the eighth.

But that's why teams acquire veteran players by August 31, the deadline for setting postseason rosters. Third baseman Luis Salazar was just such a pickup for the Cubs during the last week prior to the playoff-roster deadline in a waiver deal that brought him and outfielder Marvell Wynne to the Cubs from the Padres for pitcher Calvin Schiraldi and outfielder Darrin Jackson.

"I've got pennant fever in my blood," Salazar said of his move to the surprising first-place Cubs. "This is what you want to be in, a pennant race in a tough situation."

Manager Whitey Herzog and his Cardinals wished Jim Frey, in his latest Cubs incarnation as general manager, had never made that deal.

With 37,633 on hand, first place in the NL East was about to change hands when rookie Cubs left fielder Dwight Smith, whose enjoyed some base-running misadventures, made a big turn at first on a ball hit toward Cardinals right fielder Tom Brunansky. He continued bolting toward second.

Catcher Tony Pena had sneaked behind Smith, but Brunansky didn't throw immediately. He eventually heaved a toss that sailed wide of second for an error.

"I knew he was holding the ball on me," Smith said. "It's wet, and he was standing a long way away. I figured he had to make a perfect throw. If I screw it up, I'm going to get a lot of questions for it. But if you're scared to make a mistake, then you can't win."

"I waited too long," Brunansky admitted. "I was either going to throw behind him or to second. When he broke to second he made the decision for me."

Mark Grace fanned, and Smith then advanced on an infield out. But then Salazar tied things up 2-2 with a base hit to left off an 0-and-1 pitch by reliever Dan Quisenberry.

"It was a terrible pitch," Herzog said later.

Juiced up, Salazar struck again in the bottom of the 10th after the Cubs bullpen held the Cardinals. St. Louis reliever Ken Dayley, pitching in the situation because closer Todd Worrell was sidelined due to arm trouble, walked Andre Dawson to lead off the 10th. Then Salazar slashed an outside pitch into the right field corner. Dawson pushed his sore knees beyond their capabilities to steam around third, jump into teammate Shawon Dunston's arms, and stave off the Cardinals.

"I have never forgotten that game; two crucial hits in a come-from-behind game," said Salazar, now a minor league coach in the Milwaukee Brewers organization. "I always liked hitting in the clutch. I did well my whole career."

And it has remained the biggest Cubs-Cardinals game of modern times. The confrontation remains the closest the two teams have come to dueling for first place in September since the 1930s.

## Cubs 12, Cardinals 11, "The Sandberg Game" (11 innings) June 23, 1984, Wrigley Field

Many believe this was the mother of all Cubs-Cardinals games. And in a theatrical sense it was aired on NBC-TV's "Game of the Week" with Bob Costas the announcer, while 38,079 on a beautiful Saturday afternoon provided the perfect backdrop to entertainment at its best.

Ryne Sandberg and Willie McGee stole the show, of course. Sandberg slugged his famed two successive homers off Cardinals ace reliever Bruce Sutter, while McGee hit for the cycle. Between them, the two players drove in 13 runs.

"This kind of ballgame is thrilling for everybody, the fans and the players, and it was on national television," Sandberg said later in typical understatement. "It was one of those games where strange things happen, and I think we kind of amazed ourselves with what we did today."

"I've seen a few games like this in this park," Sutter said, remembering how, as a Cub, he was the losing pitcher in a 23-22 spectacular to the Phillies in 1979.

Cubs general manager Dallas Green summed it up best for all the witnesses: "This game left me pitted out."

Sandberg and McGee, great players in their respective franchise histories, certainly enjoyed career performances. But leave it to a relative unknown to decide the contest. Backup Cubs shortstop Dave Owen singled with the bases loaded in the bottom of the 11th to decide things.

But the game had started out like a Cardinals blowout. The Cubs had struck first as the famed 1984 "Daily Double" of center fielder Bobby Dernier and second baseman Sandberg accounted for a run with a single, stolen base and another single in the first. But St. Louis routed Cubs starter Steve Trout with a six-run second, highlighted by McGee's bases-loaded triple and a single by Cardinals starter Ralph Citarella—certainly, like Owen, a trivia buff's delight when this game is recalled.

After the Cubs closed to within 7-3 in the fifth on Sandberg's groundout and Gary Matthews' RBI double, McGee slugged a two-run homer in the top of the sixth off Dickie Noles. But, amazingly, the Cubs fought back with five in their half of the inning to close to within one at 9-8. Richie Hebner's pinch-hit single accounted for one run, then Dernier collected a two-run double, followed by Sandberg's two-run single.

Both bullpens then quieted things down until the top of the ninth, when Sandberg slugged the first of his two homers off Sutter leading off to tie it at 9-9. Yet the Cubs didn't have time to enjoy the moment. The Cardinals tallied two in the top of the 10th off future Cardinal Lee Smith on McGee's double and a grounder by pinch hitter Steve Braun.

One good turn deserves another, though. Dernier walked on a close 3-and-2 pitch by Sutter with two out in the 10th. Then Sandberg homered again, making this one for the ages.

That only tied it up. Somebody had to win it. And Owen, whose brother Spike was slightly more prominent as a shortstop in the American League, had to play the hero role pinch hitting in the 11th after three walks by Dave Rucker and Jeff Lahti loaded the bases. The last non-pitcher left on the bench for the Cubs, he slapped the single to right to officially record history.

The media mobbed Sandberg. Owen sat virtually alone by his locker.

"I was glad to make contact," he said. "I was just looking for a baseball to hit. I want to help out the team—it doesn't matter when or where," he said.

Owen's career soon faded. Sandberg's and McGee's flourished, and continued to do so deep into another decade. But they'll always have one thing in common—June 23, 1984 in the Friendly Confines.

## Cubs 10, Cardinals 10
## April 12, 1965, Wrigley Field

So many times in their team's inglorious history, Cubs fans would have gladly settled for a tie. Some 19,751 in person and hundreds of thousands of WGN-TV viewers at home did just that for the 1965 home opener against the defending world champion Cardinals.

Only darkness prevented a resolution of a wild 11-inning affair that seemed more like a victory than a mere tie to the Cubs, then entering their 19th consecutive season in the National League's second division.

This game had everything—clutch hitting, great relief pitching, unbelievably bad fielding, and the major league debuts of Steve Carlton, Glenn Beckert and Billy Williams in center field.

Huh?

With no standout center fielders in spring training camp, Cubs head coach Bob Kennedy shifted Williams, normally a left or right fielder, to center. The future Hall of Famer had decent speed at the time, and Kennedy wanted to make room for Cub-turned-Cardinal-turned-Cub George Altman in left field.

"It's better than playing left," Williams said, toeing the company line. "You're in a better position to see the game. It keeps you more alert, too, and you've got to more thinking about the different things to do if the ball is hit to you.

"I'd say he adapted himself pretty well so far," Kennedy said before the opener, predicting that Williams, then 26, would develop into a solid center fielder.

Williams had to stay alert from the first pitch. Cubs starter Larry Jackson, a 24-game winner in 1964, was way off his game as the Cardinals tallied five runs in the first. Only three were earned as rookie shortstop Roberto Pena dropped the first of two popups for errors in the game.

The Cubs came back with two in the second and two in the third, including a homer by the fumble-fingered Pena, who dropped his second popup in the top of the fourth, leading to two more St. Louis runs. Pena tried to atone with a two-run double in the bottom of the fourth, cutting the lead to 7-6.

Lou Brock, who began haunting the Cubs almost immediately after his trade to the Cardinals the previous June 15, chipped in with a double and stolen base that lead to another run in the top of the six, making it 8-6 St. Louis. Julian Javier's double and Curt Flood's single added another tally in the top of the ninth.

St. Louis was one out away from a victory with Tracy Stallard—he of the Roger Maris 61st-homer fame—on the mound, having contributed four shutout innings of relief. Ron Santo walked and Altman singled. Red Schoendienst, also a rookie as a manager on this day, summoned knuckleballer Barney Schultz, a former Cub, from the bullpen to face Ernie Banks. Of course, Mr. Cub was facing a team that he had enjoyed so much success against. Another notch on his belt: Banks slugged a 2-and-2 pitch into the left-field bleachers to tie it up 9-9 as the crowd awarded Mr. Cub a standing ovation.

A scoreless 10th preceded another act of revenge by Brock—an RBI single in the top of the 11th that gave the Cardinals a 10-9 lead. But Pena, alternating his goat and hero status almost by the inning, opened the 11th with a single. He advanced to third on a passed ball and infield grounder, then scored to make it 10-10 as Santo doubled to left center.

Rookie lefty Carlton was then called in to pitch, walking Altman. Bob Purkey then was summoned, getting Banks to fly deep to center, the runners advancing. Right fielder Doug Clemens, among the players traded to the Cubs for Brock, was intentionally walked to load the bases. Could the Cubs actually pull it out?

Not when they sent up players like Vic Roznovsky to hit. A backup catcher whose only distinction was his name, Roznovsky flied to right to end the inning—and the game. With 6 p.m. closing in on an overcast early spring day and lights still 23 years in Wrigley Field's future, the umpires called the game at the four-hour, 19-minute mark. The suspended-game rule, in which official games called on account of darkness in Chicago, would be resumed at a later date.

As a result of the tied opener and another official-but-rained-out game, Williams' and Santo's games-played log for 1965 read "164" when they did not miss any contests. But the "CF" besides Williams' name soon disappeared. He was shifted to right field, where he played regularly until 1967.

# Cubs 16, Cardinals 12
## April 22, 1980, Wrigley Field

Mix in these ingredients: a freak 90-degree day in April, ineffective pitching on both sides and career days from a couple of lesser lights, and you get a football-sized score at Wrigley Field.

A 25- or 35- or even 45-run game occurs less frequently than you're led to believe in the Friendly Confines. But when it does, the orgy of runs and attendant weird events are remembered for decades.

Both Cubs and Cardinals fans got summer fever when spring was hardly underway amid the otherwise gloomy times of baseball labor strife, near-hyperinflation in the economy and the Iran hostage crisis.

"People were on the edge of their seats," said Cubs infielder Lenny Randle. "They were taking their clothes off. They were saying, 'More, more, more.' And they got it."

"You expect things to happen like this," Cardinals catcher Ted Simmons said, "when the wind blows out."

And did that wind ever blow, gusting to 22 mph, strong even for Wrigley Field. A record-high temperature for this Tuesday afternoon—a mark that still stands—was responsible for the gales.

"I've never seen a wind that strong to right field in 25 years," said Cardinals manager Ken Boyer, a longtime veteran of the Cubs-Cardinals wars.

Boyer was prescient when he proclaimed before the game, "The team that bats last may win this game."

That's exactly what happened when Cubs catcher Barry Foote rode the jet stream out to right to end the wild affair with a ninth-inning grand slam that caught the bleacher basket.

Foote's wind-aided bomb was the last of 23 Cubs hits and completed an eight-RBI day. Cubs shortstop Ivan DeJesus hit for the cycle—a single, double, triple and homer, the latter collected when he led off the bottom of the first.

The Cardinals took advantage of the wind, too, with three homers, by Bobby Bonds, Ken Reitz and pitcher Bob Forsch.

The Cards tallied two in the first, one in the second, three in the third, five in the fourth and one in the fifth to lead 12-6 at that point. But the visitors inexplicably rested at that point, giving the Cubs a chance to catch up. The Chicago bullpen trio of Bill Caudill, Dick Tidrow and Bruce Sutter pitched four shutout innings, allowing just three hits, to aid their cause.

The Cubs cut the gap to 12-9 with a three-run fifth on DeJesus triple to the vines that capped his cycle. That knocked out Forsch, who departed on a yield of 14 hits, two walks and nine runs in 4 2/3 innings. Two innings later, DeJesus got his fifth hit of the day, preceding a Bill Buckner two-run single that cut the deficit to 12-11. Then, in the eighth, Foote belted a game-tying homer to set up his game-ending dramatics.

Two walks and a pinch single by Dave Kingman, in the middle of a malingering season that punched his ticket out of Chicago, loaded the bases for Foote in the bottom of the ninth. After Jack Brickhouse finished his guttural "Hey Hey!" on WGN-TV, Cubs manager Preston Gomez and infielder-philosopher Randle could properly sum up the afternoon.

"You could have had a heart attack," Gomez said. "It was a good game for the fans but tough for the managers."

"It was the kind of game that a retired ballplayer would love to come back and pay to see," Randle said.

## Cubs 3, Cardinals 1
## July 24, 1967, Busch Stadium

Younger fans who can remember the Cubs' divisional title seasons of 1984 and 1989, and the wild, wild-card playoff ride of 1998 can't remember just how special a Cubs' foray into first place after the All-Star break was just one generation-and-a-half ago, in 1967.

Consider the facts: Chicago had just suffered through 20 consecutive seasons in the National League's second division, with just one winning (82-80 in 1963) and one .500 (77-77 in 1952) season. In 1966, the Cubs tied a team record with 103 losses, finishing 10th in a 10-team league.

But the amazing Leo Durocher-crafted revival stunned baseball in the spring and early summer of 1967—Chicago's own version of the "Summer of Love." The culmination came on a rainy Monday night in St. Louis, when the former stumblebums dared walk with the league-leading Cardinals—at least for one day.

Cubs starter Ray Culp slipped and slid on the mud-caked Busch Stadium mound, but held firm for his best performance of his only Chicago season. He beat the Cardinals on a five-hitter before 41,337. Both the Cubs and Cardinals stood atop the National League standings with identical 56-40 records.

The mud was caking on Culp's spikes amid the downpour in the sixth inning when Orlando Cepeda tallied Lou Brock with a double and moved Roger Maris, who had singled, to third with just one out. Culp's three-run lead coming into the inning was in serious jeopardy.

But Culp got catcher Tim McCarver looking with a 3-and-2 changeup, and retired Mike Shannon on a fly to left.

The umpires then called a 51-minute rain delay, but Culp, evening his record at 8-8, came back and mowed down the Cardinals for a complete game. He walked just two and fanned six.

"I just came back feeling stronger," Culp said. "I don't know why I am throwing better this half of the season, except I did have control problems early."

"I wasn't too sure he'd come out sharp," Durocher said. "I had Chuck Hartenstein and Curt Simmons ready to go. I got to admit Ray surprised me."

Durocher wasn't entirely in a good mood. He was upset that umpire Shag Crawford wouldn't let him help clean off Culp's spikes in the sixth.

"It was the most ridiculous thing I ever heard of," The Lip said. "Ray had mud two inches thick on his shoes, and all he had to clean it off was a little broken stick.

"All I wanted to do was clean his shoes with a wire brush, and the umpire said I was trying to defy him. What kind of nonsense is that? I wasn't trying to delay the game for rain. I don't care if we play in a thunderstorm, mud up to here. All I want to do is clean the guy's shoes. And they won't let me."

The soggy, muddy victory, fueled early on by Cardinals Killer Ernie Banks' run-scoring double, a bases-loaded walk and an infield out, turned out to be the last hurrah for both the Cubs and Culp for '67. The Cardinals won the next night, and within two weeks had swept the Cubs and other competitors out of the pennant race. The Cubs still finished an upbeat 87-74 in third place, their best record up to that point since their last pennant in 1945. But Culp lost his final three decisions, entered Durocher's sizable doghouse, and was practically given away to the Red Sox, where he became a solid starter over the next three seasons.

Even though Culp's departure hurt in the long run, his route-going performance in the rain helped set the tenor for the most fondly-remembered era of Cubs baseball in modern times.

# Cubs 23, Cardinals 13
# April 17, 1954, Wrigley Field

A team batting around the order in two different innings usually produces more than enough runs to win. And the 13 tallies the St. Louis Cardinals put on the Wrigley Field scoreboard April 17, 1954, certainly would have been enough to win most games.

But that baker's dozen was still 10 short of what the Cubs amassed that windy day just three games into the new season.

"I never saw anything like it before and I'll never see anything like it again," Cardinals southpaw Al Brazle told a reporter after the 23-13 Cub drubbing. Brazle gave up four hits and five runs (two unearned) in only one-third of an inning.

The game required a then-record 3 hours, 43 minutes to play, five minutes longer than a Dodgers-Giants game played two years before. The fifth inning alone—when the Cardinals scored four times and the Cubs retaliated with 10— took 58 minutes.

"Baseball is a game that can be played by children, and the Cardinals and Cubs should have let them do it today," wrote the *St. Louis Globe-Democrat*'s Jack Rice.

Hits were plentiful—20 by the Cubs and 15 by the Cardinals. So were walks. Three Chicago pitchers put nine batters on base while a half-dozen Cardinals hurlers passed 12 Cubs. In addition to all the scoring, each team left 10 men on base.

And the Cardinals, in addition to the troubles rookie outfielder Wally Moon had with windblown fly balls that were scored hits, made five errors to the Cubs' one.

The game was a see-saw affair through four innings, the Cubs jumping off to a 2-0 lead in the first when Moon misjudged Hank Sauer's pop fly with the bases loaded. But the Cardinals, using only three hits and several walks from Cubs starter Johnny Klippstein, took a 5-2 lead in the second. The Cubs pulled to within a run in their half and the Cardinals, thanks to catcher Sal Yvars' head-first steal of home, added one to take a 6-4 advantage going into the bottom of the third.

But Chicago scored five in that frame, taking the lead 7-6 on a two-run single by catcher Joe Garagiola, once a Cardinals backstop and destined to be a Cardinals broadcaster the next season. The Cubs added three more in the fourth as second baseman Red Schoendienst and third baseman Ray Jablonski both made errors and pitcher Royce Lint uncorked two wild pitches.

The fatal fifth saw the Cardinals pull to within two at 12-10. But the Cubs came back with 10 runs and put the game out of reach. In so doing they roughed up rookie Mel Wright, who'd been acquired when the Cardinals had traded popular veteran Enos Slaughter to the Yankees just days before the season began.

"The Cards got Wright for Enos, and the Cubs got him in the slaughter," wrote Rice of the *Globe-Democrat*.

Rookie right-hander Jim Brosnan, pitching his first major league game, picked up the win for lasting the final four-and-two-thirds innings. Brosnan walked three, fanned three and gave up three earned runs on six hits. He also drove in the Cubs' 13th and 14th runs with a single in that fifth-inning explosion.

The Cubs, who'd mauled the Cardinals 13-4 on opening day in St. Louis, were 2-1 after that game, the Cardinals still winless after three contests.

At season's end, the Cardinals would limp home in fifth with a 72-82 mark, eight games ahead of the seventh-place Cubs.

Moon would go on to hit .304 and garner NL Rookie of the Year honors.

The Colorado Rockies and Los Angeles Dodgers would go on to set the record for the longest 9-inning game when Colorado won 16-15 in 4 hours, 20 minutes on June 30, 1996.

## Cubs 6, Cardinals 5 (13 innings)
## August 4, 1968, Busch Stadium

Did you know Lee Elia had another accomplishment in Cubs history besides his famous bleepin', blustering tirade against the fans in 1983?

Wind the clock back 15 years, when future manager Elia was a little-used utility infielder on the Cubs. He slapped a pinch single to left with two outs in the 13th inning off reliever Joe Hoerner to enable the Cubs to sweep a three-game series with the first-place Cardinals, who had burned up the National League most of the summer of '68.

An SRO crowd of 47,445 turned out on the hot Sunday afternoon for the unveiling of the $40,000 Stan Musial statue outside the ballpark. Many of Musial's teammates from his original Cardinals team in 1941 showed up, taking their old positions on the field. Musial, the only one dressed in a uniform, was introduced last to the roar of the crowd.

But the Cubs spoiled the afternoon for the Musial loyalists, reaching the almost unhittable Bob Gibson for five runs in an 11-inning stint. Included was a seventh-inning homer by longtime Gibson and Cardinals tormentor Billy Williams and a game-tying homer by slap-hitting Al Spangler leading off the ninth that tied the game 4-4.

The Cubs took the lead 5-4 in the 11th on a Don Kessinger single off Gibson, but the Cardinals tied it in the bottom of the inning off Cubs reliever Bill Stoneman on a double by Johnny Edwards and single by Lou Brock.

Ex-Cardinal Jack Lamabe, traded to the Cubs earlier in the season, held off St. Louis in the 12th. Then, in the top of the 13th, Randy Hundley, in the middle of a record-setting 160-games-caught season, summoned enough energy to beat out a bunt. Jim Hickman sacrificed, but Spangler fanned. Elia was the almost the last man off the bench. He had just 1 hit in 14 at bats for an .071 average. But he collected his first National League RBI on the single, sending the Cubs fans into a frenzy.

"I remember Leo Durocher telling me, 'For crying out loud, swing at a strike,'" Elia said.

St. Louis let Chicago have its fun. The victory was the 23rd in the last 30 games for the Cubs, whose hitters had buried the team in June with a 48-inning scoreless streak. But the Cubs remained 13 games behind the pace-setting Redbirds in second place, and the latter would go on to stop the challengers' forward momentum and any pretense of a late-season miracle 10 days later at Wrigley Field.

# 6

## Great Cardinals Games vs. the Cubs

### Cardinals 4, Cubs 3
### July 25, 1967, Busch Stadium

**THE Cubs had tied the Cardinals** for first place with a 56-40 record the night before, on July 24, 1967. Could baseball's surprise team of the season keep it going?

Not likely. The *"El Birdos"* Cardinals were gathering momentum that would take them all the way to the World Series title. The Cubs would just turn out to be the first obstacle they'd overcome with elan.

As the nation nervously watched reports of rioting in Detroit, more the 46,876 fans, about 8,000 less than a full house, settled into one-year-old Busch Memorial Stadium to first watch a pre-game home-run hitting contest between the clubs. The Cubs had always out-homered the Cardinals when it counted, but this time Orlando Cepeda smacked three over the distant outfield walls while Ron Santo, Ernie Banks and Billy Williams each hit two. Cepeda, en route to a Most Valuable Player season, pocketed $100.

Among the spectators was Stephen Conkovich of Granite City, Illinois, just across the Mississippi River from St. Louis. He was pictured wearing two different straw hats, depending on which team was up, the band on one proclaiming "Beat the Cards" while the other displayed the call "Beat the Cubs." He told a reporter he was really a Cardinals fan but didn't want to offend his friends who were Cubs fans.

Many Cubs fans were in attendance at the game, hoping for a continuation of their impossible-dream campaign. And with Bob Gibson on the shelf after a line drive off the bat of Pittsburgh's Roberto Clemente had broken his leg just 10 days before, many had reason to believe a Cubs leap from tenth to first was possible.

The Cubs brought southpaw Rob Gardner out of the bullpen to start this one against right-hander Ray Washburn. Cubs manager Leo Durocher wanted to take advantage of the Cardinals' 15-16 mark against lefties. Cardinals' manager Red Schoendienst countered by moving second baseman Julian Javier to the second spot in the lineup to get another right-handed bat up in the first inning.

Washburn held the Cubs scoreless for the first five frames and the Cardinals sent Gardner to the showers after only eight pitches. Leadoff man Lou Brock hit the first one back up the middle and Javier aced the next one into left. A one-out single by Cepeda, hitting .344 with 71 RBI at that moment, drove home the first run and chased Gardner. Well-traveled Bob Shaw came on to be greeted by Mike Shannon's RBI single. Tim McCarver then drove in Cepeda with a double.

Shaw settled down and lasted through the sixth. But Cardinals speed and a judgment error by Don Kessinger gave the Redbirds a fourth run in the fourth. With Brock on second and one out, Roger Maris grounded to the Cubs shortstop who threw too late to get Brock going to third, from where he scored on Cepeda's sacrifice fly.

"You throw to first and they don't get the run," Durocher said later. "I thought I could get him," Kessinger said afterwards, acknowledging that he'd thrown the ball to the wrong base.

But the Cubs didn't roll over. A single by Santo, a triple by Banks and a single by right fielder Clarence Jones made it 4-2 in the sixth, where it remained until the Cubs' ninth.

Banks opened with a single off Washburn, who then handed the ball to reliever Hal Woodeshick. The lefty, however, hit pinch-hitter Ted Savage and gave way to righty Ron Willis. Willis relieved and retired the next two hitters but then ran the count full to pinch hitter Al Spangler. That let both baserunners take off with the pitch.

Then 10-year-old Pete Cooper, now one of the operators of the large manual scoreboard installed at Busch Stadium in 1997, was listening in his bedroom to Harry Caray's play-by-play on radio station KMOX; 29 years later he remembered not just the next call but the prelude to it.

"Harry had a prescience about it," said Cooper, an aide to a congressman from the St. Louis area. "He mentioned that Savage was a fast guy who could come all the way around if Spangler got a hit."

Spangler did, into center field. Banks easily scored. Savage tore for third.

A St. Louis-area native, Savage had played with the Cardinals the past two seasons and had been so dismayed on learning he'd been traded to the Cubs in mid-May that he smashed his ukulele in the clubhouse. But he played a lot of right field for Durocher in 1967. Now a manager in the Cardinals' marketing department, he recalled what happened on the Spangler hit.

"I remember running for third base and (Cubs coach Pete) Reiser didn't give me the come-on sign until it was too late," Savage recalled three decades later. "I think I could have picked up a couple more steps."

Nevertheless, Savage still thought he had a chance to score as he tore around third and headed in with the tying run. Bobby Tolan, playing center field for an injured Curt Flood, fired the ball to relay man Javier. He wheeled and rifled it to catcher Tim McCarver blocking the plate. Here was Caray's broadcast call:

"He's gonna try . . . here's the relay . . . he is—out at the plate! Cardinals win, 4-3! Holy Cow!"

Savage, tagged across the face by McCarver, remained in the dugout for a long time. "I figured I had let the team down," he said while recreating the incident.

Tolan said afterward he'd fired the ball in to keep Spangler from taking second and hadn't figured Savage would try to score. "If he scores on the play, it's a helluva play. But if he doesn't it's a dumb play."

Caray's broadcast noted that it took a near-perfect set of relays to nail Savage. And Reiser told the press later he'd probably send in more runners like that, adding that that was how the Cubs had gotten as far as they had.

Gutsy base-running and equally daring defense had given the Cardinals the win and first place again. They would never lose it again in 1967.

## Cardinals 2, Cubs 1 (10 innings)
## June 22, 1985, Busch Stadium

What a difference a new player like Curt Ford can make. The 1985 Cardinals discovered that throughout the season.

It was the loss of one player, however—closer Bruce Sutter—that supposedly spelled doom for the Redbirds long before the season began. Shortly after he'd set the NL record with 45 saves in 1984, Sutter took a better offer from media magnate Ted Turner and joined his Atlanta Braves.

The leading sports publications predicted the Cardinals would finish last in their division in 1985.

But the nucleus of the world champion Cardinals from just three seasons past was still there. General manager Joe McDonald added slugger Jack Clark through a deal with the Giants in February. Jack the Ripper, with both his slashing, line-drive hits and towering home runs, drove in the jack-rabbits in front of him.

One of those speedsters was Vince Coleman, who'd been brought up in mid-April because the club was temporarily short of outfielders through injuries. Coleman stole every base in sight and stayed in the starting lineup.

Manager Whitey Herzog had quickly scrapped the plan to use Neil Allen as the closer, soon going to a bullpen by committee. Whether it was Jeff Lahti, Ken Dayley, Bill Campbell or Ricky Horton, they got the job done. The Redbirds had struggled the first few weeks of the season, but by Memorial Day were over .500.

The Cubs, meanwhile, seemed in great shape for a run at a second straight divisional title, relying on the veterans that had won for them in 1984. As the season neared its one-third mark, the Chicago owned a 34-19 record.

But a plague of injuries—to both pitchers and everyday players—set in. So did bad play by those who took the field. The Cardinals swept the Cubs in a three-game set in Wrigley Field June 14-16, extending the Cubs' losing streak to five and knocking them out of first place behind the Montreal Expos.

When the Cubs came to St. Louis the following weekend, their losing steak had reached nine games and they had dropped to fourth. But they were only two games behind the Expos. The second-place Cardinals, meanwhile, were 36-27 and only a half game out of the lead.

The Cardinals won the Friday night game, keeping pace with the Expos and keeping Cubs fans as blue as their apparel.

That Chicago team was without left fielder Gary Matthews, center fielder Bob Dernier and catcher Jody Davis, all out with injuries. Davey Lopes, the former Dodgers second baseman, started in center field for the Saturday night game and batted cleanup.

Before 49,231 paying fans in the seats, the two clubs battled through four scoreless innings. While Chicago runs were scarce, Cub baserunners weren't. Cardinals starter Bob Forsch walked batters in each inning but pitched out of jams.

Cubs starter Rick Sutcliffe, meanwhile, overpowered the Cardinals for the first three, not letting any ball get out of the infield. He even struck out Tom Herr, Clark and Andy Van Slyke in succession.

The Redbirds batted for 20 minutes in their fourth but didn't score, Vince Coleman's intimidating presence on the bases being the reason. After Coleman singled to open the inning, Sutcliffe threw five times to keep him close, then another five times—with four bluffed throws—after Coleman had moved to second on an infield single by fellow greyhound Willie McGee.

The Cubs finally scored in the fifth. Forsch hit catcher Steve Lake then walked Ryne Sandberg and Lopes with two out. After making a bad pitch to Leon Durham, Forsch was yanked for southpaw Horton, who walked in a run on a 3-and-2 count.

In their seventh, the Cardinals knotted the score when Van Slyke doubled and was chased home by a single from pinch-hitter Steve Braun. Braun, only 2-for-17 off the bench before that, moved to second base on the throw home but was stranded.

Dayley followed a shaky Horton to the mound in the ninth and kept the Cubs at bay. Big Lee Smith did the same to the Cardinals.

Dayley needed some defensive help from Coleman in the 10th. Lopes led off with a hit into left-center and was intent on making it a double. The Cardinals' swift center fielder, who would finish second in assists by outfielders that season, gained one there as his strong throw nailed Lopes at second base.

Ozzie Smith led off the Cardinals 10th with a single and moved to second on a wild pitch by Lee Smith. One out later he was still there and Herzog looked down his bench for someone to hit for Dayley.

The only remaining left-handed batter was Curt Ford, a 24-year-old outfielder brought up earlier that week from the Triple-A team in Louisville, where he'd been hitting .280. Herzog had determined that Ford was the best offensive player of those available for short-term help. That week Ford had sat on the bench and watched his new teammates win three of four.

But now he strode to the plate with Herzog's encouragement. He watched the first two pitches go by, then swung at the third as Smith broke for third.

A line drive leaped off his bat and toward right fielder Keith Moreland, who charged it and unleashed a throw toward the plate. But Smith was there long before it was. He and Coleman gave each other a leaping high-five as the Cardinals mobbed their newest member after he'd touched first base.

Coleman gave Ford a vigorous head rub while others patted him on the back.

"I will cherish this moment the rest of my life," Ford told Rob Rains of the *St. Louis Globe-Democrat* after the game.

The Cardinals and their fans cherished the moment long into that night. The win, coupled with Montreal's loss to the third-place Mets, gave the Cardinals undisputed possession of first place for the first time that season. St. Louis ended up outlasting the Mets in a riveting NL East race that went down to the last week of the season.

Curt Ford? He knew he'd be up only for a short time. He went six-for-12, mostly as a pinch-hitter, in 1985. He'd see more playing time over the next two seasons, particularly in 1987, when he batted .285 in 89 games for the NL champion Cardinals. He then hit .304 in that year's World Series before finishing his career in 1990 with the Philadelphia Phillies.

## Cardinals 9, Cubs 2
## September 27, 1942, Sportsman's Park, St. Louis

The 30,000 fans who went to Sportsman's Park on a sunny but chilly final day of the 1942 season realized they were seeing history in several ways.

The youthful Cardinals, whose average age of 26 was below that of everyone else in the league, had turned the tables on the Brooklyn Dodgers over the past two months. On August 6, the Cardinals were 10 games behind the Dodgers; five weeks later, the Redbirds had the lead and clung to it on the last weekend.

Going into a doubleheader with the Cubs that would close out that season—necessitated by a rainout the day before—St. Louis had won 41 of its last 50. Its 104 wins, however, were only one better than Brooklyn's total. The Dodgers would play a single game, so fans knew the two clubs could end tied and be forced to settle the issue in a first-ever best-of-three playoff.

But while the excursion to the ballpark might have provided a few hours of enjoyment, it couldn't hide news of World War II raging in both Europe and Asia. That day's *St. Louis Post-Dispatch* had carried news of government plans to ration gasoline beginning "about November 22." Owners of private vehicles would be allowed four gallons a week and be required to drive no faster than 35 mph in a nation that hadn't yet added the term interstate highway to its vocabulary. A front-page article told reader how much in armaments their household scrap iron would produce.

Those who watched the major leagues closely also wondered what the future of baseball would be next season, and beyond. The military draft had taken few front-line ballplayers during the first full year of America's participation in WWII, but that was to change.

Still, the sports sections trumpeted the importance of the twin bill. Cubs manager Jimmy Wilson, a former Cardinal catcher in the Gashouse Gang era of the 1930s, had chosen Lon Warneke and Claude Passeau to pitch. Just a few weeks before, the pair had beaten the Cardinals in a doubleheader in Chicago.

Cardinals manager Billy Southworth was countering in the opener with lefty Ernie White, a disappointment until late in the season. Rookie sensation Johnny Beazley, already a 20-game winner, would be ready for the nightcap.

One other good piece of news for the Cardinals was that veteran center fielder Terry Moore would return to the lineup for the first time in more than two weeks after a leg injury. Moore had cautioned teammates not to talk pennant until the club had clinched it.

"A festive air prevailed at the doubleheader," the *St. Louis Globe-Democrat* observed. "Many of the spectators shivering in the costlier grand stand box seats could not help envying the bleacherites who were more comfortable in the sunshine," it noted.

Blake Harper, who ran the ballpark concessions then, said it was the "eatinest and drinkenest" crowd to ever attend a game. The throng consumed 5,000 gallons of coffee and 4,000 pounds of hot dogs.

White went through the Cubs order 1-2-3 in each of the first three innings, but the Cardinals couldn't score off Warneke either. In the Chicago fourth, leadoff man Stan Hack singled and scored with two outs on a single by center fielder Don Dallessandro.

If the locals had begun to worry, their heroes relieved their fears in the home half of the fifth. Third baseman Whitey Kurowski led off with a single and went to third on an error. Pitcher White then tied the game with a single. It " . . . gave the big crowd its first chance to show enthusiasm, a chance of which the fans took full advantage," W.J. McGoogan of the *Post-Dispatch* reported.

A sacrifice moved both runners to second and third. Moore, celebrating his return to the lineup with three hits in the opener, drove both in with a single. He later scored the fourth and final run of the inning on a force out.

The Cubs countered with a run in their seventh to make it 4-2, but the Cardinals hit them in the bottom half with four more runs. For good measure, St. Louis added a run in the eighth for a 9-2 bulge.

White retired the final six in order. The last out was a fly ball to Stan Musial in left. As Musial—third in the batting race that year and labeled in print "the rookie of the year" before there was such a formal award—squeezed it, the fans erupted in the moderate way that was a hallmark of the war era.

"A few brash souls wearing straw hats lost no time in sailing them out on the field and others followed suit with felt fedoras and homburgs, but the celebration ended almost as quickly as it started," the *Globe-Democrat* noted.

Cardinals players carried White off the field on their shoulders. The two clubs fielded their bench players for the nightcap, former home-run king Jimmie Foxx holding down first base for the Cubs in that one. The Cardinals, behind a complete game by Johnny Beazley for his 21st win, took that one for good measure 4-1 and finished two games ahead of the Dodgers.

The postgame revelry also was subdued. St. Louis still observed strict blue laws in those days, which kept taverns closed on Sundays. Fans who wanted to celebrate with a drink went across the Mississippi River to East St. Louis where no laws restricted the saloons' Sunday hours.

"There were large crowds on downtown (St. Louis) streets but no great demonstration," the *Globe-Democrat* reported.

The Cardinals would go on to lose the first game of the World Series, then upended the Yankees in four straight.

## Cardinals 8, Cubs 7 (20 innings) August 28, 1930, Wrigley Field

The Cardinals have on several occasions pulled off the late-season surge that brings a team from down in the standings to the pennant. They did it in different decades, the dawn of the 1930s being one of them.

On August 1, 1930, the Redbirds were in fourth place, one game under .500, 11 games behind the league-leading Brooklyn Dodgers and nine games behind the second-place Cubs. Four weeks later, as the Cardinals and Cubs prepared for a four-game showdown in Wrigley Field, the still fourth-place St. Louisans trailed the now first-place Cubs by 6 1/2 games and were only 1 1/2 games out of second.

The Cubs were far from worried, though. They'd just whipped Pittsburgh, with burly outfielder Hack Wilson hitting his 43rd and 44th homers, already tying, then breaking, the NL record set just the previous year by Philadelphia's Chuck Klein.

Perhaps the most startling news coming from Chicago on August 28, however, was that a local "television radio station" had broadcast pictures to 200 receiver sets strategically placed throughout the city by a company financing the experiment.

"A good many thousand Chicago radio enthusiasts are ready to testify today that television—the broadcasting of motion pictures through the air by radio—is an accomplished fact and a commercially profitable form of amusement of the future," wrote the *St. Louis Post-Dispatch*'s "motion picture critic" H.H. Niemeyer, who'd seen it.

For now, however, baseball fans would follow their game mostly by reading about it the many daily newspapers in each major league city or by attending games since some team owners still forbade radio broadcasts. This was the first year of the Depression, but attendance was up in almost every NL city. The Cubs, the first NL team to draw more than 1 million fans in a season in 1927, were about to do it again for the fourth straight year.

Maybe it was the offense that was luring fans at the dawn of what would be America's toughest economic times. Hitting had become epidemic and runs were plentiful. "The guns of summer," as the *Sports Encyclopedia: Baseball*, called that year, produced in 1930 the climax of a decade-long offensive crescendo that would see the NL's collective batting average reach a staggering .303. George Fisher, a 31-year-old Cardinals reserve outfielder who hadn't played in the big leagues since 1924 and had never hit above .261, was batting .385 in late August and listed among the leaders.

Grizzled veteran Burleigh Grimes started for the Cardinals on August 28 against Pat Malone, that season the Cubs' best pitcher since he'd win 20 and be the only one to have an earned run average under 4.00. While 20,000 fans settled in, the Cardinals went down in order in their first while the Cubs blew a two- on, no-out situation in theirs. The Cardinals broke the ice right away in the next inning when cleanup hitter Jim Bottomley poled a home run into the right- field bleachers, which wouldn't have decorative ivy planted on its walls for another seven years.

Sunny Jim, as the Cardinals first baseman was called, also accounted for the second run as he drove in Sparky Adams with a sacrifice fly in the fourth.

Bottomley figured yet again in the Cardinals' scoring in the sixth. With one out, he was drilled by a Malone pitch, most probably retaliation for Grimes having hit Chicago shortstop Woody English the previous inning. There were no umpire warnings then; Malone then drilled George Fisher. Both baserunners scored, however, when right fielder George Watkins doubled and catcher Jimmy Wilson singled, making it 5-0 St. Louis.

But no lead was safe that year. With two out in their seventh, the Cubs finally reached Grimes as English doubled in a runner from first. Cubs right fielder Kiki Cuyler doubled him home and eventually scored on a ground out, cutting it to 5-3.

Grimes gave way to Jim Lindsey and the Cubs tied the game in their eighth on a one-out double by second baseman Clarence (Footsie) Blair. Blair, a 30-year-old player who'd finally made the majors just the year before, then ran the Cubs out of the inning by continuing on to third and being tagged out.

When neither team scored in the ninth, fans settled back for what would extra innings. Long extra innings, but filled with excitement and an incredible pitching performance for that season.

Right-hander Sylvester Johnson, who'd broken in with the Detroit Tigers in 1922, had retired the Cubs in the ninth and continued to mow them down for the next five innings. Meanwhile, the Cardinals could do little until they pushed over a pair of runs against Bob Osborn in the 15th. Johnson capped the scoring with an RBI single.

But the Cubs, with the shadows lengthening, weren't ready to call it a day. They scored two in their half of the inning and had runners on first and second with two out when English lined a vicious smash down the first-base line. J. Roy Stockton, covering the game for the *Post-Dispatch*, described what happened:

"It looked like a sure base hit, and (runner) Lester Bell took one look and dashed for third and home. But Jim Bottomley put all he had into a desperate lunge. Jim barely reached the ball with his head-first dive, but it stuck in his glove. Jim fell in a heap on the ground, rolled over and looked for (pitcher) Johnson at first base. Sylvester wasn't there. He didn't expect Sunny Jim to come up with that ball. He was standing on the pitching rubber. He thought he had pitched seven innings in vain and that the Cubs had won . . . But fortunately Bell was trotting toward the plate, and Bottomley, flat in the dust, had the presence of mind to throw to the plate. It wasn't much of a throw, but Jimmy Wilson finally gathered it in and dived to tag Bell before he could get home."

From there, Osborn and Johnson continuing to retire the opposition until St. Louis third baseman Andy High line a single just out of Hack Wilson's reach in center field to drive in the go-ahead run from second in the 20th. The Cubs got catcher Gabby Hartnett as far as second but didn't score.

Johnson pitched 12 innings, allowing nine hits, one walk and nine strikeouts in finishing his own victory. Osborn went the last nine for the Cubs, walking two and fanning five.

The headlines which proclaimed the great St. Louis victory and advancement in the pennant race got sour as the Cubs wiped a 5-0 deficit and won the next day 9-8. The Chicagoans, with Wilson's help, also pounded the Redbirds 16-4 in Saturday's game.

But with 47,000 both in the stands and roped off on the sidelines watching, the Cardinals took the final game of the season series between the two clubs Sunday 8-3.

Two weeks later the Cardinals would take the league lead and end the season in first, two games ahead of the Cubs.

## Cardinals 8, Cubs 6 (10)
## August 19, 1998, Wrigley Field

Sammy Sosa preferred to talk about the pennant race in which his Cubs competed while the Cardinals' Mark McGwire didn't want to discuss the home run race in which both he and Sosa were dueling until someone reached 50.

But the rest of the nation had already begun to pay more attention to those two players' chase for Roger Maris' single-season home run record than what the Cubs or Cardinals were doing in the standings. Going into the Cards-Cubs game August 19, 1998, at Wrigley Field, McGwire and Sosa were tied with 47 apiece.

Fans who'd long ago bought their tickets for the two-game series hadn't expected anything more than the usual Cards-Cubs clash. But they'd shown up the night before hoping to see history in the making, only to be disappointed as neither player hit one over the vines in a Cubs' 4-1 win.

The finale was in a "sun-sweet afternoon," as the *New York Times'* Ira Berkow called it. Berkow was one of the numerous media from outside Chicago and St. Louis who were suddenly following the pursuit of home run history.

The second-place Cubs were 69-56 and 8 1/2 games behind Houston but still hopeful for a post-season berth, probably as the wild card team. The 60-64 Cardinals were eight games behind the Cubs and had never been in contention.

Right off the bat it promised to be a different kind of game than the pitching-oriented contest the night before, when both Sosa and McGwire went hitless. With one out in the first, the Cardinals' Brian Jordan doubled off Mark Clark. McGwire brought the crowd to its feet as he flied deep to left. Ray Lankford followed with a single that gave the Cardinals the lead and then scored the team's second run as both John Mabry and recent acquisition Fernando Tatis singled.

Kent Bottenfield, a former Cub, started for St. Louis and retired the Cubs in the first. But in the second he ran into trouble. Henry Rodriguez walked and third baseman Jose Hernandez belted one out to tie the score.

Home runs by the leaders was what the crowd wanted, and it almost got its wish in the third. With two out, Sosa belted one that everyone thought would leave the park—particularly Sosa, who jogged down the first-base line as he admired it. But it hit three feet from the top of the wall, and left fielder Mabry's clean throw to second beat Sosa by so great a margin that he didn't even slide.

Meanwhile, the Cardinals continued to sit on their two runs as the Cubs came up in their fourth. Rodriguez's home run, his 31st, gave the Cubs a 4-2 lead.

Finally, in the fifth, Cubs fans had something to really shout about. With two out and Mickey Morandini on base, Sosa picked on Bottenfield's first pitch and lined it into the left-field bleachers. Cub partisans among the 39,689 jammed into Wrigley began chanting "Sammy, Sammy!" McGwire stood expressionless in his position at first base as Sosa rounded it and touched them all.

Sosa, who with 20 homers in June had barged his way onto McGwire's solo flight for the record, now had the lead. Just as importantly, the Cubs had a seemingly insurmountable 6-2 advantage.

But this was Wrigley Field and the moribund Cardinals came right back. They scored one run in the sixth the way some of the Cardinals pennant teams of the decade before had: with three singles, only one of them leaving the infield, and a passed ball.

The much-maligned John Frascatore, in the midst of a truly roller-coaster season, followed Bottenfield and retired the Cubs in order in their sixth. Then it was time for the Cardinals, who would go on to lead the league in homers for the first time since 1944, to show some muscle. Pinch hitter Delino DeShields hit a two-run homer in the seventh to bring the Cardinals within a run.

Rick Croushore put two on in the seventh but Lance Painter came on to bail him out. Sosa had been one of those baserunners, reaching on a walk. Asked later what they had talked about during that encounter, Sosa jokingly said it had been about building a golf course together and calling it Home Run Trot.

Big Mac came up with one out and nobody on in the eighth, 58 minutes after Sosa had homered. McGwire would average a home run ever 7.27 times at bat this season but had gone a week and 20 at-bats without one. Right-hander Matt Karchner ran the count to 3-and-1. McGwire belted his next pitch well beyond where Sammy had hit his, and onto Waveland Avenue, some 430 feet from the plate.

He'd tied Sammy. But more importantly, he'd tied the game, 6-6.

The bullpen had been the big reason for the Cardinals' bad record. That relief corps would blow more than 30 late-inning leads. But on this day, in a park that often broke a pitcher's heart, the Cardinal hurlers who'd coughed up so much now gave the Cubs nothing but fits. Painter got the first batter in the eighth then watched as Jeff Brantley got the last two hitters.

Cubs left-hander Terry Mullholland, meanwhile, got through the ninth unscathed and stayed in for the 10th after the Cubs had failed in bottom of the ninth against Juan Acevedo.

The wind was blowing in. McGwire came up with one out and took the two first pitches off the plate inside. Mullholland came in with one about belt high and well over the plate. The left-hander had not intended to give the big slugger anything good to hit, but got the pitch in the wrong location.

Cardinals broadcaster Mike Shannon made this call over KMOX radio: "He's trying to untie it here. Swing and there it is—into center field. Did he get enough? Forty-nine! He hit it to dead straight-away center, and there's a new leader in the clubhouse, Big Mac."

In the WGN-TV booth, Cubs broadcaster Chip Caray made this observation: "Sosa hit 48 and it woke Big Mac up."

The rest of the Cardinals would stay that way, too. Lankford, a left-handed hitter, blasted the next pitch from Mullholland into the left-field bleachers. Then the Cardinals put their trust in Acevedo.

Unlike fans in some cities, who left after what they thought was McGwire's last at-bat, the faithful in Wrigley Field hung on for the bottom of the inning. After all, Sosa would bat second.

But after Acevedo got the first batter, he disposed of Sosa easily by running a 1-and-2 pitch in on his hands; Sosa tried to check his swing but tapped back to the mound.

In the true spirit of Cardinals-Cubs game in Wrigley, the Cubs then loaded the bases on Acevedo, who threatened to make it even closer by missing with the first three pitches to Cubs second baseman Manny Alexander.

But Acevedo, a Chicago native, induced Alexander to pop up to McGwire. The Cardinals slugger squeezed it, then indulged in the new celebration rite of tapping fists with his teammates.

Afterwards, McGwire, still saying the real home run chase would begin when someone reached 50, gave the media these thoughts about the Cardinals-Cubs rivalry: "I've never been associated with a major league team that had so much excitement in a series here and in St. Louis. Last year I didn't get the gist of it. I wish the stadium was bigger so we could get more Cardinals fans in here. It would be outstanding to play 81 games here."

The next night against the Mets McGwire would reach 50, en route to his record-breaking 70. Sosa would never be far behind.

The Cubs would qualify for the wild-card spot only after beating San Francisco in a one-game playoff after the regular season. Then they'd lose to the Braves.

Acevedo would fill the Cardinals' need for a closer over the last month and a half, saving 15 in 16 tries, as the Cardinals finished a distant third.

## Cardinals 6, Cubs 4
## May 18, 1973, Wrigley Field

On May 17-18, 1973, the Cardinals-Cubs series in Wrigley Field could easily have been billed a David and Goliath matchup.

The Cardinals came to town with a 9-23 record, baseball's worst, largely the result of losing 12 of their first 13. The Cubs, meanwhile, had won seven straight, and their 21-13 mark put them three games up on the second-place Mets.

Neither Cardinals manager Red Schoendienst nor any of his players had panicked through that first miserable month, confident that things would start to come their way. The only change Schoendienst had made to a starting lineup featuring both veterans Lou Brock and Joe Torre as well as rookies Ken Reitz and Mike Tyson was to bench disappointing shortstop Ray Busse and play several others in hopes that one of them could fill the job permanently.

Cubs skipper Whitey Lockman, on the other hand, was watching Ron Santo, Glen Beckert, Billy Williams, Randy Hundley and Ferguson Jenkins again set the pace for a largely veteran team. Beckert entered that series with a 23-game hitting streak.

*Chicago Tribune* beat writer George Langford reminded Schoendienst before the first game of the series that his club would be facing the hottest team in the National League.

"Heck, we're hot, too, we've won one in a row," the Redhead quipped.

And the Cardinals, behind the brilliant pitching of starter Alan Foster and reliever Rich Folkers, had gone on to nip the Cubs 3-1 despite Beckert's two hits.

That winning streak tied the Cardinals' longest of the season thus far. But the next morning the thermometer hit a record low 37 degrees for the date, and the Cubs appeared to have chilled the Cardinals by taking a 2-0 lead after two.

But this was to be a see-saw affair. In the Cardinals third, Tyson, taking over that day at shortstop, a position he would hold for the rest of the season, slapped a leadoff single and moved to second when pitcher Jim Bibby drew a walk off Cubs starter Milt Pappas.

Brock then doubled in St. Louis' first run. Tim McCarver, subbing for Torre after the first baseman had injured his leg trying to score earlier, tallied the tying run with a sacrifice fly. Catcher Ted Simmons ended Pappas' day by hitting a triple to give the Cardinals a 3-2 lead. Simmons would go 4-for-5 against the Cubs that day and raise his three-season career mark against them to .377.

But Hundley launched a two-run homer in the home half to send Bibby to the showers and allow the Cubs to retake the lead, which they held going into the seventh.

Third baseman Reitz, who'd been struggling, stained Larry Gura's scoreless pitching line since he'd relieved Pappas by leading off with a homer to left. Reitz said later he didn't think he'd hit it hard enough to get out.

In the bottom half of the inning, Reitz showed one of the reasons broadcaster Mike Shannon would nickname him "the Zamboni machine." The Cubs loaded the bases with one out. Santo smacked the ball to Reitz, who started a 5-2-3 double play to end the threat.

"The Cardinals had shown they could play under the gun after all," wrote the *St. Louis Globe-Democrat*'s Jack Herman.

It stayed tied until the Cardinals' ninth, when leadoff man Reitz reached on an error by Don Kessinger, who'd just been inserted at shortstop for defensive reasons. Dwain Anderson ran for him. Tyson, trying unsuccessfully to bunt, then laced a single.

"At this point, the Cubs outsmarted themselves," wrote Neal Russo of the *St. Louis Post-Dispatch*. "They put on that special bunt play in which infielders are moving all over the place."

Ed Crosby smacked a single past Beckert, who was moving to cover second, and the Cardinals had the lead. Brock and right-fielder Luis Melendez followed with singles for another run.

Folkers again came out of the bullpen, again with a two-run lead. After retiring the first two he gave up a single to Beckert, who earlier had hit in his 25th consecutive game. Williams flied out to Brock, but Folkers admitted later that the Cubs' left fielder hadn't missed tying the game by much.

The Cubs resumed their winning ways the next night as Beckert brought his hitting streak to a conclusion at 26 games. But the Cardinals, despite seeing their modest three-game win streak snapped two nights later, went on to win eight straight and 13 of 14.

On July 4, the first-place Cubs had a 49-34 record and a six-game lead over the second-place Cardinals. The Cubs then folded while the resurgent Cardinals kept after them. On the day before the All-Star Game break, St. Louis edged into first place ahead of Chicago.

But after ace Bob Gibson injured himself trying to get back into first base in a crucial August series in New York, the Cards also began a slide. At season's end, they were 81-81, a game-and-a-half behind the Mets while the Cubs stumbled home in fifth at 77-84.

## Cardinals 2, Cubs 1 (10 innings)
## September 14, 1969, Busch Stadium

The 1969 season hadn't been a good one for the Cardinals. The defending NL champs had been preseason picks to finish first in the new Eastern Division created that year by expansion. But they'd stumbled out of the gate, and even by the time Cardinals broadcaster Harry Caray had started singing "The Cardinals are coming, tra-la, tra-la" in August, the gap was too much.

Still, some fans who symbolically buried a Cardinals casket the second week of September were criticized for giving up when the Redbirds still had a mathematical chance of winning. That weekend, September 12-14, the fourth-place Cardinals were to host the slumping Cubs, then take on the amazing, first-place New York Mets.

For the Cubs, their dream-come-true season was fast becoming a nightmare as they prepared for the opener of the three-game set in St. Louis. Just one week before they'd been in first place, five games ahead of New York. But since then the Cubs had lost eight straight while the Mets had gone 8-1 to move into first by two games over Chicago. Two of those victories had been over the Cubs the previous Monday and Tuesday.

Cubs manager Leo Durocher tried a little psychological strategy on his team. The Cardinals, he told them, were the team they needed to beat to get back in it. After all, the Cardinals, not the once lowly Mets, were the team the Cubs had set their sights on when the season began.

That approach worked Friday as the Cubs whipped the Cardinals, breaking the losing streak. But the Mets had won two that night over Pittsburgh by identical 1-0 scores and had picked up yet another half-game over the Cubs.

On Saturday, the Cardinals routed their rivals while the Mets again won, upping their lead over the fading Chicagoans to 3 1/2 games.

Sunday afternoon's contest at Busch had a World Series atmosphere to it, one newspaper reporter observed. More than 44,000 were in the stands to watch the Redbirds' Bob Gibson, 17-11, go against the Cubs' Ken Holtzman, 16-10. Holtzman, who'd grown up in the St. Louis suburb of University City, had thrown a no-hitter just a few weeks previously against the Atlanta Braves. But he'd been only 3-9 against his hometown team since joining the Cubs three years before.

The Cardinals seemed determined to put Holtzman and the Cubs away early. With one out in the first, Curt Flood drew a walk and scored on Julian Javier's double.

Meanwhile, Gibson was just as focused on keeping the Cubs in misery, retiring the first seven batters. In the fourth it looked like he might have pitched out of a jam by striking out Ernie Banks with runners on first and third and one out. But Jimmie Hall, one of nine Cubs center fielders that year, doubled to tie the game.

Holtzman was already in the groove. Gibson, however, was on the verge of losing it. He pulled a muscle trying to beat out a ground ball that shortstop Don Kessinger briefly fumbled in the fourth. He'd also come to realize that he didn't have his overpowering fastball or hard slider that day.

"If I tried (to throw hard) it was a fat pitch. So I took something off the slider and it kind of surprised them," Gibson told Ed Wilks of the *St. Louis Post-Dispatch* after the game.

Gibby's softer slider was put to the test the rest of the day. In the fifth, he fanned Ron Santo with Billy Williams on second and two out.

And in the ninth he made 28 pitches in foiling a Cubs scoring chance. Each of the first three hitters in that frame ran a full count, with two of them eventually being retired while the third, Jim Hickman, singled. With two out, Holtzman got his second hit of the day, moving Hickman to second base. But Don Kessinger grounded out.

Meanwhile, about that time, the Cubs noticed on the scoreboard that the Mets had finally lost, ending their 10-game winning streak. The deficit was down to three games. A win here and . . .

The Cardinals, who'd managed six hits and four walks off Holtzman for the first nine innings, still found it tied 1-1 as they came to bat in the bottom of the 10th. Holtzman returned to the mound. An admittedly tired Gibson, who'd already made 158 pitches, led off—and grounded out.

Gibson said later that he told Brock while he stepped to the plate: "I need a run, you so-and-so."

Brock, 0-for-4 that day, had 11 homers but hadn't hit one since July 16. Holtzman wanted to just show him a high curve but got it closer to the plate than he'd hoped.

"It was a curve that first was up and in, then up and away—over the fence in right field," wrote the *Post-Dispatch*'s Wilks. Holtzman stood on the mound, hands on his hips, as Brock ran the bases, the animated Cardinal on the right-field scoreboard echoing the fans' joy.

"A disconsolate group of Cubs . . . looked downhearted as they slowly walked off the field to their gloomy clubhouse," wrote Harry Mitauer of the *St. Louis Globe-Democrat*, who'd been covering the sports scene for that paper since the early 1930s.

But there was no gloom in the Cardinals clubhouse.

Brock laughed as he described what he'd been expecting from Holtzman. "Was I guessing?" he said to the press. "No. He got me on fastballs the other times."

Hope is a necessary part of a baseball player's and fan's makeup. But the next night, the Mets quickly put aside any thoughts of a miracle Cardinals pennant-race comeback. Despite striking out 19 times against Steve Carlton, the Miracle Mets used a pair of two-run homers by Ron Swoboda to win 4-3. The Cubs, meanwhile, continued their losing ways as time quickly ran out on their season.

## Cardinals 5, Cubs 3
## September 17, 1996, Busch Stadium

Cardinals and Cubs fans had long yearned to see both their clubs fighting for something other than rivalry bragging rights late in the season. The last time both teams had any shot at a playoff berth at the same time in September was in 1996.

But by default, some might argue. Since the two teams had last battled for first place of the Eastern Division, in September 1989, the National League had created a third division. Three first-place teams and a wild card in each league created the make-believe pennant race St. Louis and Chicago found themselves in as the Cubs came to Busch Stadium on September 17.

The 80-70 Cardinals, with the fifth-best record in the National League, nevertheless led its new Central Division by 2 1/2 games over the Houston Astros.

The Cardinals were run by a group of local financiers and perpetual baseball fans who'd bought the club from the Anheuser-Busch brewery the previous October. The team had plenty of new faces—power pitchers Andy Benes and Todd Stottlemyre as well as bashers Gary Gaetti and Ron Gant-along with real grass replacing the artificial turf in Busch Stadium and a catchy marketing slogan: "Baseball Like It Oughtta Be." They were in the driver's seat mainly because of their 29-11 record against NL Central foes.

The Cubs, with Ryne Sandberg coming out of retirement to join many of the same faces that had made a run for the title in 1995, trailed the Redbirds by five games. They were competing for a chance at the World Series this late in the season despite their 74-74 record.

Even some knowledgeable observers wondered about it all. " . . . the Cubs have looked like Elmer Fudd attempting to fool Bugs Bunny as their bid to join the race collapsed repeatedly with missed opportunities," wrote *Chicago Tribune* reporter Mike Kiley as the series began.

But the 29,612 who paid their way into Busch Stadium for the opener of the three-game set enjoyed it for what it was supposed to be, a series with something at stake. The Cubs-Cardinals rivalry had been particularly competitive in '96 at 5-5 going into the series.

Frank Castillo took his 7-15 record and 5.09 ERA to the mound for the Cubs against Donovan Osborne's 12-9, 3.54. Castillo actually outpitched Osborne in the first three innings, giving up only one hit and facing the minimum number of hitters. Osborne retired the side in order only once in the first four frames, but pitched his way out of each jam.

In the fourth, shortstop Ozzie Smith, about to call it quits after 15 seasons in a Cardinals uniform, doubled to lead off the inning. He took third on Ray Lankford's fly out to right and scored when Ron Gant beat out an infield single. But the Cardinals, through a single and a stolen base by cleanup man Brian Jordan, had runners at second and third with one but failed to score as Castillo fanned Gaetti and Dmitri Young.

The Cubs tied the game in their sixth as Sandberg doubled and came in on catcher Scott Servais' two-out single.

Smith prevented the Cubs from taking the lead in their seventh when he threw Rey Sanchez out at the plate trying to score from third on a ground ball with one out. Except for their fourth inning, however, the Cardinals continued to draw blanks against Castillo. In his two previous outings Castillo had given up 17 hits and nine runs in seven-and-a-third innings.

The Cubs wasted no time taking the lead in the eighth. Mark Grace led off with a single and Sandberg followed with a home run to left field. For the Cardinals, that wasted opportunity in the fourth looked all the more important.

But this was a year in which the Cardinals could come back, especially against their Central Division cousins. Light-hitting Mike Gallego, another ex-Oakland Athletic brought over to the Cardinals by manager Tony La Russa, began the Cardinals eighth with with a single to left. Royce Clayton, batting for a disappointed Osborne, flied out. That concluded the line on Castillo as Cubs skipper Jim Riggleman brought in lefty Bob Patterson to face Smith.

Now batting from the right side, Smith smacked a triple down the right field line, closing the gap to 3-2. Patterson stayed in against lefty swinger Ray Lankford and gave up another triple, also down the right-field line, tying the game.

Turk Wendell replaced Patterson. He got the first man he faced, Ron Gant, to ground out to Sandberg as Lankford held third.

That brought up right fielder Brian Jordan, the team's leading RBI man with 97. He later would remark that the excitement the fans had created helped him. On a 1-and-1 count, he hammered a 384-foot home run to left.

Jordan would later tell Cardinals broadcaster Mike Shannon in the "Star of the Game" on KMOX radio: "Actually, I was just thinking just put the, uh, ball in play. I was just looking to hit a single and I would have been happy. But, uh, I just swung hard and it went a long way."

Another ex-Oakland star, Dennis Eckersley, came on to retire the first Cub hitter in the ninth before surrendering a single to pinch hitter Scott Bullett. LaRussa summoned yet another of his former Athletic players, southpaw Rick Honneycutt, to go against dangerous lefty hitter Brian McRae. McRae grounded to third as the runner went to second.

That brought LaRussa once more to the mound, calling for T.J. Mathews, who at that point had prevented 86 percent of his inherited runners from scoring, best in the league. (Mathews the next season would go to Oakland as part of the deal that brought Mark McGwire to St. Louis.) The Cubs countered with lefty pinch hitter Robin Jennings, who flied deep to Jordan.

"It takes games like this to win pennants," Smith said as the Cardinals came out on the field to congratulate themselves and the fans hung on to see the eighth-inning triples and Jordan's homer one more time on the right-field replay board.

The next night the Cardinals won by the same 5-3 score after jumping off to a 4-0 lead. In the series finale, the two clubs engaged in a fifth-inning bench-clearing brawl. Cardinals catcher Tom Pagnozzi, who'd been in the middle of the fracas, sent everyone home with a RBI single in the 13th against a five-man infield.

The Cardinals clinched the Central Division title the next week, then blew a three-game-to-one lead in the NL Championship Series against Atlanta.

## Cardinals 11, Cubs 8
## September 8, 1989, Wrigley Field

The second weekend of September 1989 gave Cardinals and Cubs fans something they'd rarely seen—both clubs competing for first place after Labor Day and playing each other. The last time that had happened was 1945 (unless one wanted to count the tarnished race of 1973 and make allowances for their September 1969 meetings after the Cubs had blown a big lead).

Whitey Herzog's Cardinals had rebounded for a disastrous 1988, when the defending NL champs had tumbled to fifth place. But late in that season Herzog had sacrificed southpaw John Tudor, both one of his and the fans' favorites, to bring needed power in first baseman Pedro Guerrero over from the Dodgers.

Guerrero provided a solid bat all year and some needed leadership in the dugout. Entering the series in Chicago he was hitting .311 with 98 RBI.

Meanwhile, under hunch-playing manager Don Zimmer, the Cubs had a wild time of things in 1989, thanks in part to the addition of Mitch "Wild Thing" Williams, the lefty reliever who always kept batters loose. The year before with Texas, Williams had given up only 48 hits in 67 innings while striking out 61, but had also walked 47 batters.

In 1989 he was just as spectacular—and wild— while bringing 31 saves to the weekend with the Cardinals.

The Cubs had gotten out of the gate with a flourish and had taken over first place from Montreal in early August. A month later, however, they saw the Cardinals come to town only 1 1/2 games behind.

Lefty Joe Magrane, leading the league in wins at that point with 18, started against Paul Kilgus. Magrane had pitched well in Wrigley and had even shut the Cubs out there earlier in the season. But Cubs second baseman Ryne Sandberg made sure he wouldn't again as he hit a solo home run off the tall, erudite Magrane with one out in the first.

The Cardinals came right back to tie the game in the second as catcher Tony Pena doubled home second baseman Jose Oquendo. But Chicago regained the lead on an RBI single by catcher Joe Girardi. The Cubs increased it to 5-1 in the third as nine men went to the plate, capped by another RBI single by Girardi. That finished Magrane's day.

John Costello took over in the fourth and promptly gave up a single to leadoff man Jerome Walton, destined for that season's rookie of the year award. Sandberg followed with his second homer of the game—and his 29th for the year as the Cubs now seemed to cruise with a 7-1 advantage.

Among the 35,231 who packed Wrigley, some Cubs fans were heard to chant "Sweep, sweep!" The Cardinals had good reason to worry. They'd never come back that year from a deficit larger than three runs and weren't the kind of club that could depend on pulverizing their opponents.

But leadoff man Vince Coleman, who'd hit the only homer thus far in the campaign, popped one over the wall in the fifth and gave an inkling of what was to follow. Still, that made it only 7-2, and the Cubs came to bat intent on scoring for the fifth straight frame.

Costello, who'd started off so shakily, limited Chicago to a hit and a walk over the next two innings. Entering the seventh, it was still 7-2. But then Zimmer made a mistake in handling his pitcher. Southpaw Kilgus, who had been largely ineffective in 1989, had not started a game in many weeks. Despite that fact, Zimmer tried to stretch out Kilgus beyond the sixth instead of patting him on the back and thanking him for a good afternoon's work as he sent him to the showers.

Todd Zeile batted for Costello and singled in the seventh off a tiring Kilgus. Coleman followed with a single. Shortstop Ozzie Smith doubled, scoring Zeile and chasing Kilgus. Smith said later he'd considered stopping at first to prevent the Cubs from walking Guerrero, already two for two. But Cubs manager Don Zimmer had new hurler Les Lancaster pitch to Guerrero, and the Pedro smacked a single that scored both runners. Guerrero then moved up on an error by shortstop Shawon Dunston and closed out the rally by scoring on a single by Jose Oquendo. The Cardinals had jumped back into a game in which they had been left for dead.

After Harry Caray led the crowd in "Take Me Out To The Ballgame," the Cubs' Vance Law looked like he'd provided the needed momentum breaker with a sacrifice fly to make it 8-6 Chicago. Then the rains came and halted things for 44 minutes. Cardinals fans fretted. But the skies cleared.

The Wild Thing was warming up when Coleman reached on a single off Law's glove at third and Smith walked. Williams replaced Paul Assenmacher on the mound as Guerrero limbered up in the on-deck circle.

While Guerrero was hot, Williams was not. He hadn't saved a game since August 17. The last time he'd pitched, three days before, he'd given up a game-winning homer on an 0-and-2 pitch to the Mets' Juan Samuel.

Guerrero didn't allow any suspense to develop. He went the other way with Williams' first pitch and put it five rows deep in the right field bleachers to give St. Louis a 9-8 lead. Guerrero had been cheerleading when the team had been down by six runs. Guerrero had said to them: "This game isn't over. Boys, don't give up."

Third baseman Terry Pendleton later said, "I don't think that anyone wanted to let him down after all he'd done for us this season." He backed up his words. After Williams walked the next hitter, Tom Brunansky, Pendleton also homered, extending the lead to 11-8.

Dan Quisenberry, who'd started his career under Herzog's direction in Kansas City 10 years before, stifled the Cubs over the last two innings. The Cardinals were only a half-game from the top.

But that's as close to the prize as they would get in 1989. The Cubs won the next two games, starting their final push to the NL East title.

## Cardinals 5, Cubs 4
## July 28, 1974, Wrigley Field

Cardinals catcher Ted Simmons was never one to back away from a confrontation. The scrappy catcher could mix it up with the best of them —opposing players, umpires and even enemy fans.

Most importantly, though, Simmons usually let his bat speak loudest, and had done so consistently in his first three seasons as the Cardinals' starting backstop. He'd hit a solid .300 in 1971, 1972 and 1973.

But Simmons was in a 2-for-32 slump as he and the Cardinals came to Chicago the last weekend of July 1974, and his batting average was barely above .250. The Cardinals, too, had recently gone through their own bad times, losing 13 of 14 right before the All-Star Game and dropping out of first place.

But a 5-1 spurt starting right before and continuing right after the break, including a win over the Cubs in the first game of the series, had drawn the Cardinals to within a game of .500. It also put them within three games of the first-place Phillies, who were atop a weak Eastern Division.

Simmons had contributed two hits in that Saturday opener, a 3-2 Cardinals win before 29,000. Now in the Sunday matchup, he was catching right-hander Sonny Siebert. The last-place Cubs countered with a young Steve Stone, both his Cy Young Award and color-analyst role on WGN telecasts far in the future.

Another good crowd of 30,425 witnessed a scoreless game for the first four innings. In the fifth, Simmons, the runner at first, broke up a sure double play with a stand-up block on Cubs' second baseman Billy Grabarkewitz. As Cubs manager Jim Marshall came out to argue with the umpire, Simmons, while running off the field, got an earful from a fan in the fourth row of the grandstand.

Simmons related later to *St. Louis Post-Dispatch* sports editor Bob Broeg that that particular fan had been heckling him in Wrigley Field ever since he'd come up to the majors. " . . . he's, oh, maybe 35 to 40, usually well-dressed . . . he delights in letting me have it and at times I let him have it right back," Simmons said later.

One inning later Simmons would do just that—with his bat. Trailing 1-0, the Cardinals put two men on for Simmons. He got a fastball away and drove it over the right-field wall for a three-run homer, his 13th of the season, that gave the Cardinals the lead.

"When I hit the home run, I gagged him," Simmons said after the game of his adversary in the stands.

In the bottom half of that inning, Simmons had to quickly change roles and become peacemaker. Siebert threw one high and tight to Billy Williams. The veteran left fielder, who had spent most of his 14 full Cubs seasons tormenting the Cardinals, started toward the mound, convinced Siebert had thrown at him. Siebert walked off the mound and toward the plate. Both benches emptied.

Simmons, however, got between batter and pitcher, appealing to Williams to get mad at him because he'd called for the pitch. Why, Simmmons asked Williams, would the Cardinals want to rile the great hitter when they had a 3-1 lead?

It prevented a brawl, but not a rally. Williams got back in the box and smacked a single. Andre Thornton followed with a hit. Cardinals left-hander Rich Folkers came out of the bullpen to face Cubs center fielder Rick Monday, who slugged a three-run homer deep into the right-field bleachers to put the Cubs back on top 4-3.

The Cardinals continued to hit Chicago pitching—six hits off Stone in a little over five innings and five hits off reliever Oscar Zamora in a little less than two—but only managed to tie the score in the eighth on three singles and a sacrifice fly.

Simmons again came to the rescue in the bottom of the eighth, throwing out pinch runner Matt Alexander trying to steal. Reliever Al Hrabosky, developing his reputation as the "Mad Hungarian" (and the lifelong enmity of Cubs fans), took care of the other two in that frame by striking them out.

In the Redbirds' ninth, second baseman Ted Sizemore, not known for his power, got a pitch up around the letters from Cubs southpaw Ken Frailing and drove it out of the park to give St. Louis a 5-4 lead. Five years later Sizemore would wear Cubs pinstripes, but for now he was a St. Louis hero.

When Hrabosky gave up a hit to the first man he faced in the ninth, manager Red Schoendienst summoned hard-throwing Mike Garman, who fanned Grabarkewitz, then got pinch hitter Chris Ward to pop up.

But pinch hitter Jose Cardenal singled and dangerous rookie Bill Madlock, with two already, stepped to the plate. Madlock popped a foul that first baseman Joe Torre tried to track down. But Torre had trouble with the late-afternoon sun, stumbled and dropped it.

Steadying himself, Garman then got Cardenal to hit a high hopper to Ken Reitz, and the sure-handed third baseman got a forceout to end the game.

Simmons, with his four hits, raised his average to .266 — and .500 against the Cubs for the season.

The next day the Cards would complete a three-game sweep before nearly 19,000. The three games would draw 78,000—nearly 8 percent of the Cubs' total attendance that year.

The Cardinals used the series as a springboard to re-entering the NL East race, one they would lose at the wire to the Pirates when the Cubs would blow a 4-0 lead against the Buccos in the final game of the season.

# 7

# Great Cubs Player Performances vs. the Cardinals

## Don Cardwell's no-hitter
## May 15, 1960, Wrigley Field

**"WATCH it...There's a drive on the line** to left field, C'mon, Moose . . . He did it! He did it! Moryn made a fabulous catch . . . It's a no-hitter, a no-hitter . . . And what a catch that Moryn made! Oh, brother, what a catch he made!"

— Jack Brickhouse, WGN-TV, May 15, 1960

What are the odds of pitching a no-hitter? 1,000-to-1? 100,000-to-1?

They're astronomical, and for future inclusion in the no-hitter list in the Hall of Fame, you need great stuff and a lotta luck. Chicago's Don Cardwell had both in the gathering twilight of May 15, 1960 in the only no-hitter ever pitched in a Cubs-Cardinals game.

Adding to Cardwell's distinction was his status as the only pitcher ever to throw a no-hitter in his first start with his new team after being traded. The hard-throwing North Carolinian came over from the Phillies just two days previously in a deal for Cubs second baseman Tony Taylor.

Cardwell will forever be linked with two other interesting baseball characters in his hitless gem. Joe Cunningham, who would go on to serve the Cardinals in community-relations roles, was all set to ruin his no hitter with a low liner to left with two out in the ninth when . . . otherwise lumbering Cubs left fielder Moose Moryn, charging in at his own version of Warp 9, made a dip-glove catch by snatching the ball virtually off a tall blade of grass.

Moryn's catch, ending the second game of a doubleheader, touched off a celebration normally reserved for World Series triumphs. More than 5,000 happy fans poured onto the field, mobbing Cardwell as he was being interviewed on TV and radio immediately after the game.

It's all preserved for posterity. The eighth and ninth innings, along with the postgame hoopla, comprises the oldest sports videotape known to exist. So many countless hours of great games that were taped and then discarded somehow—including the White Sox's American League pennant clincher, aired on September 22, 1959 on WGN-TV, and the Sox's subsequent World Series—last ever played in Chicago-broadcast both on WGN-TV and Chicago's NBC affiliate, WMAQ-TV.

St. Louis fans never saw the Cardwell game on TV. KPLR-TV broadcast only the first game of the doubleheader. So the lucky ones were the hundreds of thousands of homebound fans within the 75-mile range of WGN's signal in these pre-game cable days. The original telecast was aired in color in the first season of tinted WGN baseball broadcasts, but recorded in black and white.

Countless fans have told Cardwell himself that they attended the game. Actual attendance at the doubleheader was 33,543, a huge crowd by the Cubs' 1960 standards.

The no-hitter provides constant grist for conversation for Cardwell in his rounds as a car dealer in Winston-Salem, N.C. But if you wind the clock back almost 40 years, he hardly expected to be facing Cunningham at Wrigley Field with a no-hitter on the line. He used an automotive term to describe his reaction to the trade on May 13, just after the then-24-year-old thought he had established himself in the Phillies rotation.

"It was like a sticker shock, because it was on a Friday," Cardwell recalled. "We had just gotten in early in the morning from a road trip, and I was supposed to pitch against Cincinnati that night. I got a call early in the morning and they said they want you in Chicago today."

Cardwell dutifully arrived in town, and Cubs manager Lou Boudreau slotted him to pitch immediately in the second game of May 15's doubleheader. The pitcher was on edge waiting to take the mound.

"You're a little nervous, since it is your first start. You get a little edgy," he said. Cardwell even expressed his feelings to National League president Warren Giles in the dugout just before he took the mound. "He told me, 'I never felt quite so nervous before. I wish I was out there this minute,'" Giles told Jack Brickhouse during a postgame TV interview.

Boudreau and the Cubs needed a quality Cardwell start desperately. Even by Cubs standards, the team had floundered at the start of the 1960 season with a 6-13 record coming into the four-game weekend series with the Cardinals. Beginning an era of utter management confusion, Cubs owner P.K. Wrigley 11 days earlier had arranged a unique "trade" — Cubs manager Charlie Grimm, long in the tooth in his third tenure in the Wrigley Field dugout, changed jobs with WGN-Radio baseball color analyst Boudreau. Broadcasters like Larry Dierker have come down from the booth to manage, but never were swapped one-for-one for the previous manager.

The Cardinals treated the folks watching on TV back home to a 6-1 victory in Game 1 as Ken Boyer slugged two homers and Larry Jackson hurled a four-hitter. That was cause for celebration in St. Louis. The Cardinals had lost their previous 13 road games starting off the 1960 season, the main reason for their 9-15 record coming into the doubleheader.

Determined to use his fastball as the afternoon shadows began to creep across the infield, Cardwell mastered the Cardinals from the start. Cardwell had thrown the heater in his warmups; coach Elvin Tappe reported he had a swollen hand from catching him on the side. Cardwell walked the second batter he faced, Alex Grammas, on a close 3-and-2 pitch, but the rest of the lineup went down in order. With the shadows reducing visibility, the Cardinals were also fooled through Cardwell's empty-handed windup, in which he would go through his motion without the ball, placing the ball in his glove at the last moment before release.

Ernie Banks provided Cardwell all the runs he needed with a two-run homer in the sixth to make the score 3-0 after the Cubs had broken the scoreless duel in the fifth on an infield forceout against Cardinals starter Lindy McDaniel.

By now fans in back of the dugout were starting to keep track of the outs. They'd vocally let the pitcher know. Cardwell couldn't block them out.

"When you came off the mound into the dugout, people were sitting awfully close," he said. "In the seventh and eighth, these people were getting more vocal about the game. But the players didn't say much. I just sat on the bench and concentrated on what I was going to do."

Cardwell had retired 20 in a row by the time Cubs second baseman Jerry Kindall made a great stop to his right, handling a tricky hop to throw out the Cardinals' Darryl Spencer to lead off the eighth. The right-hander then retired Leon (Daddy Wags) Wagner on a grounder to first baseman Ed Bouchee.

Pinch-hitting for Curt Flood next was Stan Musial, who came into the 1960 season with a lifetime average of .337, but was hitting just .264 at that moment. By now the crowd was roaring on every pitch. Musial broke up two budding no-hitters in 1959 and 1960, but Cardwell fanned him on four pitches.

"Strike three! Holy mackerel!" Vince Lloyd screamed on WGN-TV.

Musial later said he barely saw Cardwell's pitches.

"I just swung at the sound," he said. "This guy had great stuff. I never saw anything like it."

Viewers at home couldn't wait for the action to resume. They didn't have to. In 1960, between-inning breaks were just one minute, enough for only one TV commercial. By this time, Oklahoma Oil Co.'s message of putting a tiger in your tank, complete with a tiger strolling through a gas station in the last commercial prior to the top of the ninth, couldn't have sold too much petrol to the excited, hitless gem-anticipating fans.

Carl Sawatski pinch hit for catcher Hal Smith leading off the ninth. He put a charge into a 1-and-2 Cardwell fastball, sending a liner deep toward the right field wall. George Altman backpedaled and tracked it down one-handed, his back brushing up against the wall. "Caught by Altman. Oh brother!" Brickhouse intoned on video. "Whooo, man!"

Few could have realized Altman's challenge. "In Wrigley Field, late in the day, you have problems seeing the ball in right field," he said. "That's what you practice for. You have instincts for where the ball would be. There was some tension, you want to make sure your teammate gets the no-hitter. At that point, you feel you'd run through a brick wall to help him."

Did Cardwell believe Sawatski's drive was going to bang off the wall, or worse?

"Nah. I knew it wasn't going to make it," Cardwell said, laughing. "A lot of times as a pitcher, you tell how well a ball is hit. The ball just didn't sound like it had enough carry to it. When George got back to the warning track, I said, 'OK, that man is out.'"

George Crowe then pinch hit for Cardinals starter Lindy McDaniel. Like Musial, he was experienced breaking up no-hitters, slugging a homer to ruin Cubs pitcher Warren Hacker's 1955 bid in Milwaukee. Crowe slashed a 2-and-1 pitch to right center, where center fielder Richie Ashburn tracked it down. Two out.

Joe Cunningham was the last barrier between Cardwell and all-time fame. The Wrigley Field throng rose to its feet as one mass of cheering humanity.

"Del (Rice) put down one finger (fastball), and that's all I was thinking about, one finger," Cardwell said.

Fastball, outside. Ball one. Foul ball into the screen, 1-and-1. Inside, 2-and-1. Another fastball, high and inside, 3-and-1. Next a borderline inside pitch. Other umpires might have called ball four, but Tony Venzon thought otherwise. Cunningham argued to no avail. "I got pretty upset," he said. "I usually didn't get that upset."

Cardwell then went for the clincher.

"I made a good pitch," he said. "The ball was sinking, going down and away from Joe. He went right out after it, made contact with it."

"I just hit the ball where it was pitched," Cunningham said. "I thought it was a base hit when I hit it."

The crowd groaned as the liner apparently headed for a safe landing in front of left fielder Moose Moryn. The closest spectators in the Cubs bullpen didn't think Moryn had a shot. All the way across the field, Altman just hoped Moryn could get to the ball.

"I never saw Moose drop a ball," he said. "Moose was a pretty good outfielder (despite his lack of speed)."

It may have been mind over matter for Moryn. Ernie Banks had heard the left fielder act psyched up on the bench a few minutes earlier.

"I thought Moose was going to get it," Banks said, and not because he had a good view from his vantage point at shortstop. "Moose was really excited about the whole thing. He knew it was a no-hitter. He reached inside of himself and did more. He was so inspired. We all wanted to do more."

Moryn dropped his glove. He snared his prize. Triumphantly, he held up his glove for all to see as he continued running toward the infield and his suddenly-celebrating teammates.

"Moose, bless his heart, made a great catch coming in," Cardwell said. "He got a good jump on the ball."

After the game, Moryn said, "If I'd have missed that last catch, I'd have been begging for an error," he said.

Thousands poured out of the box seats or lowered themselves down the 10-foot ivy-covered walls from the bleachers. Seeing the mass of humanity, Altman shifted into high gear.

"I was pretty quick then and made a beeline for the dugout," he said.

But Cardwell couldn't escape so quickly.

"My main concern was to get into the clubhouse, to get off the field," he said. "You see all the people coming out of the stands. You knew the clubhouse was down in the left-field corner. Knowing I had baseball spikes on, I didn't want to spike anyone coming off the field, even though they were happy and elated about being there to see the no-hitter."

But first Cardwell had to submit to a postgame TV interview with Lloyd near the third-base dugout, amid the pushy, happy mob. A cordon of Andy Frain ushers could hardly keep the well-wishers back. Arne Harris, then a young assistant director, screamed at the crowd to give his interview quarry some room. Somehow Lloyd managed to get the gasping Cardwell to talk for five minutes.

"I don't know what to say. I'm just lucky," Cardwell told Lloyd.

"What were you thinking about when they sent in Musial?" Lloyd asked.

"I was scared. He's always hit me so good," the pitcher replied.

"What about Cunningham?" Lloyd queried.

"He's too tough to pitch to. He's too rough," Cardwell said.

The crowd pushed in closer. "I'm going to have to get out of here," Cardwell said. "I want to be sure this guy has a real good convoy of ushers. Don, I'm a little afraid to let loose of you right now," Lloyd said. "Let me go, I'm going to get hurt here," Cardwell said, signing off as he was hustled down the line to the safety of the clubhouse as the crowd surged with him down the third-base line. Lloyd then pulled his mike closer and found plenty of slack. An exuberant fan had snapped the cord.

Warren Giles, in town to present Banks his 1959 Most Valuable Player trophy between games, was pleased with the fans' demonstration.

"I've never seen such a demonstration of enthusiasm at a baseball park, whether it was at the World Series or winning a pennant or anything else," Giles told Brickhouse in the TV booth after the game.

Cubs general manager John Holland then stepped to the WGN mikes, beaming over the immediate spectacular results of his trade with the Phillies.

"He's young, had great stuff and in a class with (Bob) Anderson and (Glen) Hobbie," Holland said. "He fits into our program. Most of all, we felt that he was a fellow who could pick our staff up. This is out of this world. I'm so happy I can hardly talk about it."

Brickhouse touted the drama of baseball. "This is a memory now that every guy out there can take to his grave with him," he said, then praising the "*esprit de corps*" of the WGN staff in corralling Cardwell in the middle of the maelstrom of joy.

Cardwell could digest some impressive numbers as he celebrated afterward. He threw just 93 pitches in a game lasting one hour, 46 minutes. He had hurled the first no-hitter against the Cardinals since Hod Eller of the Reds on May 11, 1919. And his distinction as the only pitcher to toss a no-hitter in his first start since being traded to a new team would follow him beyond his baseball days.

The no-hitter would prove to be the high point of Cardwell's 1960 Cubs season, by light years. He finished 8-14 with a 4.37 ERA on a 60-94 team that avoided the NL cellar by just one game. He rebounded with a respectable 15-14, 3.82 season for another lousy Cubs team in 1961, but then nose-dived to 7-16, 4.92 for an even worse club (59-103) in 1962.

So where do you think Cardwell, Moryn and Altman, heroes of the no-hitter, ended up? Just one month later, on June 15, 1960, Moryn, pushed out of a regular's job in Wrigley Field, was traded to—you guessed it—the Cardinals for outfielder Jim McKnight. Then, on October 17, 1962, Cardwell himself was sent packing to St. Louis along with Altman and catcher Moe Thacker for—this makes perfect sense—McDaniel, the losing pitcher in the no-hitter, and Jackson, the Game 1 winner for the Cardinals. Catcher Jimmie Schaffer also was sent to Chicago. Cardwell never did spent any playing time in a Cardinals uniform, though, as he was traded a month later to the Pirates for shortstop Dick Groat.

The strange synergy continued at the end of the 1960s. Cardwell spent his baseball dotage as a fifth starter for the 1969 Miracle Mets, which snatched the NL East title away from the Cubs. He said 1969 was the high point of his career.

But people still mention his no-hitter more than his secondary role on the Mets. And Moose Moryn, a pretty good hitter for a few years with the Cubs, always was known for his famed catch as he ran a liquor store in suburban Cicero and appeared annually at the Cubs Convention. One day he came back to St. Louis and called Cunningham, then a prominent St. Louis front-office man. "I gave him some great seats. I was honored," Cunningham said. Moryn died in 1996.

A no-hitter is indeed a special event. If the author of such a feat is good enough to get Stan Musial swinging at sound, folks don't forget too easily.

## Sandberg's two homers vs. Sutter
## June 23, 1984, Wrigley Field

What kind of blessed event would cause Whitey Herzog to proclaim Ryne Sandberg "Baby Ruth?"

Better yet, another Whitey-ism: "He's the best baseball player I've ever seen. That's right, the best all-around player I've ever seen."

Cardinals dugout guru Herzog had just seen Sandberg slug not one, but two, homers in successive at-bats against Bruce Sutter, possessor of the trickiest split-finger fastball ever invented. If Sutter gave up a homer a month, he was doing poorly. Never two in one outing—to the same player.

Leave it to Cardinals announcer Mike Shannon, in his own special way, to have summed up the day in an instant analysis.

"Whatever happens from here on out, you can write this sumbitch down in your book and keep it there," he said. "Two homers off Bruce Sutter. How many guys do that in a career? And back-to-back . . . "

Sounds too strange to be true. Even with the passage of years, the feat seems unbelievable. But Sandberg actually did it, tying up a wild, wild game twice against Sutter. In doing so, the quiet Cub made his reputation and kick-started into high gear both an MVP season and a Hall of Fame-bound career as one of the greatest second basemen ever.

"A once-in-a-lifetime game for me," Sandberg said from the vantage point of 15 years later.

Sandberg's spree was the climax—but not the final result—of one of the wildest Cubs-Cardinals games ever played. Fittingly staged before a national TV audience, the Hollywood-script outing ended with the Cubs winning 12-11 in 11 innings. But we still don't believe it happened.

Sandberg warmed up for his date with destiny with an RBI single in the first inning. He singled again in the third, then was retired on a grounder to short in the fifth. That would be the only time he would not hit safely this afternoon. And if the truth be known, nothing the Cardinals could have thrown Sandberg, not even Sutter's best splitter, could have gotten him out during his best-ever hot spell.

The Cubs had fallen behind 7-1, but had cut the deficit to 9-8 with a five-run sixth that included a two-run single by Sandberg. Amazingly, that was the last scoring until the bottom of the ninth, when Sandberg led off against ex-Cub Sutter. Remembering Cubs manager Jim Frey's spring-training advice to muscle up in clutch situations instead of slapping the ball to the opposite field, Sandberg drove Sutter's pitch into the left-bleachers to tie up the game.

The Cardinals' tallying of two runs in the top of the 10th only set up Sandberg perfectly. Sutter retired Larry Bowa and Richie Hebner. Then Sutter thought he had Bob Dernier struck out on a close, hair-outside 3-and-2 pitch. Dernier took it and catcher Darrell Porter didn't hang on to it.

"That makes it tough for the umpire to call it a strike," Herzog said later.

Given an extra shot, Sandberg jumped on Sutter's 1-and-1 pitch and sent it soaring to nearly the same spot in the bleachers. Sutter threw a fit on the mound, Bob Costas went nuts in his broadcast perch and sheer bedlam erupted in Wrigley Field.

Just think what the normally composed Sandberg was thinking.

"I'm speechless . . . sort of in shock," he said afterward. "I don't even know what day it is. I was going up there thinking about pulling the ball against Sutter. I wasn't even thinking about hitting one out.

"To go up there and think I'm going to hit a homer run again is unbelievable. Both of the homers were off split-fingered fastballs. I was looking for it."

Sutter couldn't believe it, either.

"I made two bad pitches and both went out of the park," he said. "Except for those two pitches, everything was hit on the ground. If I throw good pitches, he doesn't hit them out. He's a fine player."

Sandberg's goal for 1984 was 15 homers, his total combined for 1982 and 1983. The 5-for-6 afternoon that included seven RBI made it a cool 24-for-his-last-48 (.500) for him. He would go on to exceed that and every other projection. Sandberg had 19 homers, 19 triples, 36 doubles, 84 RBI, 114 runs scored, a .314 average and 32 stolen bases, an all-around offensive portfolio that easily nailed the NL MVP award for Sandberg. His power simply grew over the years to where he led the NL with 40 homers in 1990, finally ending his career in 1997 as the all-time leading home run-hitting second baseman.

"As an all-around player, he doesn't have to take a back seat to any-body," Frey said, echoing Herzog.

All-around players need defining moments, and this day was Sandberg's. Surprisingly, on quiet nights in his south Phoenix home, the now spring-training instructor for the Cubs does little time-tripping to those glorious moments.

"I think I've seen the tape just once," he said. "I have a lot of tapes, and I have that on tape, but just I haven't gotten to the point where I sit back and watch some of those games."

Maybe the memory, through one's own heart and soul, is the best medium to re-live one afternoon as "Baby Ruth."

## Castillo one strike from a no-hitter
## September 25, 1995, Wrigley Field

To show you just how hard it is to pitch a no-hitter, Frank Castillo had 13 strikeouts in this game compared to Don Cardwell's seven 35 years previously. He was totally unhittable, just like Cardwell.

The difference was simply timing. Castillo couldn't get one last pitch past Bernard Gilkey. Like Joe Cunningham, Gilkey went the opposite way with the pitch. But unlike Moose Moryn, Sammy Sosa at his diving best couldn't come up with the two-out-in-the-ninth triple that would have enabled Castillo to match Cardwell in end results. And instead of a near-full house at the Friendly Confines, just some 5,000 fans on a Monday night tried to make the racket of a much bigger throng.

Nearing the end of a good season in which he ranked as a tough-luck pitcher who often didn't get run support, Castillo spun his best game as the Cubs were trying to stave off mathematical elimination in the NL wild-card race. He totally baffled the Cardinals with his curveball.

In fact, the entire game was a strikeout spree. The Cubs fanned 12 times against Alan Benes, Brian Barber, Doug Creek and John Frascatore.

The Cubs amassed a 7-0 lead by the fifth, providing Castillo with a huge cushion in which he could concentrate. No exceptional plays were made until Mark Grace snared a hard grounder by John Mabry toward the hole between first and second in the eighth. Grace "led Frankie on a fly pattern" as the pitcher covered first for the out.

Castillo truly was in a groove like never before-or since.

"I told myself, 'Don't get too excited, stay focused, keep the ball down and just hit the glove,'" he said. "It was the best control I had all year."

Castillo retired the first two Cardinals, and looked like he'd get his no-hitter. He got Gilkey to whiff at a first-pitch slider, then threw a beautiful changed for strike two. Castillo then threw two wide ones.

Gilkey was determined not to give up. "I was involved in a no-hitter in the minor leagues and it wasn't a good feeling," he said. "I thought back to that. I didn't want to be part of another one. The whole world would know about it."

Cubs catcher Scott Servais, figuring Gilkey was sitting on Castillo's slow stuff, called for a fastball. But it caught too much of the plate.

"I'm going to kick myself a little (on the pitch)," Servais said.

Gilkey laced the ball toward the right field gap. Sosa used all his considerable speed, but came up a few feet short in a diving try. Moose Moryn he wasn't on this night, despite the difference in athleticism.

"Any time a ball is hit like that, I'm going to dive for it, but this one I couldn't get," he said. "Believe me, if I'd had a chance, I would have caught it. I wanted that ball hit to me so-o-o-o bad."

Castillo was thankful for the effort.

"Sammy tried, but there was no way," he said. "I've got to give Gilkey credit. He stayed in there."

Castillo then retired Tripp Cromer to complete the one-hitter to raise his record to 11-10. That's where it finished for the year. The near-gem also seemed to signal the end of Castillo's effectiveness. He nose-dived to 7-16 in 1996 and was dumped off on the Rockies in mid-season 1997. Castillo spent an injury-plagued 1998 season with the Tigers and showed up in the Diamondbacks' camp in 1999.

Maybe he wouldn't have had to pack his bags if he had thrown another pitch, or the fastball in a different location to Gilkey, or if Gilkey had sliced the drive more toward Sosa. We'll never know. Such is the pattern of almost no-hitters—and the game of baseball as a whole.

## Foote drives in 8 runs
## April 22, 1980, Wrigley Field

Like Castillo, Barry (Big) Foote's biggest day at the Cub preceded a huge drop-off in his performance and his near-future exit from Wrigley Field.

But, oh, did he have fun at the expense of the Cardinals in the memorable 16-12 victory on a freakish 90-degree April day in Chicago.

A former Expo, oversized catcher Foote had won the starting catching job in 1979, amassing a decent season with 16 homers. He seemed to set the stage for another good campaign with a two-homer outburst, including a game-winning, opposite-field grand slam in the bottom of the ninth.

"It was a great individual performance," Foote said. "But it was also a team effort. Baseball is a game played by individuals."

With the wind blowing out a gale on the unbelievably warm day, the Cardinals had zoomed out to an 11-6 lead by the top of the fourth. But Foote had single-handedly tried to keep the Cubs in the game with a second-inning RBI single and a two-run double in the third. The Cardinals scored one more run, then the Cubs closed the gap to 12-11 in the seventh.

With one out in the eighth, Foote homered to tie it 12-12. Then the Cubs put together their winning rally in the bottom of the ninth.

With one out, pinch hitter Dave Kingman singled. Lenny Randle pinch-ran for him and stole second. Bill Buckner was walked intentionally. After Larry Biittner struck out, a wild pitch from Cardinals reliever Mark Littell moved the runners up. Jerry Martin then walked to load the bases.

Foote then jumped on the first pitch—"a slider out over the plate"—catching the wind toward right center. The ball carried all the way to the basket below the right-field bleachers for the game-winning grand slam.

But amid the postgame celebration, Foote was more proud of throwing out the Cardinals' Garry Templeton trying to steal second in the top of the ninth.

"Throwing out the runner overshadowed the homer," Foote said.

A bad back soon cut Foote's production and playing time. He finished 1980 with just six homers and 28 RBI, batting .238. Early the following season, he found himself shuttled out of Chicago in Cubs owner Bill Wrigley's budget-cutting spree that preceded the sale of the Cubs to Tribune Co. Foote finished up his career with the Yankees at age 30 in 1982.

# DeJesus hits for the cycle
## April 22, 1980, Wrigley Field

Adding to the more unlikely element of that windswept 1980 game was Ivan DeJesus' greatest batting spree in his career. Foote and DeJesus. You wouldn't have picked them for the muscling-up heroes of a win, but that's the crazy nature of the game.

"A great day in my life," is how the Cub of 1980 (eventually a Cardinal of 1985) described hitting for the cycle while Foote was busy amassing eight RBI. But in the fifth inning, DeJesus had to be virtually convinced he had just accomplished the rare batting feat.

DeJesus, then in his fourth season as the Cubs' shortstop, was dusting off his pants after sliding into third on a triple to the vines in right center. Third-base coach Joey Amalfitano told him, "Congratulations."

"Congratulations? What for?" a puzzled DeJesus asked.

"You just hit for the cycle," Amalfitano replied. "That's a single, double, triple and home run, all in the same game."

DeJesus got off to a rousing start for his cycle, belting a homer off Cardinals starter Bob Forsch in the first inning. He doubled in the third and singled in the fourth before completing the cycle with the three-bagger in the next inning.

For good measure, DeJesus singled in the seventh. He finished his afternoon 5-for-6.

"It's like pitching a no-hitter," DeJesus said. "It's something you've never done before . . . and maybe never will do again. But if I go 5-for-6 in the game, and we lose, it's not the same."

DeJesus attributed his fast start to abstaining from winter baseball in Puerto Rico. He had played in the winter league every season for the previous nine years. He had gotten off to slow starts as a Cub, so he decided to change things up.

But if DeJesus started fast in '80, he finished slowly. Normally a .280-range hitter, he finished at just .259, then nose-dived to .195 in the Cubs' horrid 1981 season. DeJesus, though, had one more lasting contribution to Chicago baseball history. He was the man traded after the 1981 season to the Phillies for Larry Bowa and a young player named Ryne Sandberg.

Eventually, DeJesus made his way to the Cardinals, where he was a valued utility player on the 1985 World Series team.

## Williams hits for the cycle
## July 17, 1966, Busch Stadium

DeJesus' cycle had been the first by a Cubs since Billy Williams against . . . you guessed it, the Cardinals.

Williams had made a career within a Hall of Fame career of feasting on St. Louis pitching. But he made the second game on a hot Sunday afternoon doubleheader at the newly-opened Busch Stadium memorable. It's a wonder Williams had any energy left, after the Cubs had dropped what the newspapers called a "nerve-tingling" 11-inning game in the opener. Williams had gone 2-for-4 in the opener, including the go-ahead RBI single in the 10th. But the Cardinals rallied to tie and then won 4-3 in the next inning.

With veteran Art Mahaffey pitching, Williams singled in the first inning of the nightcap. He opened the third inning with a double off Don Dennis. He tripled off the right-field wall against Dennis in the fifth, driving in Lee Thomas. Then, with lefty Hal Woodeshick on the mound in the seventh and Cubs manager Leo Durocher urging him to "go out there and hit one out," Williams slugged a 2-and-0 pitch into the right center-field bleachers, underneath the scoreboard.

"I was tired," Williams said. "I'd be running the bases all day and didn't want to run any more. I wanted to walk."

Williams' heroics enabled the Cubs to win 7-2 on the fine starting pitching of Ken Holtzman, who was relieved by Fergie Jenkins. The latter would not move into the starting rotation for another few weeks. Williams finished 1966 with 29 homers and 91 RBI, part of a competitive lineup that nevertheless could not prevent the Cubs from finishing 59-103, in 10th place in a 10-team NL.

Almost another three years would pass before Williams would go down swinging trying for another cycle against St. Louis—and be cheered for it.

## Williams comes through on his "Day"
## June 29, 1969, Wrigley Field

Very rarely do players come through magnificently on special days in which they were honored.

Cal Ripken, of course, was one, homering on the night he played in game No. 2,131. Speaking of ironmen, Williams played two for the price of one while spraying baseballs all over Wrigley Field on the afternoon he broke Stan Musial's old National League record of 895 consecutive games played.

With 41,060 jamming Wrigley Field to overflowing for a Sunday doubleheader, and between 10,000 and 20,000 more turned away at the gate to see the first-place Cubs duel their archrivals, Williams was honored between games.

The man of the day set up the good mood with an eighth-inning double that helped break a scoreless deadlock between Fergie Jenkins and Bob Gibson. The Cubs tallied all their runs in that inning on their way to a 3-1 victory.

During the intermission, Williams was showered with gifts, including a car, a fishing bat, a Weimaraner puppy for his hunting expeditions, a pool table and a washer-and-dryer combination. To show how different the times were, the Chicago baseball writers chipped in to give Williams an elegant fishing pole for deep-sea jaunts.

"I want to thank the Almighty God for giving me the ability to play major league baseball," Williams said during the ceremonies. "I want to thank God for protecting me over all the games I played."

Williams actually had been hobbled somewhat in the week prior to the doubleheader with a bad foot. Dutifully, manager Leo Durocher kept finding ways to get Williams in either in the starting lineup or as a pinch hitter.

Williams had last rested on September 22, 1963, when then-manager Bob Kennedy sat him down in a Wrigley Field game against tough Braves lefty Warren Spahn. Why didn't he leave the lineup over the next seven years? The old player's sense of insecurity—if you rested when you were available to play, someone might take your job.

That included doubleheaders during summer's dog days. No problem for the Cubs, who were full of ironmen in the 1960s. Ron Santo also played every day. In 1968, Randy Hundley set a record for catchers that probably won't ever be broken—160 games played. So there was no way Williams would have benched himself against nightcap starter Jim "Mudcat" Grant, a formerly top right-hander nearing the end of his career. With the glow of the ceremonies still fresh, he went out to dismantle the Cardinals practically by himself in the Cubs' 12-1 victory.

Williams singled in the first, doubled in a run in the second, slashed an RBI triple to left center in the fifth, and triple again, this time good for two RBI, in the sixth. Then, in the eighth against reliever Dave Giusti, Williams swung from the heels, trying to complete the cycle. But he struck out while the crowd stood in a final ovation.

"I really wanted that home run, but it was a beautiful day. Beautiful," Williams said.

"You know, I get paid for playing ball, paid well. It's something you want to do and like to do. But this day was something extra. It shows me how the fans really appreciate me for the job I do in Chicago."

The fans continued appreciating Williams for years. He went on to play 1,117 consecutive games before he took himself out of the lineup on September 2, 1970 at Wrigley Field in the middle of his greatest season-42 homers, 129 RBI and a .322 average. But his NL consecutive games record eventually was broken by Steve Garvey a decade later. And it paled, of course, in comparison to Cal Ripken's 2,630, the endurance-feat equivalent of 70 homers.

## Dawson's parting shot
## September 27, 1987, Wrigley Field

The ultimate strong, silent type, Andre Dawson never, ever would call a homer. Instead, the Wrigley Field crowd called it for him.

With his dream season nearing its conclusion, Dawson had 46 homers to his credit on the final home game of the 1987 season as 33,912 watched on "Fan Appreciation Day." But the appreciation instead was turned toward the classy Dawson's way, as well it should have.

Coming to bat for the last time in the bottom of the eighth with the Cubs leading the Cardinals 6-3, Dawson was welcomed by a standing ovation and chants of "MVP! MVP! MVP!" "Andre's Army" tried to will one more homer out of their hero.

"The fan support has enabled me to relax and play to the best of my ability," Dawson said of the end result of signing a blank contract as a free agent during the collusion era in order to play for the Cubs the previous spring training. "But it would have been out of context if I'd stepped out and tipped my hat to them. I just figured I'd wait until after the game or when I went back out (to right field) in the top of the ninth."

Dawson didn't wait at all, giving the roaring fans a last sample of what came oh-so-naturally to him in '87. He tomahawked a 3-and-1 pitch from Cardinals reliever Bill Dawley onto Waveland Avenue for his 47th homer and 132nd RBI.

"He threw me a changeup," Dawson said, "the ball happened to be out over the plate, and I was able to get the bat head through the strike zone. The ball didn't have much movement on it, so I was able to see it pretty well."

In defeat, the Cardinals were as magnanimous as possible toward Dawson, who evoked admiration from opponents with his old-fashioned baseball virtues and unparalleled tolerance of pain from his surgery-scarred knees.

"It was beautiful. He's that kind of player," shortstop Ozzie Smith said.

"God Almighty," exclaimed manager Whitey Herzog. "I don't know how you do any more than Dawson's done."

"There's only one Andre Dawson. Everyone admires him," slugger Jack Clark said.

Dawson won his MVP award, a rarity for a player on a last-place club, with season final totals of 49 homers and 137 RBI. Playing through more knee operations and the attendant pain, but giving all a clinic on how a major leaguer should conduct himself on and off the field, Dawson stayed with the Cubs through 1992. He left as a free agent, and experienced some bad feelings toward the Chicago organization in the process.

He finished up on with the Red Sox and Marlins, but apparently is leaning toward wearing a Cubs cap when he's eventually inducted into the Hall of Fame. Hawk has patched it up with the Cubs, and remains one of the team's most popular players of modern times.

# Kessinger goes 6-for-6
## June 17, 1971, Wrigley Field

The game began with a kid named Burt Hooton, fresh off the University of Texas campus as the Cubs' No. 1 draft pick a few weeks previously, striking out Lou Brock. That was the first man Hooton ever faced in the majors. But the contest didn't end until Don Kessinger came across the plate with the winning run in the 10th in the 7-6 Cubs win in front of 22,749 on a Thursday afternoon.

Nobody else besides Kessinger deserved to tally the winner. The Cubs shortstop (and future Cardinal) enjoyed his career day with a 6-for-6 performance, his final hit leading off the deciding rally.

"Some days you're just lucky, I guess," said Kessinger, who relied on more than luck to craft a long, productive career. A poor hitter as a rookie in 1965, he took up switch-hitting at the suggestion of manager Leo Durocher the following season. That enabled him to develop into a decent hitter instead of the All-American Out, as was the status of many good-field, no-hit shortstops of the era.

The former Ole Miss basketball and baseball star, who grew up as a Cardinals fan in Arkansas, led off a two-run first with a single. He drove in another run with a single in the second. Two more singles preceded his only extra-base hit of the afternoon, a double that led off the eighth and sprouted into the run that tied the game 6-6.

Kessinger's single in the 10th came before an intentional walk to Billy Williams and a Ron Santo single to left for the game winner.

You're no slouch if you get six hits in one game. And you usually need extra innings to accomplish it. Frank Demaree had been the last Cub to collect that many, in a 14-inning game in 1937. Only five more years would pass before Jose Cardenal would match Kessinger with six hits. Sammy Sosa also got six hits against the Rockies at Mile High Stadium in Denver in 1993. The record in one game is seven, by several players. Rennie Stennett of the Pirates collected that lucky number against the Cubs in 1975.

Despite his outburst against the Cardinals, Kessinger hit a modest .258 in 1971. He played for the Cubs through the 1975, the last of the Leo Durocher-era players to serve as a Chicago regular, before being traded to the Cardinals for reliever Mike Garman. Oddly enough, Kessinger's big-league career ended back in Chicago-as player-manger for the White Sox in 1979.

## Banks belts 5th grand slam
## September 19, 1955, Sportsman's Park

If there was a record to be set, Ernie Banks would do it against the Cardinals.

Author of so many career milestones against St. Louis, staring with his first career homer, the budding Mr. Cub passed up Babe Ruth, Lou Gehrig and a host of other greats on a Monday night before just 4,953. His fifth grand slam homer of the 1955 season bettered by one the former big-league mark for a season, shared by Ruth, Gehrig, Ralph Kiner, Rudy York, Vince DiMaggio, Sid Gordon, Al Rosen, Tommy Henrich and Ray Boone.

Banks connected in the seventh against future Cubs teammate Lindy McDaniel, a Cardinals "bonus baby" making his first big-league start at just 19. Singles by Dee Fondy, Gene Baker and Gale Wade had loaded the bases for Banks.

"They told me not to get the ball inside against Ernie," McDaniel recalled. "But I was young. I didn't know the hitter. Later I was able to get him out inside."

Banks, then a slim shortstop with quick-silver wrists, had belted grand slams earlier in 1955 off Russ Meyer of the Dodgers on May 11, Lew Burdette of the Braves on May 29, Ron Negray of the Phillies on July 18, and Dick Littlefield of the Pirates on August 2.

A lot of his best power feats went to waste, though, during this dark period in Cubs history. The September 19 game against the Cardinals was no different. Banks' 44th and final homer of '55, gave the Cubs a 5-0 lead, short-lived when the Cardinals came up with two runs in the bottom of the seventh and three in the eighth on Harry Eliott's homer. The Cardinals finally won 6-5 on Rip Repulski's homer off Jim Davis in the 12th.

The bases-loaded blast virtually completed the first of a number of great seasons that made Banks the most prolific power hitter in the NL through 1960, even better than Hank Aaron, Willie Mays and Frank Robinson. Banks finished with 117 RBI in 1955. After a dip to 28 homers in 1956, he followed up with 43, 47, 45, and 41 in succession the next four seasons before a knee injury slowed him and caused a shift to first base in 1961.

Banks went on to connect for 12 grand slams out of the 512 homers he amassed in a career that finally ended in 1971. His final bases-loaded shot came against the Padres' Jack Baldschun in 1969.

# 8

---

# Great Cardinals Player Performances vs. the Cubs

## McGwire passes the Babe, Maris with Nos. 61, 62
### September 7-8, 1998, Busch Stadium

**NO baseball player had ever entered a season** with such expectations—from the fans and himself.

The baseball world hoped—demanded, some might say— that in 1998 Cardinals slugger Mark McGwire would break the single-season home run record.

And from Day One he did his best to comply. Cardinals fans who couldn't be at Busch Stadium or in front of a television on opening day, March 30, heard the longtime voice of the Cardinals, Jack Buck, make this fifth-inning call over flagship station KMOX:

"Bases loaded, two out, the pitch to McGwire: Swiinnng and a high fly ball into left. That ball carries to the track, (voice rises) might leave the park—he did it, a grand slam and it's four to nothing! McGwire with number one."

Roger Maris, the man who'd set the mark of 61 in 1961, hadn't been considered a threat to do so entering that season. Maris required 10 games to hit his first homer and had drawn the hatred of many fans for topping the record of 60 set by Babe Ruth. Few had expected Ruth to hit 60 and break his own record of 59 as 1927 began, but they rejoiced when he did so.

McGwire's 1998 quest would keep the memory and accomplishments of both those sluggers alive. And it would dominate the front pages of daily newspapers and the lead stories of TV news unlike any sports story ever had.

Hitting monstrously long home runs early in the season that put him on a pace for 80, McGwire often dwarfed the accomplishments of the rest of the Cardinals, who floundered and never were serious contenders.

But Big Mac's accomplishments drew thousands of lukewarm fans to the park wherever the Redbirds played. Those fans didn't care about the game but about the four or five plate appearances of this modern Paul Bunyan.

Television often showed, with poignant commentary by play-by-play and color announcers, the exodus of fans after what looked like McGwire's last time at-bat even though the game was still going on and its result still in the balance.

Briefly overtaken by the Cubs' Sammy Sosa, McGwire had reasserted his leadership in a see-saw game in Chicago in August. On Labor Day, thanks to a spurt that had seen him hit 13 home runs in a 19-game stretch, McGwire was on the doorstep of immortality with 60.

So was Sosa, who had 58. The two would face each other in a two-game series, Labor Day afternoon and the following evening.

Mostly overlooked in the hoopla over McGwire's and Sosa's run for the record was that the Cubs were still battling for a post-season berth. Second-place Chicago entered the day 10 games behind the Houston Astros in the Central Division but in the three-dimensional standings that now existed were one game ahead of the second-place Mets of the Eastern Division for the NL wild-card spot. In the opener, the Cubs sent to the mound much-traveled Mike Morgan, doing his second tour of duty with the Cubs after having toiled for the Cardinals as well.

While 50,530 were in Busch Stadium, hundreds of thousands others in the St. Louis area watched the game on KPLR-TV. While the cameras panned the crowd, showing someone with a sign proclaiming Sosa and McGwire to be "Two Nice Guys," announcer Bob Carpenter noted that Cardinals fans had given a warm hand to Sosa his first time up. "Now they want him to strike out," Carpenter said with a laugh, and Sosa popped up to his rival at first.

When McGwire stepped to the plate in the home half, Carpenter and sidekick Ozzie Smith allowed the camera and the crowd to tell a familiar story—a standing ovation amid an air of anticipation.

McGwire, looking like a modern warrior with his red left-arm elbow pad and his black left-leg shin guard, intently watched the pitcher, waving his bat slowly back and forth until he cocked it behind his head as the pitcher started to draw his arm back. It was a ritual McGwire had used in every plate appearance that year.

The first pitch from Morgan was a slider; thinking fastball, McGwire waved at it and missed. The next was an up-and-in fastball. McGwire didn't flinch, but the fans booed, as they long had done for any pitch outside the strike zone since opponents had begun walking him intentionally early in the season.

Back in the TV booth, Carpenter and Smith were discussing Morgan's talkative nature as Morgan came in with a fastball about belt high but closer to the middle of the plate than he'd wanted. Smith completed his sentence but viewers weren't listening: their attention was captured by McGwire's quick and majestic swing as it caught the pitch and sent it screaming toward the Stadium Club just below the upper deck in left-field. The ball was hooking but had been hit so hard it didn't have time to go foul. It startled the well-dressed diners inside the Stadium Club as it ricocheted off the protective glass in front of them and dropped to the fans below.

McGwire threw both hands up as he ran down the first-base line. In right field, Sosa smiled and applauded by patting his glove. Waiting for him just after he stepped on the plate and gave a forearm smash salute to next batter Ray Lankford was McGwire's 11-year-old son, Matthew, in a Cardinals batboy uniform. He'd just arrived at the park. McGwire picked him up and carried him toward the dugout.

He went into the dugout but quickly emerged to point: to his heart, to the fans, to his father, celebrating his 61st birthday, to Sosa and to the family of Roger Maris sitting in a first-base box.

And the game went on. The Cardinals had a 1-0 lead. They'd make it 2-0 then hold off the Cubs for a 3-2 win. In his other three appearances, McGwire singled and flied out twice. Sosa was 1-for-5 and struck out with the tying run on third and two out in the ninth.

Thousands of fans stayed afterwards to watch the post-game media conference on the big screen above the right field bleachers. "I don't think I will ever let go of the moment," was one of the many things McGwire said.

The next evening, September 8, Busch Stadium again was packed. It was the final game of the homestand, and Big Mac, as well as Cardinals fans, wanted that record-setter this night. The same supporting cast—son, father, Maris family, even Cardinals legend Stan Musial—were in their places as a national audience tuned in to watch on the Fox Network.

That broadcast kept up the almost surreal atmosphere that at times had pervaded the great chase. At the commercial break between innings after McGwire grounded out in the first, the main character of the "King of the Hill" animated series, which was pre-empted for tonight's broadcast, was shown in his living room armchair. "Mr. McGwire," the character began, "we know you're having a pretty good season, but we'd like to start our season. So why don't you don't you do me a favor and try to hit a home run tonight. OK?"

McGwire couldn't comply his first time up. But in the fourth, with the Cubs leading 2-0 behind Steve Trachsel, he again approached the plate to a standing, screaming ovation. Preparing himself with the intense watch of the pitcher and slow back-and-forth waving of the bat, he was the only one oblivious to the popping of pocket-camera flashcubes all over the stadium, another ritual that had accompanied his every swing in a night game as he neared the record.

Trachsel's first pitch was knee high and over the plate. McGwire attacked it and sent a laser shot headed for the left field corner. Fox broadcaster Tim McCarver would later say he thought it had enough force to go through the wall if not over it.

But as main Fox announcer Joe Buck and thousands of viewers wondered in that split second if it would clear the wall, fans in the box seats along the left field line assured them it had as they raised their arms in a triumph. It would be McGwire's shortest homer of the season, a computer measurement of 341 feet, but it would have the longest impact.

McGwire, not sure either if had enough height, had torn out of the batter's box. When he saw it go over, he became so excited he hopped over first base, missing the bag entirely.

"Touch first base, Mark, you are the new single-season home run king," Joe Buck said over the airwaves as first-base coach Dave McKay made sure McGwire came back and did so.

What followed was a home-run trot unlike any other, even Henry Aaron's when he'd broken Babe Ruth's career mark nearly a quarter century before. McGwire was congratulated by every Cubs infielder, especially Gary Gaetti, who'd seen many of those early-season Mac blasts while still a member of the Cardinals. As he trotted down the third-base line, McGwire pointed to "the man upstairs," as he'd often described it. Like a

**Mark McGwire's** individual battle with Sammy Sosa in 1998 added to the aura of the Cubs-Cards series. [Photo courtesy of St. Louis Cardinals]

Though he fell short by four in the 1998 home run race to Mark McGwire, the Cubs' **Sammy Sosa** was a runaway favorite for the National League's MVP Award. [Photo courtesy of Brace Photos]

The Cardinals picked up future Hall of Fame pitcher **Grover Cleveland Alexander** on waivers from the Cubs in 1926. Ol' Pete came back to haunt his former teammates on June 27th when he spun a four-hitter at Sportsman's Park. (See page 122) [From SPI photo archive]

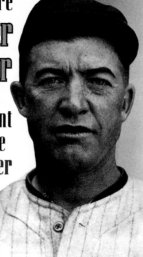

Two of the game's greatest players, **Rogers Hornsby** (left) and **Hack Wilson** (right), were Cubbie teammates in 1930. Hornsby played and managed both the Cards and the Cubs during his legendary career.

[From SPI photo archives]

Cardinal pitcher **Dizzy Dean** mowed down a record 17 Cubs on strikeouts in 1933. In 1938, Dean was traded to Chicago, helping the Cubbies win the National League pennant. (See page 120) [From SPI photo archives]

**Mordecai "Three Finger" Brown** was traded by the Cardinals to the Cubs on December 12, 1903 for Jack Taylor and Larry McLean. (See page 178) [From SPI photo archives]

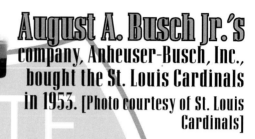

**August A. Busch Jr.'s** company, Anheuser-Busch, Inc., bought the St. Louis Cardinals in 1953. [Photo courtesy of St. Louis Cardinals]

**Philip K. Wrigley** (left), longtime owner of the Cubs, visits with Chicago manager and longtime Cardinals standout Frankie Frisch (right). [From SPI photo archives]

Future baseball broadcaster **Joe Garagiola** played for both the Cubs and the Cardinals. [From SPI photo archives]

The Cardinals' **Stan "The Man" Musial** collected his 3,000th career hit against the Cubs at Wrigley field on May 13, 1958. (See page 112) [Photo courtesy of St. Louis Cardinals]

**Lou Brock's** arrival in St. Louis in 1964 set off a chain reaction of success for the Cardinals. He ended his Hall of Fame career with 3,023 hits and a record 938 stolen bases.
[From SPI photo archives]

Cardinals pitcher **Ernie Broglio**, who compiled an 18-8 record for the Redbirds in 1963, was traded to the Cubs for Lou Brock on June 15, 1964. He eventually was released by Chicago in 1966. (See page 157)
[From SPI photo archives]

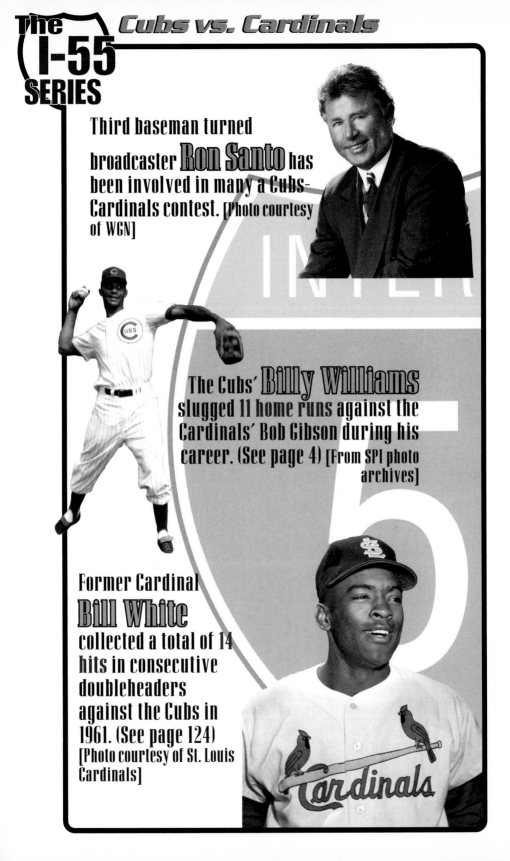

Third baseman turned broadcaster **Ron Santo** has been involved in many a Cubs-Cardinals contest. [Photo courtesy of WGN]

The Cubs' **Billy Williams** slugged 11 home runs against the Cardinals' Bob Gibson during his career. (See page 4) [From SPI photo archives]

Former Cardinal **Bill White** collected a total of 14 hits in consecutive doubleheaders against the Cubs in 1961. (See page 124) [Photo courtesy of St. Louis Cardinals]

On the fourth of July, 1969, the Cubs' **Ferguson Jenkins** struck out 10 Cardinals in 10 innings, beating Bob Gibson and the Redbirds, 3-1. (See page 147) [From SPI photo archives]

**Bob Gibson** shut out the Cubs, 1-0, on June 20, 1968, extending his scoreless innings streak to 38. (See page 144) [Photo courtesy of St. Louis Cardinals]

**Harry Caray** (center) teamed with **Lou Boudreau** (left) and **Vince Lloyd** (right) on the Cubs' broadcast team...

...and with **Jack Buck** (left) in the Cardinals' booth. (See page 31) [Top photo courtesy of Bill Wills, bottom photo from SPI photo archives]

Chicago's **Don Cardwell** pitched the only no-hitter in Cubs-Cards series history on May 15, 1960. (See page 89) [From SPI photo archives]

The Cardinals' **Mike Shannon** (left) and the Cubs' Glenn Beckert (right) had a major collision on April 16, 1969, at Busch Stadium. (See page 224) [Photo courtesy of St. Louis Cardinals]

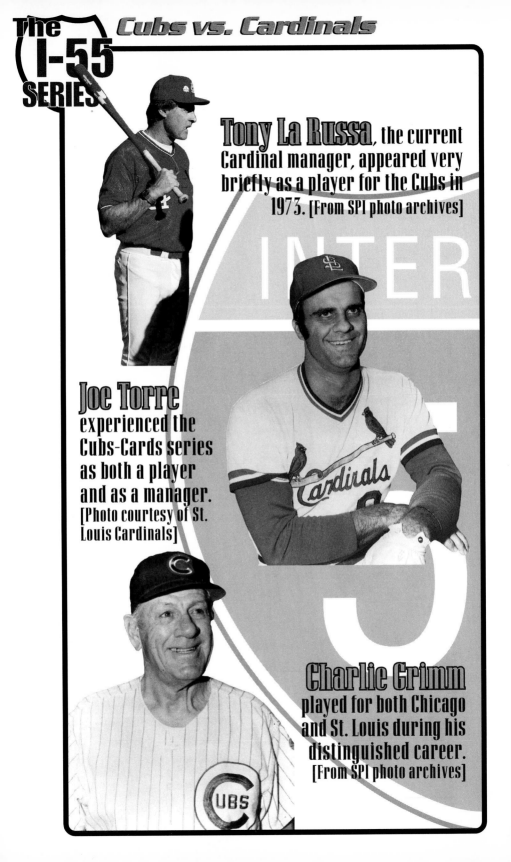

**Tony La Russa**, the current Cardinal manager, appeared very briefly as a player for the Cubs in 1973. [From SPI photo archives]

**Joe Torre** experienced the Cubs-Cards series as both a player and as a manager. [Photo courtesy of St. Louis Cardinals]

**Charlie Grimm** played for both Chicago and St. Louis during his distinguished career. [From SPI photo archives]

**Whitey Herzog** came to understand the Cubs-Cardinals rivalry during his colorful career as the St. Louis manager. (See page 3) [Photo courtesy of St. Louis Cardinals]

As a Cardinal player and as the Cubs manager, perhaps no one personified the series rivalry better than **Leo Durocher**. [From SPI photo archives]

The I-55 SERIES

Both **Bruce Sutter** (left)...

...and **Lee Smith** (right) were standout relief pitchers for the Cubs and Cardinals. [Photos courtesy of Chicago Cubs and St. Louis Cardinals]

**Mark Grace's** 1989 battle with former teammate Frank DiPino on the pitching mound at Busch Stadium caused the Cubs' star to miss much of the month of June that season. (See page 228) [Photo courtesy of Brace Photos]

Two consecutive home runs off reliever Bruce Sutter on June 23, 1984, will always be recognized as one of **Ryne Sandberg's** greatest single-game accomplishments. [Photo courtesy of Brace Photos]

**Gary Gaetti** began the 1998 season as a Cardinal, but ended it as a Cub. No one had a more unique view of the McGwire-Sosa home run battle than he did. [Photo courtesy of St. Louis Cardinals]

**Al Hrabosky**, the Cardinals' "Mad Hungarian", had some fun with the fans in Wrigley Field's left-field bleachers before a 1977 doubleheader. [Photo courtesy of Jim Rygelski]

One of the most colorful members of Wrigley Field's bleacher crowd is Jerry Pritikin, **"The Bleacher Preacher."** [Photo courtesy of Jerry Pritikin]

Two of the most famous venues in baseball are St. Louis' **Busch Stadium** (top) and Chicago's **Wrigley Field** (bottom). [Photos courtesy of St. Louis Cardinals and Chicago Cubs]

rerun of the day before's celebration, he picked up Matthew, this time holding him much higher.

Fireworks went off. He and his teammates then indulged in numerous slaps on the back, forearm smashes and hugs. One unexpected hug came from Sammy Sosa, who'd trotted in from his right-field position while a bewildered Trachsel stood near the mound.

McGwire then vaulted the railing and hugged the Maris family. Nearly breathless when he got back to the dugout, he took a wireless microphone and uttered such phrases as "unbelievable," "class" and "thank you, St. Louis."

The shirt-sleeved crowd continued the party, applauding and bouncing to the music piped in. They admired the new poster of McGwire swinging a bat and the number 62 in the background.

Ten minutes after McGwire had ventured where no major league batter had ever gone before, the game resumed. The Cardinals used that homer as a springboard to come back and beat the Cubs again 6-3. Again Sosa didn't homer, and the big hand-operated scoreboard in center field noted that the race stood 62-58 in McGwire's favor.

And nearly everyone stayed around at the conclusion to watch the big-screen message board in right field and listen to what their hero said at the post-game media conference.

Still in his Cardinal jersey but wearing a red cap proclaiming the number 62, a keyed-up McGwire sipped at his bottle of water and listened to the long, ponderous questions from the media. His answers were short, sometimes grasping for the right words to fit the asker's expectations.

"It was a sweet, sweet run around the bases," he said to one question, though to another he said he would have to see the tape since the whole experience was such a blur.

His eyes watered as he described holding earlier that day the bat Maris had used to belt number 61. He then smiled as he thanked a friend for the hug he'd gotten from him over the phone earlier in the day.

McGwire said it was special to have hit the homer in St. Louis. Sensing that the fans saw him, McGwire then spoke directly to them. "I truly wanted to do it here, guys. Thank you, St. Louis."

A final question asked for him to pose with both his bat and Maris'. Someone asked what final number for his season's output would be put next to that bat in the Hall of Fame.

"I guess we'll find out September 27," he said. The magic number would turn out far greater than McGwire and anyone ever could imagine.

# Musial first Cardinal with 3,000 hits
## May 13, 1958, Wrigley Field

Following a St. Louis win in Chicago on May 12, 1958, Cardinals star Stan Musial had 2,999 career hits after smacking a double in four plate trips.

Manager Fred Hutchinson announced that Stan wouldn't start the Chicago series finale the next day so he'd have a better chance of getting that 3,000th hit—something accomplished then by only seven other players—before the home folks.

"It means more to the fans back home than it does here," Hutchinson said before the game. "After all, only 5,000 people showed up today. And besides, I know Stan wants to get it at home, before his friends."

Hutchinson, however, added, "I'll call on Stan as a pinch batter if we need him."

Cardinals coach Terry Moore told the *St. Louis Globe-Democrat* that Musial, too, wanted to achieve No. 3,000 at home. Musial had confided to his former teammate on two previous pennant winners that if he played he hoped the Cardinals would win but that he would walk four times.

The Cardinals, thanks to an unusual home-and-home series with the Cubs, had snapped out of the early-season doldrums that had seen them lose 14 of their first 17. They'd swept a four-game weekend set from the Cubs in Busch Stadium, then immediately journeyed to Chicago, taking the first game Monday. The surprising Cubs, meanwhile, had won 13 of their first 21—before coming to St. Louis.

Musial, 37, ever the standard of consistency, was pounding the ball at a .483 clip (42 for 87) after having led the league the year before with a .351 batting average.

In beautiful weather, only 5,692 fans paid their way into Tuesday's game for the matchup between ex-Cub Sam "Toothpick" Jones and the Cubs' Moe Drabowsky.

The hosts took a 1-0 lead in their first as right fielder Lee Walls doubled, moved to third on a wild pitch and scored on a sacrifice fly by Ernie Banks.

The Cardinals tied it in their third. Joe Cunningham, starting at first base that day in place of Musial, reached on an error to load the bases with two out. But the Cardinals could manage only one run.

Walls blasted his 10th homer over the left field wall in the Cubs half of the third to give the Cubs the lead back ,then gave the Cubs a 3-1 lead with a sacrifice fly two innings later.

With wife Lil watching in the box seats, Musial sunned himself in the Cardinals bullpen just beyond the dugout along the first-base side as the sixth began. Right fielder Gene Green led off with a double. Catcher Hal Smith grounded out, Green staying at second.

Hutch summoned The Man, as he'd been known for the past decade since Brooklyn fans had given him the nickname for the way he battered their Dodgers in Ebbets Field. The fans gave him a standing ovation as he went to hit for Jones.

Drabowsky, born in Poland, was a gritty competitor who'd later achieve fame as a reliever for the Baltimore Orioles before finishing his long career with the Cardinals. He'd had some success against Musial in previous encounters and ran the count to 2-2 as Stan fouled three pitches off.

Drabowsky later remembered the next pitch: "It was a curve ball on the outside part of the plate. He looked like it just about fooled him. But he was still able to hit it."

Cardinal broadcaster Harry Caray's call on KMOX radio: "Line drive—there it is—into left field—hit number 3,000! A run has scored — Musial around first, on his way to second with a double. Holy Cow, he came through!"

Green scored. The game stopped, a rarity in those days. "The scene that followed looked a bit like one from Mack Sennett's old Keystone Kops," Bob Broeg of the *St. Louis Post-Dispatch* wrote in describing how photographers, usually barred from the field, came pouring out and gathered near second, shooting away.

"The fans cheered wildly, forgetting he had wounded their Cubs," wrote Edward Prell of the *Chicago Tribune*.

Umpire Frank Dascoli retrieved the ball and gave it to Musial with a handshake. Hutchinson, after vigorously pumping Musial's hand, waved in pinch-runner Frank Barnes. It was a move later questioned by the writers, noting that the game was only in the sixth and that Musial might have been depended on to help with a rally later.

But Hutchinson said later he wanted the Cardinals' meal ticket to fully enjoy his day. As Musial, basking in the fans' reaction, walked off the field, he kissed a blonde leaning over the wall next to the dugout.

A photographer at the impromptu press conference in the Cardinals locker room asked if Musial had known the woman. "I'd better," Musial said with a laugh. "She was my wife."

In that meeting with the press, though, Musial was more interested in what was happening on the field. "Please turn up the radio. What's the score?" he asked at one point.

Jones, the pitcher he'd batted for, came by, pulled a trademark toothpick out of his back pocket and said, "We're ahead 5-3."

Musial's double had sparked a four-run rally. Reliever Billy Muffet came on to limit the Cubs to two hits and no runs over the last four innings to preserve the Cardinals' sixth straight win by that same 5-3 score.

Musial acknowledged relief that he'd reached the plateau and that the pressure to achieve it was now off. Always humble about his own achievements, he nevertheless admitted he wanted to retire as the National League's all-time hit man and would now look to surpass Honus Wagner's record of 3,430. He downplayed any speculation that he could hit .400 for the season.

But he did say he wanted to play at least two more years.

This was one of the last years for major league teams to travel by train. The Cardinals train ride from Chicago to St. Louis' Union Station was likened to a whistle stop tour by a victorious political candidate, crowds waving to it as it cut through the heart of Cardinals-Cubs territory in Illinois.

"Even Cubs fans came up along the tracks to greet Stan," recalled then-Cardinals broadcaster Joe Garagiola.

Upon reaching St. Louis, Musial said, "I never realized that batting a ball around could cause such a commotion. I know now how (Spirit of St. Louis aviator Charles) Lindbergh must have felt when he returned to St. Louis (after being the first man to successfully pilot a trans-Atlantic flight)."

Musial finished 1958 at .337. The Cardinals and Cubs tied for fifth with 72-82 records.

The Man lasted another five seasons, retiring with the then-NL. record of 3,630 hits—exactly half of them before the hometown fans who'd always loved him.

# Brock joins 3,000-hit club
## August 13, 1979, Busch Stadium

Lou Brock had faced pressure situations many times before and done so with style and grace, as when he'd broken Maury Wills' single-season stolen base record and later topped Ty Cobb's career mark for thefts.

But as the Cardinals prepared for the finale of a five-game series against the Cubs on August 13, 1979, the 40-year-old Brock faced yet another tense situation: the eyes of the baseball world were on him because he had 2,998 career hits.

His relaxed attitude under the media microscope was an inspiration to his teammates, especially young pitcher John Fulgham, who said Brock was teaching all the Redbirds a lesson.

To the Cardinals' speedster, gaining entry to the exclusive 3,000-hit club was important for a very personal reason. He wanted to be remembered as a hitter as well as a base stealer. Often overlooked in the discussions of his base stealing prowess was that he'd had four seasons of 200 hits or more, and another four with at least 190. In his earlier days he'd hit the ball for distance, being one of only three people to have hit a home run into the distant center field section of the old Polo Grounds in New York.

But that had been with the Chicago Cubs, who'd traded him in June 1964 to the Cardinals for pitcher Ernie Broglio. Brock hit and ran the Cardinals to a pennant and World Series title that year.

Fifteen years later, he was wrapping up a wonderful career as a Cardinal, playing before St. Louis fans who'd always idolized him as fans of the Cubs could only ask themselves, "What if?"

A banner unfurled at Busch Stadium during the August 13 game read: "Cards thank Cubs for best years of our lives, '64-'79."

While Brock had maintained a .300 average for most of his career, he'd slumped to .221 in 1978, and many wondered if he was through. A teammate's sarcastic remark—Brock wouldn't tell the media who it had been—that he was hitting off his back rather than front foot had helped him turn things around. He entered 1979 needing 100 hits for 3,000, but announced the season would be his last.

In addition to the media hoopla and fans frenzy over seeing history in the making, the Cardinals and Cubs were in a pennant race as they neared the middle of August. They'd split the first four games of this series, the Cardinals taking a doubleheader Friday while the Cubs had won Saturday's and Sunday's games. The third-place Cubs had a record of 61-52, four games behind Pittsburgh, while the Cardinals were right behind at 59-55.

For some curious reason, Cardinals officials had expected a crowd of only about 25,000, half of Busch Stadium's capacity. But nearly 45,000 showed up, some lining up for bleacher seats as early as 9 a.m. To accommodate the masses, the game started 20 minutes later than scheduled.

Gritty Pete Vuckovich started for the Cardinals against Dennis Lamp. The Cardinals reached Lamp right away as leadoff man Garry Templeton bunted safely. Brock, batting second in the order, strode to the plate as Busch Stadium organist Ernie Hays played some bars from the film "Close Encounters of the Third Kind" since Brock had told him this would be his last close encounter. The crowd chanted "Lou! Lou! Lou!"

On a hit-and-run, Brock singled into left, sending Templeton to third. Keith Hernandez followed by grounding to third as Templeton scored, but Brock tried to go all the way to third and was thrown out as first baseman Bill Buckner quickly returned the throw he'd just received from third baseman Steve Ontiveros.

In the fourth, the electricity of expectation surrounded Brock as he led off. Lamp had given up three hits but hadn't walked any while striking out two. He got ahead of Brock with a 1-2 count then tucked one under his chin. Brock bent way over backwards to get out of the way as the crowd unleashed a torrent of boos. Brock later told the press that the knockdown "jarred me back to reality" and made him realize he hadn't been concentrating as much as he should have been.

Cardinals broadcaster Jack Buck, calling the game on KMOX radio, described what happened next: "The two-two pitch: breaking ball— hit off the pitcher (voice rises) to the third baseman. (voice rises even more) No play! Base hit . . . (voice quivers with excitement) 3,000 for Lou Brock!"

While Lamp knelt to the third-base side of the mound, wringing his pitching hand, which had taken the brunt of that smash right back at him, Brock touched first and was mobbed by his teammates. The game halted for a 16-minute ceremony in which Brock received a salute from Cardinal great Stan Musial then thanked Cardinals fans and his family for their support. Just 21 seasons before, Musial had gotten his 3,000th hit, also against the Cubs.

When play resumed, Doug Capilla replaced the injured Lamp, and Keith Hernandez forced Brock at second. Hernandez was picked off first but made it to second on Buckner's error. One out later, George Hendrick singled him home to give the Cardinals a 2-0 lead.

Brock trotted to his position in left field for the fifth inning, but upon reaching it was called back by manager Ken Boyer. Jerry Mumphrey moved over from left to take Brock's place as Brock trotted off to another standing ovation.

The Cardinals had lost both Brock's previous record-setting games. They wanted this to be a win. But in the seventh, the Cubs chased Vuckovich with two runs to tie the score.

It stayed that way until the ninth. Willie Hernandez, the fourth Cub hurler, had kept the Cardinals in check for two innings and retired the first batter in the ninth. But Ken Reitz singled, the 1,000th hit of his career. Tom Herr, just brought up from the minors, ran for him. Ken Oberkfell was hit by a pitch, causing Cubs skipper Herman Franks to summon Bruce Sutter from the bullpen.

Sutter was on his way to the Cy Young Award and in those days was often called in with the score tied. Dane Iorg batted for the pitcher and admitted later he'd never until that plate appearance hit a fair ball off the Cardinals nemesis, who'd saved seven earlier Cub wins that year over St. Louis.

This time Iorg lashed a single, but Herr went only to third. Leadoff man Templeton lofted a fly ball to Cubs slugging left fielder Dave Kingman, and Herr easily beat the throw, giving the big crowd one more thing to celebrate.

Brock had joined a select club, entered previously by 13 players and since by only six others. But his thoughts went quickly back to the daily task.

"I'm prepared to play every game the rest of the year," he said after the game, noting that the Cardinals were still in the hunt.

He'd get 23 more hits that year and finish with a .304 average in his final season.

## Cards' pitchers blank Cubs three in a row
## June 18-20, 1968, Busch Stadium

As the first-place Cardinals prepared to host the Cubs in mid-June 1968, St. Louis manager Red Schoendienst was most concerned with getting better punch from his right fielders.

"I just wish somebody would get hot in right field," Schoendienst said before the opener of a three-game series.

But Schoendienst had no concerns over the pitching staff, which had paced the Cardinals in their recent 16-4 run that taken them to a 38-25 mark and 4 1/2-game lead.

Over the next three games, that pitching staff would shut down a powerful Cubs lineup like never before.

Right-hander Nelson Briles, who'd come out of the bullpen in 1967 when ace Bob Gibson had suffered a broken leg, took off the beads he'd worn eight times— all Cardinals' victories—during the recent surge. He said later he wanted to see if the club could win without his wearing them.

On June 18, Briles scattered eight hits. He was helped twice by striking out Cubs slugger Ron Santo on curveballs with baserunners in motion. Both times Cards catcher Johnny Edwards and his infielders turned a double play to thwart rallies.

Bobby Tolan, starting in right for an injured Roger Maris, smashed a fifth-inning solo home run off Cubs starter Bill Hands for the only run of the game.

Briles' closest call came with two outs in the ninth. Outfielder Lou Johnson caught a pitch both he and Briles thought was headed out of the then-cavernous park, but birthday boy Lou Brock caught it for the final out.

"Fortunately, we were playing here and not at Wrigley Field," Briles, then 8-5, said after his snappy two-hour, five-minute victory before 28,235.

On June 19, tall southpaw Steve Carlton took his 7-2 record to the mound for the Cardinals. His one-hit performance brought to many people's minds comparisons with famed Dodgers lefty Sandy Koufax, who'd dominated the National League from 1962 until his premature retirement after the 1966 season.

Cubs second baseman Glenn Beckert, who got the only hit off Carlton that night, a clean single in the fourth, said of him afterwards: "His curveball is the closest to Koufax's I've ever seen."

Carlton fanned nine and walked none in a 4-0 victory that lasted exactly two hours and was viewed by 27,577. He got all the runs he needed when cleanup man Orlando Cepeda launched a 400-foot home run to the left-field bleachers with two aboard in the third off Rich Nye.

Carlton then had yet to develop the devastating slider that would earn him four Cy Young Awards with the Phillies during the following two decades. And he'd yet to develop his aversion to the press, freely discussing his success afterwards.

"The pitch that Beckert hit was a fastball down and in," Carlton said afterwards. "I wanted to jam him but I didn't get it inside enough. But I'm happy to settle for just that hit."

Carlton also attributed his success to the experience he'd gained in the Cardinals' world championship season the year before. And, he added, a contributing factor was his gaining 10 pounds over the last year.

Catcher Johnny Edwards said Carlton's fast ball had always been moving. He added that Carlton's curve was so great that Edwards could often feel it still moving in his glove.

The shutout by the Cubs was their 12th of the season, exactly twice as many as they'd suffered the year before. It was their third straight shut-out, including a 1-0, 11-inning loss to Atlanta the previous Sunday. The Cubs hadn't scored since the first inning of their game Saturday, meaning their scoreless streak had reached 37 innings.

As Cubs manager Leo Durocher groused about how he'd shake up the lineup for the series finale, he mused on how the Cardinals two years before had discussed a trade that would have sent Carlton and Nelson Briles to the Cubs for Billy Williams.

The finale was a Businessman's Special, a 12:30 p.m. starting time in muggy 90-degree-plus weather. That day's mound opponents, however, Chicago's Ferguson Jenkins and St. Louis' Bob Gibson, seemed determined that the 26,550 in the stands not swelter too long, wrapping up their business in a brisk two hours, five minutes.

Jenkins was only 6-7, Gibson 7-5 entering that game, both victims of lack of support. But it was the kind of matchup that made 1968 "The Year of the Pitcher."

Jenkins went eight innings, giving up only four hits and two walks while striking out 11. Gibson in nine innings surrendered five hits and one walk while fanning six.

The game was decided in the Cardinals third. After light-hitting shortstop Dal Maxvill and Gibson went down on strikes, Lou Brock slashed a triple into the right field corner and scored when Curt Flood ripped a single into left to plate the game's only run.

The Cards had only one other scoring chance while the Cubs had only one in the game. Cubs right fielder Lou Johnson stranded the tying run on third in the fourth inning, and from then on Gibson continued his mastery. In the ninth he disposed of the Cubs third-, fourth- and fifth-place hitters—Billy Williams, Al Spangler and Ron Santo—on a strikeout and two popups, in that order.

"That first man who faces Gibson in the ninth inning is in trouble. Gibson just won't let that first man get on base," Cardinals third baseman Mike Shannon said. Shannon had admired Gibson's prowess for years, but especially that season rated him "the best ninth-inning pitcher" he'd ever seen.

Gibson with his fourth shutout lowered his earned run average to 1.21. The *Post-Dispatch* noted that Gibson could start thinking about the club season ERA of 1.72 by Bill Doak back in 1914.

The loss brought the Cubs' scoreless streak to 46 innings and allowed them to top by one the old record for futility held by the Cincinnati Reds.

The win allowed the Cardinals to maintain a 5 1/2-game lead in a pennant race that was already all but over several weeks before the All-Star Game.

Gibson went on to pitch 13 shutouts in a 22-9 season that saw him break not only the Cardinals' record for ERA but also the league's when he finished at an unbelievably stingy 1.12, the top symbol of 1968's "The Year of the Pitcher."

Briles finished 19-11 with four shutouts and a 2.80 ERA while Carlton slipped to 13-11 and 2.99 as the Cardinals won their second straight pennant.

The Cubs went on to tie the major league record of 48 straight scoreless innings before putting a run over in their next game on June 21, 1968 against Cincinnati.

## Dean sets K mark with 17 vs. Cubs
## July 30, 1933, Sportsman's Park, St. Louis

The Cardinals were hot. They'd won four straight since second baseman Frankie Frisch had been promoted to manager and now were to take on the defending NL champion Cubs in a Sunday doubleheader at Sportsman's Park.

The crowd of 29,500 came close to filling the north St. Louis ballpark. They possessed good timing. They'd see Dizzy Dean, the Cardinals' brash, 23-year-old pitcher, write his name into the history books.

The Cardinals, in fourth place, had defeated the third-place Cubs the day before, moving to within two games of them.

A workhorse who would pitch in a league-leading 48 games that year— including 26 complete games in 34 starts—Diz had recently worn himself out. Shortly before he'd been fired, manager Gabby Street had decided to give Dean a rest which Frisch had continued. Dizzy had pitched only the previous Sunday and a short relief stint on Thursday, so he was well refreshed by his standards as the Cubs series started.

But it didn't look good for Dean when he struggled with the first two hitters. Cubs third baseman Mark Koening doubled and scored on Billy Herman's single. Dean fanned two batters that frame, adding one in the second and two more in the third as he prevented Chicago from scoring any more runs.

In the home half of the third, with the Cardinals still trailing 1-0, Dean took offensive matters into his own hands. He doubled off starter Guy Bush and moved to third on leadoff man Pepper Martin's scratch hit. From there, Dean scored the tying run on Frisch's fly ball (which counted as a time at bat since the sacrifice fly rule had been abolished in 1932 and wouldn't return until 1939).

Dean then retired the Cubs in the fourth without a strikeout, the only inning without a whiff. But he didn't stop them from scoring as the Cubs pushed over another run on an error and a double to take a 2-1 lead.

While the Cardinals bats stayed cool, Dizzy's pitching got hot. He struck out the side in the fifth and added two in the sixth, bringing his total to 10.

The Cardinals, however, still trailed 2-1 going into their half of the sixth. When Cubs starter Guy Bush walked the leadoff man, the Cardinals' bats came alive, helped by an error. Center fielder Ernie Orsatti doubled with runners on second and third to give the Cardinals the lead 3-2. Catcher Jimmy Wilson singled him home, then shortstop Leo Durocher doubled, scoring Wilson, and moved up on a wild pitch by new hurler Burleigh Grimes. Dean ended the scoring with his second hit, a single.

Dean batted .181 that season on only 19 hits. His third hit of the game, a double, drove home St. Louis' eighth and final run in the eighth.

But he was paid a modest Cardinals salary to pitch. On this day, he did it with a flourish. After fanning one Cub in the seventh, Dean recorded the last six outs of the game on strikeouts. He saved his best K rations for the end, retiring the final four batters on strikes.

Of his 17 strikeout victims, 12 went down swinging. Curiously, the only Cub who didn't fan was Dean's mound rival, Bush.

Reports of post-game interviews were rare in those days, and there were no comments from Dean in the St. Louis papers. Eleven years later, however, he'd recount the event for a Chicago journalist and remark that if he had been aware he was setting a strikeout record he would have gotten more.

The writers then debated the nature of the record, showing the growing distance between the game and its 19th century roots that began about that time.

"Musty records also show that Charles Sweeney of Providence fanned 19 batters way back in 1884 and that Frank L. Shaw of the Boston club of the old Union Association (a major league for one season) fanned 18 in 1884, but those feats were accomplished in the days of the distant past, before baseball had become a big business and before Babe Ruth's big bat had started a reign of terror for pitchers," wrote sports editor J. Roy Stockton of the *St. Louis Post-Dispatch*.

Better to count Dean's performance as the record since it topped by one strikeout the mark four pitchers had achieved in this century. For sure, it had been the most strikeouts in a game since 1909. It also enabled catcher Wilson to establish a record for putouts by a catcher with 18.

Dean's accomplishment was considered the modern record for a quarter century, until the Dodgers' Sandy Koufax struck out 18 San Francisco Giants in 1959. Steve Carlton pushed the record to 19 in 1969. Roger Clemens fashioned the first of his two 20-strikeout performances to establish the present record in 1986, a feat matched by Cubs wunderkind Kerry Wood in 1998.

For the rest of 1933, Dean won seven more games to end at 20-18. The Cardinals finished fifth, two places behind the Cubs.

Dean wouldn't have much success against the Cubs for the rest of his career, though, going 13-17. Chicago was the only team against which he didn't hold a winning career mark.

Diz eventually joined the Cubs in 1938 after a line drive in the 1987 All-Star Game broke his toe. He hurt his arm by trying to rush back into action. Pitching only part-time, though, he'd help the Cubs win the 1938 pennant.

## Ol' Pete wins first for Cardinals
## June 27, 1926, Sportsman's Park, St. Louis

Sometimes a loss today results in big wins later.

That's what the Cardinals discovered after they'd been pasted 18-11 by the Pittsburgh Pirates June 21. Had the Cardinals won they'd have replaced the Bucs in second place. But by remaining in third the Redbirds —rather than Pittsburgh or first-place Cincinnati—were able to claim famed pitcher Grover Cleveland Alexander when the Cubs put him on waivers that day.

All three contenders had wanted Alexander, but he went to the Cardinals since they were the lowest of the three in the standings.

"This must be the Cardinals' year," wrote *St. Louis Post-Dispatch* sports editor J. Roy Stockton. "Even in defeat they profit."

Yet wins were what the Cardinals brass wanted when they shelled out the $4,000 waiver price and signed Alex the Great, also known as Ol' Pete. While only 3-3 in limited use by Chicago manager Joe McCarthy that season, Alexander came to St. Louis with a lifetime 318-168 mark. The Cardinals, starting to reap the benefits of the farm system general manager Branch Rickey had started six years before, were enjoying the heady air of the first division for one of the few seasons in this century. They wanted the veteran Alexander to strengthen their chances of remaining there.

The 39-year-old Alexander had feuded with rookie skipper McCarthy all year. McCarthy had never played major league ball, and Alexander resented such a person telling him how to retire major league batters. This led to other personality clashes between the two men.

McCarthy had recently suspended Alexander for breaking training rules and said right before the transaction that sent him to St. Louis: "Alexander hasn't pitched for a month and recently has been no help to the team."

But Alexander had his own version of things after the deal. "I'm in condition and ready to pitch right now," he reportedly told his old battery mate, Bill Killifer, now a Cardinals coach. Alexander and Killifer had helped the Phillies win the 1915 pennant and had many good games for the Cubs after being traded to Chicago together in 1918. Alexander's regular catcher in St. Louis would be Bob O'Farrell, who'd also caught Alexander in Chicago.

Cub fans were dismayed. "His release was a particular shock to a group of North Side fans, who only 10 days ago presented him with an expensive automobile," wrote sports editor Joe Foley of the *Chicago Journal*.

Alexander wouldn't have to wait long for his first start. The sixth-place Cubs, struggling with a 31-32 record but only 7 1/2 games behind the Reds, were scheduled to play the Cardinals in a doubleheader in St. Louis on Sunday, June 27. Manager Rogers Hornsby announced that Alexander would start the first game for the Cardinals, who by that weekend had climbed into second with a 37-28 record.

Whether it was because of the notoriety surrounding Alexander or the draw of a pennant race, advance ticket sales were brisk for the doubleheader. Fortunately, Sportsman's Park, which the Cardinals then rented from the American League Browns, had been dramatically upgraded in the off-season to accommodate the tenants. Its capacity had nearly doubled, to 33,000, with a new right-field pavilion, new bleachers and double deck for the grandstand. When the gates opened at 10:30 a.m. that Sunday, three-and-a-half hours before the first pitch, a record 37,146 fans started filing in. That total eclipsed the previous record 20,626 which had watched a Browns-Cardinals exhibition in 1922.

The largely partisan St. Louis crowd gave Alexander a tremendous ovation as he walked to the mound to face his former teammates. He responded by retiring the Cubs in order.

But Alexander's mound opponent, rookie Bob Osborn, was just as tough, matching goose eggs for four innings.

Cardinals right fielder Billy Southworth opened the scoring by driving one of Osborn's pitches into the pavilion in the fifth for a 1-0 Cardinals lead. Chicago took the lead in the seventh when St. Louisan Charlie Grimm, the jovial Cubs first baseman, popped a two-run homer into the pavilion. The Cardinals came right back in their half as shortstop Tommy Thevenow singled home third baseman Lester Bell, tying the score.

After giving up Grimm's homer, Alexander was as stingy as he'd been before it, not allowing another baserunner. After retiring the side in order in the 10th, Alexander watched from the bench as Southworth drew a leadoff walk from Osborn and was sacrificed into scoring position by Bell. The Cubs walked catcher Bob O'Farrell and Alexander strolled to the plate, Hornsby giving his pitcher the chance to win his own game. Alexander hit a long foul to left then struck out.

But leadoff man Ray Blades topped the ball to Grimm at first and Osborn raced over to take the toss at the bag. He dropped it—the scorer ruled it a hit—as Southworth touched on the plate for a Cardinals' 3-2 win in only one hour and 48 minutes.

"Alec appeared the master of old," the *St. Louis Globe Democrat* proclaimed after the win. Alexander's totals: 10 innings pitched, four hits, two runs, both earned, one walk and five strikeouts.

The Cardinals lost the second game 5-0 on a one hitter by Chicago's John "Sheriff" Blake as the crowd became more unruly, occasionally littered the field.

But Alexander had silenced any skeptics. He went on to go 9-7 with a 2.92 ERA for the Cardinals, helping them win their first ever pennant by two games over the Reds and seven over the fourth-place Cubs.

Alexander would be even better in the World Series, winning two and saving the final game with two-and-a-third brilliant relief innings.

## White gets 14 hits in back-to-back twin bills
## July 17-18, 1961, Busch Stadium, St. Louis

On the day Ty Cobb died, Cardinals first baseman Bill White went on a two-day hitting binge that would see him tie one of the Georgia Peach's more esoteric records.

Not mentioned in the July 18, 1961, obituaries was that Cobb had collected 14 hits in consecutive doubleheaders July 17 and 19, 1912.

Back-to-back doubleheaders, especially against the same team, were rare. But because of earlier rainouts that had to be made up, the Cardinals faced such a pair of twinbills against the Cubs July 17-18 at old Busch Stadium.

Even as baseball fans paused to mark the passing of one of the greatest hitters—and most unpopular players—who'd ever lived, their attention was focused more on another hitting feat going on in the American League. Both the New York Yankees' Roger Maris, with 35 homers, and Mickey Mantle, with 32, were on pace to break Babe Ruth's legendary single-season home run mark of 60. July 17 also marked the day Commissioner Ford Frick ruled that Ruth's record would have to be broken in 154 games, not the 162 that American League teams began playing that year because of expansion.

In St. Louis on Monday night, July 17, 13, 647 fans settled in for the first of two consecutive doubleheaders between the sixth-place Cardinals and seventh-place Cubs. Separated by only a half-game, neither sub.-500 club was headed toward contention. The Cardinals were 5-4 under new manager Johnny Keane, who'd replaced fired Solly Hemus just before the halfway point of the season; the Cubs, meanwhile were still operating under the bizarre College of Coaches system that rotated field direction among different people.

Keane was determined that these upcoming four games not destroy his already shaky pitching staff. So the starters understood their job was to go as long as they could. Those Cardinals pitchers would have one advantage, however. Cubs shortstop Ernie Banks would miss both days while having his eyes tested in Chicago for depth perception problems.

With White in his customary No. 3 spot in the lineup and singling four times, the Cardinals banged out 17 hits, overcame a 6-0 deficit with four runs in the seventh and six in the eighth and won the opener 10-6. In the second game, White again went four-for-five—three singles and a double—and drove in two runs to help the Cardinals again come back to win 8-5.

But rivaling White for the fans' affection that first night was second baseman Julian Javier. He'd returned to the lineup just the day before after being out a month with a groin injury, and he, too, rapped out four hits in five times to the plate in each game. The crowd chanted "go, go" when Javier reached base, and he thrilled them with two stolen bases as well as a triple that gave the Cardinals the lead for good in the first game.

Giving up those hits for Chicago were the likes of Don Cardwell, who'd held the Cardinals hitless the year before, and Barney Schultz, who two years later would help the Cardinals win the World Series. The Cardinals' Lindy McDaniel relieved weary starters Curt Simmons and Ernie Broglio in the ninth of each game.

White and Javier were within four of the NL record for hits in two consecutive doubleheaders, achieved by several players.

The July 17 doubleheader had taken nearly seven hours to complete, and didn't end until nearly 1 a.m. White didn't get to bed until nearly 3 a.m. But he couldn't sleep, mindful of having to lead a kids baseball clinic at 10 a.m. at Heman Park in the St. Louis suburb of University City.

He did lead the two-hour clinic then headed for Busch Stadium to prepare for that night's two games. The only sleep he got, he said later, was a 45-minute nap in the trainer's room.

If White was tired, however, he didn't show it, rapping out three more hits in the opener off Cubs starter Glen Hobbie. White's ninth home run of the season, a two-run blast to the pavilion roof in right field in the sixth, made it 7-3 in what turned out to be an 8-3 Cardinals win. Javier, meanwhile, went hitless.

In the nightcap, White again banged out three hits, this time two triples and a double. His second double, in the seventh, keyed a three-run rally that gave the Cardinals the final margin of victory 7-5. Starter Bob Gibson went all the way, duplicating the route-going performance of Larry Jackson in the opener. Javier chipped in with two hits.

White's totals for the four contests: 18 at-bats, seven runs scored, 14 hits, two doubles, two triples, one homer and six RBI. The binge raised his season's average from .289 to .317.

"I've felt bad before and still had a good game. Never anything like this, of course," he said, mustering enough energy to talk after another six hours of baseball before 12,889 fans.

But White downplayed the importance of the record. "I guess there are records for just about anything, aren't there?" he said. "I know it feels good to win two more ballgames."

The Giants came to town the next day and White proved his hitting wasn't a fluke as he went 2-for-5 in a Cardinals win over San Francisco.

White ended the season at .288. Banks soon returned to the Cubs lineup and finished with 29 homers. The Cardinals played much better under Keane than they had under Hemus and finished 80-74 and up a notch to fifth. The Cubs slumped to seventh, 64-90.

## Sutter saves both ends of twin bill
## June 26, 1982, Wrigley Field

The Cardinals entered the last Saturday of June 1982 in first place, but even their most devoted fans must have wondered how much longer they'd remain there.

Closer Bruce Sutter had been getting hammered a lot recently, and his earned run average entering a weekend four-game series with the Cubs in Wrigley Field was an astounding 4.78. In a recent stretch of 13 appearances, the battered and bearded ex-Cub had displayed a most unlucky 7.11 ERA.

"Cardinal reliever's split-fingered fastball no longer impervious to assault by hitters," read the sub-headline on a column that morning by *Chicago Sun-Times* sports editor Ray Sons.

In his six previous big-league seasons, Sutter had relied primarily on his baffling split-fingered fastball. To batters it seemed to make an almost 90-degree drop as it neared the plate, and many hitters had virtually tied themselves in a knot fishing for it.

Sutter had ridden that pitch to a Cy Young Award while pitching for the Cubs in 1979. He'd led the league in saves—when the rules granting them were much stingier—in three seasons, including the 25 he'd registered for the Cardinals in strike-torn 1981. (The Cubs, irritated at his doubling his salary to $700,000 in an arbitration case, had dealt Sutter to the Cardinals for hitters Leon Durham, Ken Reitz and Tye Waller after 1980.)

But, as sports editor Sons pointed out, hitters nearing mid-season 1982 were no longer intimidated. The Mets had ripped Sutter's pitches for five earned runs in an inning and a third the week before, and catcher John Stearns had been quoted as saying Sutter had relied too long on that one pitch.

Sutter acknowledged he would have to change. "If you throw the same pitch all the time, all the time, all the time, they just get so they totally disregard everything else," he told Sons.

He described how, since he didn't knock batters down—that not being his style—opponents would lean over the plate and be able to reach pitches off the plate. They'd foul off the bad ones until he'd had to bring one up, and they'd tee off.

"I gotta make an adjustment," Sutter said. "I used to be bullheaded. I'd never change. Now, I gotta change."

Cardinals manager Whitey Herzog, however, wasn't worried about his ace. "When the game is on the line, he'll still be in there," the White Rat said.

Nevertheless, Herzog had brought in Mike Roarke, Sutter's former pitching coach with the Cubs, who took time off from his insurance business for a consultation with his former protégé. Roarke concluded that Sutter had simply been throwing the ball too hard.

Sutter had spent the Friday, June 25, game in the bullpen but as a spectator, watching the Cardinals' old nemesis, Fergie Jenkins, continue to celebrate his return to the Cubs. Behind the 39-year-old Jenkins, Chicago whipped St. Louis 5-3. The Cardinals, however, backed into first place by themselves as the Montreal Expos lost a doubleheader to drop a half-game behind.

On a raw, windy, damp Saturday the Cardinals prepared for a doubleheader of their own. They sent youngster Dave LaPoint to the mound in the opener and followed that by pitching a relic of their own, Jim Kaat, in the nightcap. Doug Bird opened for the Cubs and Lee Smith came out of the bullpen to start the second game for the pitching-weary Chicagoans.

The nearly 30,000 fans who shivered through these two rather quickly played games (2:11, 2:37) saw little offense. The Cubs outhit the Cardinals in both games, though even then Chicago managed only 15 hits to St. Louis' 10.

But the Cardinals, without a real power hitter, played the kind of old-fashioned baseball known as "Whitey Ball" that made them a winner that year. The few men who did reach were moved along by sacrifices or moved themselves up by swiping a base. As it did all year, the defense sparkled when it had to, as when rookie center fielder Willie McGee and shortstop Ozzie Smith cooperated to throw out what would have been the tying run at the plate in the first game.

After the Cardinals scored two in the ninth—the most runs in any inning that day—to take a 4-1 lead, Herzog summoned Sutter when the Cubs leadoff man reached base. He retired the side one-two-three to register his league-leading 16th save. Only two of the pitches had been split-fingered fastballs.

Between games a Cubs fan barged into the men's room in the bleachers, chanting, "Cardinals suck, Cardinals suck, Cardinals suck . . . "

"Hey," growled a Cardinals fan, "we're in first place."

Without missing a beat, the Cubs fan continued, " . . . first place sucks, first place sucks, first place sucks . . . "

The second contest was just as much a nail-biter as the late innings rolled around. The Cardinals had erased a 1-0 Cubs lead when third baseman Ken Oberkfell and catcher Gene Tenace had hit back-to-back doubles in the second. In the next inning, left fielder Lonnie Smith had singled, stolen second and scored on Keith Hernandez's single.

Kaat, making only his second start in the past two years, pitched six credible innings, then surrendered to Doug Bair. When two men reached off him, however, the call again went out to Sutter.

He walked the first man he faced but then induced Larry Bowa to tap back to the mound to end the threat. Sutter gave up a hit but fanned a man in the ninth to preserve the 2-1 victory. He used more split-fingered fastballs in the second game but had still mixed his pitches.

Tenace, who caught those deliveries, said the two saves were "a big lift for him (Sutter)."

Sutter was happy with the performances and said he'd overcome a hurdle. "I got to where I was choking the ball," he said of his troubles the past few weeks. "If I can relax, my pitch will break more."

## Worrell closes out Cubs
## September 19, 1987, Busch Stadium

One thing Cardinals manager Whitey Herzog liked about closer Todd Worrell was that he could shake off an occasional bad game and come back with a great one.

Worrell had demonstrated that in 1986 when he'd earned NL Rookie of the Year honors. He'd lost 10 games in relief—but also saved a league-leading 36 for a club that had never been in contention.

In 1987, Worrell was the bullpen mainstay for a Cardinals club in the thick of a pennant race as summer gave way to fall. The start of a weekend series against the fifth-place Cubs September 18 found the Cardinals clinging to a 1 1/2-game lead over the New York Mets and three games over the Montreal Expos.

The Cubs had an offense, most notably Andre Dawson, who would hit 49 homers that season and take the Most Valuable Player award. They'd pounded Cardinals pitching in the first game, winning 8-1. Fortunately for the Redbirds, the Mets had also lost. Meanwhile, the Expos had won.

On Saturday night, September 19, the Cardinals, without slugger Jack Clark, who'd injured himself the week before sliding into first, sent rookie Joe Magrane to the mound. Chicago countered with veteran Scott Sanderson as 50,460 sat in to watch.

St. Louis drew first blood in the third as Ozzie Smith drove in Vince Coleman from first with a triple that rattled around the right-field corner. First baseman Dan Driessen, whom the Cardinals had acquired for just such a situation as they now faced without Clark, kept the rally going with two out by smacking an RBI single. Crowd favorite Willie McGee then drove a home run into the right-center field seats.

Magrane, a 6-foot-6 southpaw who batted right-handed, added to his own 4-0 lead the next inning by hitting his first-ever home run. The often-witty Magrane noted that the pitch was a "hanging something," and said he could have written the word "Voit" on it as it neared the plate. It was a reference to a basketball manufacturer and hence the ease with which he was able to handle the pitch.

For good measure, Magrane took a one-hitter into the sixth.

But as Cubs and Cardinals matchups often evolve, this one didn't become a rout. The Cubs came back, aided by a Terry Pendleton error, scoring three times off Magrane in the sixth. With a 7-7 record, Magrane was trying for just his third victory in his last 16 starts, though Herzog noted Magrane had pitched well in four of his previous five outings.

When the Cubs loaded the bases in the seventh, Herzog made the call for Worrell. Just five days before, Worrell had been unable to protect a 2-0 lead for Magrane; now there was no room for error, especially with the two batters awaiting him—Ryne Sandberg and Andre Dawson. Magrane anxiously watched from the bench.

Worrell put a couple of fastballs under Sandberg's chin. Then, after seeing him foul off a couple others, he struck out the Cubs' second baseman with a low slider.

Up came Dawson, with his 44 homers and 123 RBI. He'd launched his MVP season off Worrell back in April with a grand slam that had left Busch Stadium like a cannon shot. Later in the season Worrell had fanned Dawson in Wrigley Field with the game on the line, as it was here.

"You can't think about what happened two months ago or even yesterday," Worrell said that night, showing the maturity that Herzog so admired.

Reflecting on that confrontation some 11 years later, Worrell said the book on Dawson then was that one could strike him out on a slider low and away. "I had a nasty slider until I hurt my arm (much later in his career)," he said recently.

But Worrell suspected that to get Dawson out this time he'd have to try something different. "I needed to get one in on him tight to strike him out," Worrell reflected recently about his approach. "I had to get a good, hard pitch inside, out of the normal sequence for getting him out."

There was a caveat: not getting it inside enough would be fatal.

Worrell got two strikes on Dawson. Then Worrell got his fastball just where he wanted it, in on Dawson's hands. Frozen, the batter could only watch it cross the inside corner for strike three.

Worrell called it his best pitch of the season.

He gave up a hit in the eighth but finished the game. His line: two and two-thirds innings, one hit, no runs, no walks, three strikeouts.

It was his 30th save. It was also Magrane's eighth victory.

"As long as I'm around here I know Todd is going to come in and get me out of jams," an appreciative Magrane said.

Most importantly, it let the Cardinals retain their 1 1/2-game lead over the Mets on their way to the NL East title and eventual World Series date with the Minnesota Twins.

## Rookie Miller blanks Cubs in debut
## August 13, 1952, Wrigley Field

Cardinals manager Eddie Stanky was concerned. It had been nearly two weeks since one of his pitchers had finished what he'd started.

It was an era that still saw a high percentage of complete games—the fewest by any NL staff in 1952 would be 43 by last-place Pittsburgh and the most 80 by the fourth-place Phillies.

As the Cardinals prepared to take on the Cubs in Wrigley Field on August 12, Stanky was sending rookie right hander Stu Miller to the mound against Cubs veteran Bob Rush.

It was the last contest of a 22-game road trip that had taken the Cardinals to the ballparks of all seven NL opponents. Going into the finale of that swing, the third-place Cardinals were 12-9 to climb to 63-48, but still 11 games behind the Dodgers. The Cubs, who'd pounded four Redbird pitchers the day before in winning 10-2, were in fifth with a 55-53 record.

A paid crowd of 18,457 was joined on this Ladies Day by more than 10,000 women admitted free.

Miller, 24, was 5-foot 11 1/2 and—on his first day in the big leagues—about 155 pounds. He had just been brought up from the Cardinals' farm club in Columbus of the American Association. After winning eight of his last 10 starts, including a 1-0 game the previous Friday, he'd been pronounced ready for the big leagues by Columbus manager Johnny Keane.

On the eve of Miller's first start, veteran southpaw Harry Brecheen dined with him and went over the Cubs' starting lineup. Brecheen later told Bob Broeg of the *St. Louis Post-Dispatch* that Miller had "ice water in his veins," meaning he wasn't intimidated. But the rookie acknowledged he'd be nervous at least until after the first pitch.

The Cardinals did their best to take the edge off for the newcomer in their first. With one out, second baseman Red Schoendienst singled to left. Center fielder Stan Musial followed with a single up the middle. When the Cubs unsuccessfully tried to get Schoendienst going to third, Musial took second. The Cubs then intentionally walked right fielder Enos Slaughter, but left fielder Hal Rice foiled that strategy by singling to left for an RBI. Musial, however, overran third and was tagged out.

Little did Miller know that would be his offense for the day. Little did the Cubs know what he'd be throwing at them.

"I have just three pitches, a fast ball, a slow one and another slow one that's slower than the other. I guess they would call that one a change-up, and it's my most effective pitch," Miller said.

Others would later say that Miller had three pitches: slow, slower and slowest.

The Cubs, meanwhile, sensing they might have a rough day against Miller, tried rattling him as early as the second inning by complaining that he was violating the rules by wetting his fingers. After what was described as "a mild rhubarb," Miller walked a man and gave up a single to another with two outs but pitched out of the jam.

Fred Heger of St. Louis, a retired phone company executive, was in his early 20s and had just completed Army Reserves duty when he and a friend went to Chicago for a week. He was at that game.

"We sat on the third-base side. We'd read about Miller that he was junk-ball pitcher. You'd think you or I could hit him. He really baffled the Cubs that day."

One thing Heger noted that day about the Wrigley Field crowd's treatment of their hero, Hank Sauer, the Mayor of Wrigley Field, who'd hit two home runs against the Cardinals the day before: "We couldn't get over the way they cheered him, like he was Babe Ruth. Musial didn't even get that much applause here."

Sauer was the only one to consistently hit Miller that day, going 3-for-4 and collecting half the Cubs' hits. Each time, however, he was left stranded.

One of the better chances the Cubs had to score came in the sixth. Right fielder Gene Hermanski popped one into center field but Musial made a diving catch for the second out. Luckily so, because Sauer followed with a pop fly double to right field then took third on a passed ball. But Miller induced the next man to ground out.

The Cardinals in the meantime got to Rush for 10 hits in his eight innings but were unable to push any more runners across.

While the Cardinals bullpen started throwing in the ninth, Stanky said later he'd intended to win or lose it with the kid. And Miller certainly earned his victory with his ninth-inning performance.

With one out, Sauer was credited with his third hit when he smashed one off the glove of third baseman Tommy Glaviano, who'd just replaced Vern Benson for defensive purposes. Catcher Toby Atwell then singled, sending Sauer to second. First baseman Dee Fondy forced Atwell, sending Sauer to third with the tying run.

Second baseman Bill Serena, who'd already gotten one hit off Miller, walked to the plate and nearly to first base as Miller missed with the first three pitches. But after a strike and a foul ball, the count was full. Serena, guessing a changeup, was paralyzed by Miller's fastest pitch of the day, a low fastball across the inside corner for a called strike three.

Miller's line: nine innings pitched, six hits, two walks and four strikeouts.

Five days later Miller would come within one out of being the first NL hurler since 1898 to pitch shutouts in his first two starts as he beat the Cincinnti Reds 2-1.

Miller, 5-3 for the rest of that season, would become primarily a reliever in 1953. He pitched three more seasons for the Cardinals before being dealt to the Giants, then later to the Orioles, becoming an ace reliever for both clubs and helping each win a pennant.

During the 1961 All-Star Game in San Francisco's new Candlestick Park, Miller gained notoriety after being charged with a balk when his lithe frame was literally blown off the pitching rubber by the famed Candlestick winds. But he righted himself to get the win.

These rookies also turned in complete game shutouts in their first-ever starts: King Cole of the Cubs over the Cardinals, 8-0, October 6, 1909; Jackie Collum of the Cardinals over the Cubs, 6-0, September 21, 1951; and Jim Cosman of the Cardinals over the Cubs, 2-0 on October 2, 1966.

# 9

---

# A Dual Great Player Performance

## Both pitchers go 18 innings in 2-1 Cubs win
### June 24, 1905, League Park, St. Louis

**FEW games better symbolize the dead-ball era**—when pitching and defense far outshined offense—than the 18-inning 2-1 game the Cubs won from the Cardinals on June 24, 1905.

Pitching took the headlines as both starters, Cubs rookie Ed Reulbach and cagy Cardinals veteran Jack Taylor, each went the distance. Taylor pitched better but Reulbach's defense helped him out repeatedly in extra innings.

Pitching the equivalent of two games in one day was not unheard of. It had been done six times before, going back to 1882. Taylor had hurled 19 innings for the Cubs in beating Pittsburgh 3-2 in 1902.

In that era, most starters finished (the Cubs summoned a reliever in only 20 of 153 games that year while the Cardinals went to the bullpen just 19 times in 154 games). But Taylor went well beyond the standard. As he took the mound that day in St. Louis, he was continuing a streak he'd begun in 1901 that would reach a record 187 consecutive complete games the following season.

Reulbach wouldn't put up the career complete-game numbers of his mound opponent, yet he, too, would blossom into a dependable starter.

As they took the field June 24 following a rainout the day before, the Cubs and Cardinals were teams heading in dramatically different directions.

The fourth-place Cubs were nine games behind the New York Giants and would finish second to New York. But Chicago already had in place the Tinker-to-Evers-to-Chance nucleus that, with excellent pitching from people like Reulbach and Mordecai (Three Finger) Brown, would reel off four pennants in the next five years.

The Cardinals were headed toward a distant sixth place and would finish no higher than seventh during the five years the Cubs dominated the league. Taylor, who'd won 21 games the year before, was on his way to a 21-loss season.

The game, as was then the custom, started at 4 p.m. in hopes of attracting the mercantile class that could get off work early enough to attend. The Cardinals played their games in League Park in north St. Louis, on the site of the present-day Beaumont High School.

Neither club scored until the Cubs in their fourth pushed a run over in a style typical for the times: right fielder Billy Maloney singled and stole second. First baseman and soon-to-be manager Frank Chance reached on an infield single, sending Maloney to third. Shortstop Joe Tinker then scored Maloney with a ground ball to the shortstop.

Meanwhile, Reulbach kept the St. Louis hitters off stride until the bottom of the ninth. The Cardinals tied the score when right fielder Josh Clarke led off with a single then came round to score on manager-third baseman Jimmy Burke's double. Catcher Jack Warner, on whom the Cubs stole six bases that day, then sacrificed the winning run to third. But Tinker put out the next two batters, one on a pop up and the other on a ground ball, to send it to extra innings.

"Reulbach and Taylor both accepted the gage of battle and fought on with bull-dog determination as inning after inning passed without a run crossing the plate," reported the *St. Louis Globe-Democrat*. "Neither was willing to give an inch, though both were tired and showed the effect of their long-continued labors. Taylor stood up under the strain better than his younger opponent, and it looked for the final four or five innings that Reulbach was fighting on his nerve."

The Cardinals hit Reulbach in nearly every one of the extra innings, but each time Chicago's defense bailed out the young pitcher. The Cubs pulled off five double plays in overtime, including: a conventional Tinker-Evers-Chance one which ended the 10th; Chance to catcher Johnny Kling back to Chance to cut down the winning run at the plate with none out in the 11th; Tinker to Chance which ended the 13th; Chance to Tinker to Chance in the 15th, and an unassisted double play by Tinker in the bottom of the 17th as he snared a line drive and stepped on second before the runner could get back.

St. Louis center fielder Dave Brain nailed a Chicago runner trying to score in the 10th for a St. Louis double play.

But someone had to win, and Chicago found a way in the 18th. With one out, left fielder Frank (Wildfire) Schulte tripled and scored on a sacrifice fly by Maloney. St. Louis put a man on in its half but got the last man to foul out.

"Then the crowd wended its way home in the fast gathering dusk," the *Globe-Democrat* concluded. The game took 3 hours and 10 minutes, a length registered by some modern, nine-inning 2-1 games.

The pitching line for the day:

|          | IP | H  | R | BB | SO |
|----------|----|----|---|----|----|
| Reulbach | 18 | 14 | 1 | 6  | 6  |
| Taylor   | 18 | 11 | 2 | 4  | 7  |

Reulbach wasn't finished with herculean feats. Just two months to the day after this performance, he pitched all 20 innings in a 2-1 Cubs win over the Phillies. In the 1908 stretch-drive pennant, he pitched and won both games of a doubleheader against Brooklyn.

In eight full seasons with the Cubs, Reulbach was 136-64.

Taylor, who had been traded to St. Louis for Mordecai "Three Finger" Brown back in 1903, returned to Chicago two years later. He would help the Cubs win the pennant in 1906 and 1907 and retire with a 151-139 record.

# 10

# Jenkins vs. Gibson

**RUN-hungry fans were advised to stay away** from the famed pitching duels between Fergie Jenkins and Bob Gibson.

Matching perhaps the two greatest pitchers in both the Cubs' and Cardinals' franchise histories, the nine games in which Jenkins and Gibson linked up between 1967 and 1972 were a baseball purist's delight.

The pace of the game was the snappiest possible; two-hour games, or less, were the norm. Jenkins used to run to and from the mound. Gibson pitched, got the ball back, and was ready to go again. No dawdling. There were a minimum of walks and a maximum of 1-and-2 counts. If a batter made hard contact, he was fortunate. The mix was a winning formula over long, 17-season careers. Jenkins won 284 games with a 3.34 career ERA. Gibson nailed 251 wins with a 2.91 ERA.

Possessing unbelievable endurance and stamina, Hall of Famers Jenkins and Gibson were all-around athletes. Both were excellent hitters as pitchers. Both executed fundamentals expertly, rarely beating themselves with a fielding faux pas. They were so coordinated that they could have played other sports—and did.

Both had stints in the off-season for the Harlem Globetrotters. Both Jenkins and Gibson were good amateur basketball players. Jenkins didn't stop there. He played hockey in his native Chatham, Ontario, throwing his 6-foot-5 frame around the rink. He also played football in high school.

While both played at a high level of competitiveness, they offered contrasting personalities. Jenkins was the affable "Fly," a people person who'd talk to anybody, anytime. Although a wicked clubhouse cutup, Gibson, nicknamed "Hoot," was far more serious, rarely talking to an opponent, displaying a hiss-and-vinegar side sometimes even decades later when questioners approached him.

Jenkins ended up on the positive side of the ledger with a 5-3 lifetime mark against Gibson.

But barely. Almost all their matchups were close, low-scoring affairs. And if the truth be known, each hurler did not go into the game relishing the duel. They knew that had bring their best stuff and maximum concentration level to the mound.

"I was aware, of course. He was the enemy pitcher," Gibson said.

"The problem was, everyone thought I loved to pitch against Fergie and I liked the competition. Not really. You'd rather pitch against somebody you know you're going to get four or five runs off of. We weren't going to get but one or two runs off of him, and that made it tough."

Ditto with Jenkins.

"I knew if I was pitching against Gibson, runs would be at a minimum," he said. "Same with (Juan) Marichal, (Gaylord) Perry. Bobby was one of the top five in the National League in the time before I got established. If I gave up two or three runs, I was a loser."

Jenkins and Gibson really never talked to one another off the mound during their golden era.

"I felt that hitters just love to get comfortable with you," Gibson said. "The more you consorted with them, the more you talked with them, the more comfortable they get with you. I felt that if I just stayed away from them and they didn't have any idea of what I was about, it would work in my favor. I still believe in that."

"I didn't care what he (Jenkins) was thinking. I knew I was going to have to be on my best game in order to beat him. I wasn't concerned about how he did it. He did it differently than me. I was a high fastball pitcher; he was a sinkerballer. We both had a pretty good slider. He was in and out more than me; I tried to overpower the guy most of the time."

Jenkins understood Gibson's standoffishness.

"Bobby was always fielding ground balls at short or third; that's how he got his exercise in," he said. "He was the kind of guy who concentrated on what he had to do. We might exchange glances and say 'hi.' But when the game started, we're all business. Both of us knew that if we let up, we'd be in trouble."

The embargo against conversation ended with the ebbing of Jenkins' career in 1984. Gibson had retired after the 1975 season. The pair saw each other frequently at Randy Hundley's fantasy camps and old-timers' games. Then they had more grist for conversation when both joined the coaching staffs of their old teams in 1995.

Such meetings evoked the old feelings of competitiveness. And, looking back, Jenkins rates Gibson the toughest competitor he had ever seen along with the best modern-day Cardinals pitcher.

"By far," he said. "When Bob was on the mound, he was all business, he didn't mess around. That's very important. When you're out there, your concentration is 100 percent pitching, no foolishness. That's how you win ballgames."

We won't see pitchers of their kind ever again. What they started was often what they finished. During Gibson's 1.12 ERA Cy Young Award season in 1968, he completed 28 of 34 starts. Coupled with his 22 victories, Gibson ended up with six complete-game defeats. Ditto with Jenkins during his own Cy Young campaign in 1971. Jenkins finished 30 of 39 starts, amassing 325 innings pitched. He won 24.

But when they pitched against each other, matters sometimes weren't decided at the end of nine innings. Jenkins and Gibson had to pitch into the 10th and the 11th innings at times, in the near-100 degree heat of Busch Stadium, a feat of endurance that you won't see in today's game.

"I doubt that we'll ever see that happen again," Gibson said. "It's really sad that everybody blames the pitchers for not completing ballgames. It really has nothing to do with the pitchers. It has to do with the way the game is played today. They have the setup men and the closers, and that's who they look to in the sixth, seventh and eighth innings."

But, surprisingly, Gibson had no personal code that anything less than a complete game was unacceptable.

"What it was, was the press would criticize you if you didn't finish ballgames," he said. Jenkins agreed, remembering post-game questions over why he didn't finish the game, particularly against an opponent he should have beaten.

In contrast, Jenkins believed that if both he and Gibson had the luxury of multi-layered bullpens and ninth-inning-only closers, "we both probably would have won 300 ballgames."

When Gibson and Jenkins both tutored younger pitchers in recent years, it was a "do as I say," not "do as I do" style.

"I think the mental approach was what I was concerned with," Gibson said. "You did that by talking the game, talking about setting guys up. As far as mechanics, most of them have pretty good mechanics, otherwise they wouldn't be here."

And, in many cases, present pitchers don't enjoy their craft enough— or the sheer adrenalin of hooking up in a duel with one of the best.

"We both had a lot of fun doing it," Jenkins said. "It's too bad that some of these guys now don't reach back and think about how the game was really played."

Following is how Jenkins and Gibson played the game, start by start, in their matchups.

## Cubs 7, Cardinals 5
## June 3, 1967, Busch Stadium

Gibson already was the longtime Cardinals ace—and a certified Cubs Killer—when Jenkins, in his first full year as a starter, took the mound in their first matchup before a huge Saturday night crowd of 46,670.

Neither pitcher was at his best. Jenkins was touched up for two runs in the first on doubles by Lou Brock and Tim McCarver, sandwiched around a walk to Roger Maris. A notoriously slow starter in games, Jenkins held the damage tot he two spot and then settled down.

The Cubs uncharacteristically bombed out Gibson with a five-run fifth, highlighted by a three-run homer by Billy Williams, Gibson's top Cubs nemesis. Gibson was so off his game that Cardinals manager Red Schoendienst didn't allow him to work out of the fifth, pulling him in favor of reliever Nelson Briles.

But Jenkins had no rocking-chair outing, despite two more Cubs runs in the ninth off Cards reliever Hal Woodeshick. He had to work for his sixth win. With one out in the eighth, Jenkins hit Orlando Cepeda with a pitch, then served up a double to Tim McCarver that just barely missed clearing the right field wall. Cepeda thought the ball was gone, trotted around the bases and had to hold up at third when the ball came back into play. Re-energized, Jenkins fanned Mike Shannon and got Julian Javier to pop up for the third out.

In the ninth, Jenkins retired pinch hitters Curt Flood and Dave Ricketts. But Lou Brock, forever exacting revenge on the team that traded him, homered into the right-field seats to cut the Cubs lead to 7-3. Then Bobby Tolan singled and scored on Maris' triple. Cubs manager Leo

Durocher gave Jenkins the hook. Another Cardinals run tallied on Cepeda's single as Durocher employed three relievers—Cal Koonce, Bob Hendley and Bill Hands—to finally nail down the victory.

Jenkins would not have a chance to face Gibson again in 1967 after the latter broke his leg while pitching and missed much of the season's second half. He finished with a 20-13 record and 2.80 ERA, while Gibson—13-7 with a 2.98 ERA—recovered in time to become the Cardinals' World Series pitching hero with three complete-game victories over the Red Sox that included just 14 hits and three runs with 26 strikeouts in 27 innings.

|  |  | IP | H | R | ER | BB | SO |
|---|---|---|---|---|---|---|---|
| Jenkins, | (W, 6-3) | 8 2/3 | 10 | 5 | 5 | 3 | 6 |
| Gibson, | (L, 6-5) | 4 1/3 | 7 | 5 | 5 | 2 | 2 |

## Cubs 5, Cardinals 1
## April 20, 1968, Busch Stadium

The second consecutive Saturday Night Special involving the two aces ended up in Jenkins' favor, with the first double-complete game performance of the duels.

A decent spring night crowd of 29,348 saw Jenkins get within one out of a shutout, the only Cardinals run coming on Curt Flood's homer in the ninth. A Jenkins' characteristic—a walkless performance—enabled him to master the Cardinals on a three-hitter.

"Last year I gave up far too many walks (83 in 289 innings)," Jenkins said after the game. "I got hurt a lot when I'd give up a couple in front of a hit. So this year I'm determined to make them hit their way on base. I'm going to try to pitch 100 innings before I hand out a walk."

McCarver and Shannon reached on singles in the second and eighth, respectively. In between, Jenkins retired 18 in a row.

"After that hit I was determined to make it nothing more than a one-hitter," Jenkins said of McCarver's single, one pitch after the pitcher thought he had McCarver struck out on a checked swing. Umpire Tony Venzon ruled McCarver had checked in time.

Once again, Williams touched up Gibson. He slugged a two-run homer with Glenn Beckert aboard in the first. In the fifth, Williams touched up Gibson for an RBI doubled to right center, capping off a two-run inning. Lou Johnson accounted for the final Cubs run with a two-out double off the left-field fence in the ninth. Overall, the Cubs reached Gibson for 10 hits in the two-hour, three-minute game.

"Everything was working for me tonight," Jenkins said. "My best pitch probably was my curve."

|  |  | IP | H | R | ER | BB | SO |
|---|---|---|---|---|---|---|---|
| Jenkins | (W, 2-0) | 9 | 3 | 1 | 1 | 0 | 7 |
| Gibson | (L, 0-1) | 9 | 10 | 5 | 5 | 1 | 8 |

## Cardinals 1, Cubs 0
## June 20, 1968, Busch Stadium

Two streaks collided on during the hot, humid Thursday afternoon "Businessman's Special" game.

With the momentum growing for his memorable 1968 season, Gibson had hurled three consecutive shutouts with a scoreless innings streak of 29 going into the contest. Meanwhile, the Cubs had gone 37 scoreless innings themselves. And Jenkins had been shut out in five of his seven defeats coming in, while enduring a 10-inning no-decision in his previous start in which the Cubs had been blanked over 11 innings against the Braves.

You know who won this one. Gibson prevailed when the motivated Brock tripled into the right-field corner with two out in the fourth for the only extra-base hit of the contest. Curt Flood then followed with a single to left for the only run of the game. Jenkins fanned 11 in a usually winnable performance, but one run often was one too many in his duels with Gibson.

The Cardinals ace allowed just one Cubs scoring chance in the top of the fourth when, with two out, Ron Santo walked and advanced to third on Dick Nen's single. But Lou Johnson grounded out to third to end the threat. Gibby also helped himself by holding the usually tough Williams hitless in four at-bats.

Durocher tried to shake his lineup up with a strange order that included popgun left-handed hitter Al Spangler batting cleanup and playing center field while the little-used Nen, father of present-day Giants closer Robb Nen, played first base in place of Ernie Banks. But results were not forthcoming; Gibson held the Cubs to five singles. Game time was two hours, five minutes.

The Year of the Pitcher was in full swing. Don Drysdale had gone

58 scoreless innings. Gibson ran his total to 38 with the win. Jenkins' tough luck would continue.

|  | | IP | H | R | ER | BB | SO |
|---|---|---|---|---|---|---|---|
| Jenkins | (L, 6-8) | 8 | 4 | 1 | 1 | 2 | 11 |
| Gibson | (W, 8-5) | 9 | 5 | 0 | 0 | 1 | 6 |

## Cubs 6, Cardinals 5 (13 innings)
## August 4, 1968, Busch Stadium

Gibson was dominating like few others ever in baseball coming into the game. He had won 12 in a row and possessed an 0.50 ERA over his previous 108 innings.

But neither Gibson nor Jenkins was around for the finish as the Sunday matinee crowd of 47,445, partly attracted by ceremonies unveiling Stan Musial's statue outside Busch Stadium, enjoyed a 13-inning thriller.

Normally sure-handed shortstop Don Kessinger put Jenkins in a hole in the third when he failed to touch second on what should have been a routine out. He was charged with an error. Soon after, center fielder Adolfo Phillips let a pop single fall in front of him in center. The Cardinals pushed a total of three runs across with the benefit of three other singles.

Removed for a pinch hitter in the fifth, Jenkins was not around when Spangler tied the game with a homer off Gibson to lead off the ninth. Earlier, in the seventh, Williams bedeviled Gibson again with a solo homer that tied the game 3-3. Gibson continued pitching through the 11th, when the Cubs got the go-ahead run on a Kessinger single. But the Cardinals bailed out Gibson, who left for pinch hitter Phil Gagliano in the bottom of the 11th. He had pitched almost two games on a yield of 12 hits, three walks and 10 strikeouts. The Cubs finally pushed across the winning run in the top of the 13th.

The Cubs had managed to make Gibson toil in two of his three duels against Jenkins in 1968. But they were merely blips on the way to a never-to-be duplicated season. Gibson's 1.12 ERA was accompanied by 22 wins — including 13 shutouts — along with 268 strikeouts in 304 2/3 innings and just 198 hits yielded.

Jenkins did not have too shabby a season either with a 20-15 record and a 2.63 ERA. He actually could have won more games than Gibson with a trifle more run support. Jenkins held the dubious record of losing five 1-0 games in '68.

| | IP | H | R | ER | BB | SO |
|---|---|---|---|---|---|---|
| Jenkins | 4 | 6 | 3 | 2 | 1 | 2 |
| Gibson | 11 | 12 | 5 | 4 | 3 | 10 |

## Cubs 3, Cardinals 1 (Game 1 of a doubleheader) June 29, 1969, Wrigley Field

The Jenkins-Gibson duel played a secondary role on this Sunday before an SRO Wrigley Field crowd of 41,060. Almost everyone focused on Billy Williams Day, as the honoree broke Musial's old National League consecutive game streak of 895 games in grand style, going 5-for-9 in the doubleheader.

But the Cubs' sweep-they won the nightcap in a laugher 12-1-wouldn't have been accomplished without another stellar Jenkins outing to outpitch Gibson in Game 1.

Gibson started off hot with seven strikeouts in the first three innings. Hoot also pitched out of two bases-loaded jams in the fifth and sixth. Jenkins matched him almost pitch for pitch in a scoreless standoff.

But Gibson finally weakened in the eighth when Williams doubled into the left field corner. Banks singled through the middle for the game's first run, then Willie Smith homered into the right-field bleachers to make it 3-0.

Vada Pinson broke Jenkins' shutout with a one-out homer in the ninth. Mike Shannon came up as the tying run with two out after a Tim McCarver single, but popped to second to end the game.

Jenkins fanned just three Cardinals, working more craftsman-like without his best strikeout stuff. The Cubs helped him out with two double plays as the Cardinals left just five men on base. Meanwhile, Gibson punched out 10 Cubs total.

Game time was two hours, six minutes, enabling the spectacular between-games ceremonies honoring Williams to get under way quickly.

| | | IP | H | R | ER | BB | SO |
|---|---|---|---|---|---|---|---|
| Jenkins | (W, 10-5) | 9 | 8 | 1 | 1 | 2 | 3 |
| Gibson | (L, 10-5) | 8 | 7 | 3 | 3 | 3 | 10 |

# Cubs 3, Cardinals 1 (10 innings)
# July 4, 1969, Busch Stadium

Cool-customer Jenkins was famed for seemingly not perspiring in the most brutal heat. He was put to the test over 10 innings in the 95-degree holiday afternoon sauna before 28,177 in St. Louis, and passed (not passed out) with flying colors.

Jenkins' gray flannel road jersey hardly looked stained as he again matched Gibson pitch for pitch in a quick rematch from their Billy Williams Day duel. "The heat was so oppressive that it seemed remarkable that both Jenkins and Gibson were able to continue pitching," reported Jerome Holtzman of the *Chicago Sun-Times*. Plate umpire Shag Crawford had to leave the game after six innings due to heat exhaustion.

Each team's hitters tried to wear out the opposing pitcher by taking their time strolling to the plate, forcing both Jenkins and Gibson to stand out in the mound amid the broiling air waiting for the hitter. It could have been worse. Busch Stadium's first heat-trapping artificial turf was not installed until the next season.

Kessinger tripled and scored on a sacrifice fly in the third. In the bottom of the fourth, Vada Pinson singled in Lou Brock, who had walked and advanced to third on Curt Flood's single. That 1-1 tie lasted until the top of the 10th, when singles by Kessinger and Beckert brought up Williams to face Gibson, who privately couldn't have liked the matchup. Williams doubled to center for one run, and Beckert then scored on Ron Santo's single.

Jenkins kept on truckin' through the 10th, finally ending the exhausting day by fanning Curt Flood for the last out. The winning pitcher raised both of his hands over his head in triumph.

Need to get somewhere fast even after extra innings have kept you? This contest ended in two hours, 32 minutes.

Jenkins pitched superbly through the end of August, but was rocked in September as the Cubs pulled off their famous fold under the onslaught of the Miracle Mets. He finished 21-15 with a 3.21 ERA. Gibson wasn't far off his 1968 pace with a 20-13 mark and 2.18 ERA, sometimes beset by lack of run support from his teammates.

|         |          | IP | H  | R | ER | BB | SO |
|---------|----------|----|----|---|----|----|----|
| Jenkins | (W, 11-5) | 10 | 7  | 1 | 1  | 2  | 10 |
| Gibson  | (L, 10-6) | 9  | 10 | 3 | 3  | 3  | 9  |

## Cardinals 2, Cubs 1 (Game 1)
## September 23, 1970, Busch Stadium

If the Cubs had roughed up Gibson at times in his games against Jenkins, then Gibson fashioned the best kind of payback in the first game of a twi-night doubleheader in St. Louis.

Gasping for breath with just a week left in the National League East pennant race, the Cubs headed for life support when Gibson shut them down on two hits and set the tone for a Cardinals sweep. Chicago fell to 2 1/2 games behind the first-place Pirates as Gibson stopped a homer-laden Cubs lineup cold on two hits, inspiring rookie Jerry Reuss to hold down the Cubs by an identical 2-1 score in the nightcap.

The Cardinals staked Gibson to all the runs he would need in the second. The Cubs mishandled the cutoff play, enabling one run to score. Julian Javier then tallied Ted Simmons on a bloop single.

Williams, making good contact off Gibson as usual, accounted for the only Cubs fun in the fourth with a sacrifice fly after Glenn Beckert tripled. But Gibson allowed just one other hit, a seventh-inning single by Joe Pepitone.

Meanwhile, Jenkins pitched yet another winnable game. He fanned 12 and walked two. Inexplicably, Leo Durocher allowed Jenkins to bat for himself leading off the eighth inning down one run to Gibson. But Jenkins would not show he was a good hitter on this day. Gibson fanned him for the third time in a row. He had seven strikeouts for the game.

Gibson also kept the ball in the ballpark. Williams had 42 homers, Jim Hickman had 32 and Ron Santo 26, but Cub Power was short-circuited for the night-and for the season.

Jenkins ended up 22-16 with an ERA of 3.39, setting a Cubs team record of 274 strikeouts, in an offensive-oriented year. Gibson had his last monster season with a 23-7 record and 3.12 ERA. In a coincidence, he had the exact same number of strikeouts for the season as Jenkins, setting a career personal best for himself at age 34.

|  |  | IP | H | R | ER | BB | SO |
|---|---|---|---|---|---|---|---|
| Jenkins | (L, 21-16) | 8 | 7 | 2 | 2 | 2 | 12 |
| Gibson | (W, 23-6) | 9 | 2 | 1 | 1 | 3 | 7 |

# Cubs 2, Cardinals 1 (10 innings)
## April 6, 1971, Wrigley Field

This could have been the consummate Jenkins-Gibson matchup. Opening Day, 39 degrees, 41,121 in attendance, and both pitchers sawing off the bats of the frigid players. And, of course, Billy Williams making the difference against Gibson in the end.

Jenkins was particularly economical. In eight different innings, he faced the minimum three batters. Only Joe Torre, by know a Cubs Killer, touched him up, with a seventh-inning homer for the only Cardinals run.

Gibson allowed just a scratch run to the Cubs in the fourth. Williams singled to lead off. Santo singled to right center, sending Williams to third. Pepitone then hit a potential double-play grounder to third baseman Torre. But instead of going around the horn, Torre fired to the plate to cut down Williams for just the one out. Given one last shot, Johnny Callison then popped a double down the first-base line for the Cubs' tally.

Getting more chilled by the minute, Williams decided to end it all. He slugged a homer with one out in the 10th halfway up the right field bleachers. Unbowed, Gibson held his head up high as he walked off the mound.

Gibson had started seven consecutive Opening Days. Williams provided him with his first loss. Jenkins, too, was noted for his Opening Day prowess. "Darn it," Cardinals manager Red Schoendienst said, "that Jenkins is a great pitcher, too.

Can you imagine an extra-inning game at the turn of the millennium going so quickly? Almost 10 full innings, game time: one hour, 58 minutes.

The game set the tone for Jenkins' Cy Young Award season: 24-13, 2.77 ERA, 263 strikeouts, and a measly 37 walks in 325 innings. Gibson missed out on a 20-win season for the first time in four years, but hurled his first career no-hitter, against the Pirates, as he finished 16-13 with a 3.04 ERA.

|         |          | IP     | H | R | ER | BB | SO |
|---------|----------|--------|---|---|----|----|----|
| Jenkins | (W, 1-0) | 10     | 3 | 1 | 1  | 0  | 7  |
| Gibson  | (L, 0-1) | 9 1/3  | 7 | 2 | 2  | 4  | 5  |

# Cardinals 1, Cubs 0
## May 31, 1972, Wrigley Field

Gibson was aging but still determined when he took the mound for the last time against Jenkins on a spring afternoon in Chicago. And it was virtually the same ol' result. One run meant everything.

Gibson stopped the Cubs on three singles while Lou Brock, in his 10th season of making the Cubs pay for trading him, singled over shortstop in the fifth for the only run after light-hitting Dal Maxill singled and Gibson sacrificed.

The victory was Gibson's 51st career shutout, a tidy affair in which he faced only three batters over the minimum. Asked if he felt any significance in yet another matchup against Jenkins, Gibson replied, "Only that you know you've got to pitch a good game to win."

Jenkins allowed the Cardinals more opportunities on an eight-hitter and admitted he "was beaten by a better pitcher."

Both pitchers practically outdid themselves in pacing. Game time was just one hour, 47 minutes. They had saved their quickest work for last.

Jenkins would amass his sixth consecutive (and final) 20-win season as a Cub, with a 20-12 record and 3.21 ERA. Recovering from a 1-5 start, Gibson showed some flashes of his old dominance with a 19-11 record and 2.46 ERA.

|  |  | IP | H | R | ER | BB | SO |
|---|---|---|---|---|---|---|---|
| Jenkins | (L, 5-5) | 9 | 8 | 1 | 1 | 2 | 5 |
| Gibson | (W, 2-5) | 9 | 3 | 0 | 0 | 2 | 4 |

The 1972 season was the last hurrah of both pitchers as Cubs and Cardinals aces. Jenkins would be traded in a major housecleaning after the 1973 season, eventually working his way back to Wrigley Field for the final two seasons of his career in 1982-83. Gibson spent two more years in the St. Louis rotation, but limped home in his final season as a part-time pitcher in 1975.

Both left a legacy that won't be forgotten by anyone who ever saw them pitch head to head: four one-run games, three extra-inning pitching stints and two 1-0 contests. Their final pitching lines head to head:

|  | IP | H | R | ER | BB | SO |
|---|---|---|---|---|---|---|
| Jenkins | 65 2/3 | 48 | 15 | 14 | 12 | 53 |
| Gibson | 68 2/3 | 52 | 21 | 20 | 19 | 52 |

They don't make 'em like they used to.

# 11

# McGwire vs. Sosa: A Year-After Viewpoint

**YOU'D figure that almost every pundit in baseball** would rank the Mark McGwire-Sammy Sosa home-run duel that captivated half the world in 1998 as the crowning event in the Cubs-Cardinals rivalry.

But instead you get disagreement as to the power push's place in or even out of the timeline of Chicago-St. Louis baseball.

"It's a nice footnote to a great rivalry," Cardinals manager Tony La Russa said.

But was it even a part of the rivalry itself?

"It's almost like it was a separate game going on," Cubs pitcher Steve Trachsel, who served up McGwire's No. 62 homer. "You had the Cubs-Cardinals game, then you had the game with Sammy against Mark. You had fans split four different ways. It was almost as if when Sammy or Mark came to the plate, the other game took a back seat as people waited to see what would happen."

Back seat or not, baseball benefited from the duel that went down to the final day of the season—three weeks after McGwire broke the hallowed Roger Maris record. With the action firmly back on the field instead of the negotiating table, the attractions that made baseball our most traditional—and, deep down, beloved—sport came to the forefront. Record-breaking achievement was the headline, not labor disputes or salary arbitration or free-agent defections over salaries to which the average person could never relate.

And after a decade in which the more-manufactured, scripted glamour of the NFL and NBA dominated the Q ratings, the natural flow of the duel between McGwire, favored as the record breaker, and Sosa, a true rags-to-riches story, won over millions. For the first time in memory, the betting-oriented angles of all Sunday NFL games in September had to take second billing to McGwire-Sosa.

"Now Sammy and Mark are the two biggest celebrities in our game, possibly two of the top five in sports," said John McDonough, the Cubs' vice president of marketing and broadcasting. "Their duel will just add to the legend of the Cubs-Cardinals rivalry."

Forevermore, McGwire and Sosa will always have 1998, even if McGwire, a reticent man by nature, wanted to put his other-worldly achievement of 70 homers behind him by the start of the '99 season.

Both are better men for the experience, even if McGwire used every ounce of his considerable strength to run the gauntlet of pressure of the home-run chase.

"Nothing could be any worse than what I went through the last few months of the season," he said. "I don't think there's ever been another athlete to be singled out in one sport like I was singled out for the last two months of the season. Every move you make was being watched.

"My life's definitely going to change."

McGwire's personality definitely changed for the better. Standoffish and often curt with the media prior to mid-season, the red-bearded giant seemed to loosen up when he saw how much fun Sosa had with the chase. Sosa, almost always a playful people person before he hit the limelight, handled multiple media sessions daily until the Cubs started controlling access, the better to keep the slugger on his daily routine.

It was one of the friendliest personal rivalries ever seen in sports, an example of sportsmanship rarely seen in today's dog-eat-dog world.

"I really believe they pushed each other and made each other great," Cubs broadcaster Chip Caray said.

Suddenly, McGwire could offer up a smile here, a quip there, and life wasn't so unbearable after all. Sosa clasped his new-found role-model life close, and globe-trotted through the winter of 1998-99 to enjoy the fruits of his NL Most Valuable Player season, be it barnstorming through Japan or at Hillary Rodham Clinton's side during her wandering husband's State of the Union address.

Nobody had any questions, though, that McGwire and Sosa had their priorities straight. Their achievements were bigger than life, perhaps once in a lifetime, but their places on their teams were secure—one man on a 25-man roster.

"I didn't come back to show up my teammates," Sosa said. "I have a lot of respect for my teammates. I'm a team player. Whatever happens in the past, I don't have any kind of ego. I'm the same guy."

But if both McGwire and Sosa insist they haven't inflated their self-importance, they at least handle their game differently, through a combination of maturity and environment. Busch Stadium and Wrigley Field may have been the best place for each of them to thrive and not only break the Maris record, but utterly demolish it.

McGwire had been earmarked as Maris-mark conqueror as an Oakland Athletic in 1997. But he had become increasingly unhappy. Cardinals manager Tony La Russa and general manager Walt Jocketty knew they could get the best out of McGwire, having worked with him in Oakland. They also took a good gamble that he'd respond well to the mid-American, baseball-crazy surroundings of St. Louis and sign a long-term deal after coming over in a trade near the end of July 1997.

"Putting Mark in that environment was a big factor," Jocketty said of the reach for the record. "Once we acquired him, there was a lot of negative reaction, that we gave up too much for a guy to have for only two months.

"But we knew Mark was a baseball purist, and loved the game. Tony and I cherished the opportunity to work in a city that had so much history, and the support of the fans. The history and the support, there isn't a better place to work and play. It was something Mark would embrace. The fans helped him out."

And the crazy factor was McGwire thrived like nobody else in a ballpark that formerly was death to power hitters. A slash-and-run Cardinals style had to be patented for Busch Stadium with its former 386-foot power alleys and heavy night-time air. The ballpark was re-tailored to be more hitter- and fan-friendly just prior to McGwire's arrival, but Jocketty said his moon-shot homers would have garnered him the record in Busch Stadium's spacious old days.

"No question, Mark would have broken record in the old (dimensions) ballpark," he said.

Sosa had long been comfortable in Wrigley Field and among the ever-loyal Cubs fans. He felt that when he arrived in 1992 after his career went south as a Chicago White Sox, he had been there all his life.

The fans cheered Sosa, even "salaamed" to him en masse in the bleachers after his power feats—and despite his spectacularly inconsistent play in his first few Cubs seasons. He could heave a baseball nine rows into the box seats or strike out on a ridiculously bad outside pitch. It didn't matter. The fans, and spiritual leader Harry Caray knew they had a potential superstar on their hands. Not even backbiting by some team-mates and a torrent of media criticism—one local talk-show host called him "Roberto Clemente without a brain"—changed Sosa or soured him on life. Instead, he'd sit atop the Cubs dugout, yoga-style, signing auto-graphs before games. "Nobody can take my game away from me," was his only retort to critics.

Sosa thus was in good position to ride the crest in 1998 when he combined maturity at 29 and a few new wrinkles in his batting stance, especially a "tap step" suggested by Cubs hitting coach Jeff Pentland. The slugger never really cut down on his big swing or whiff-king tendencies; he still fanned 171 times in '98. But he made pitchers work to strike him out, carrying the hurlers to full counts many times. And he played the short game enough to amass an astounding 158 RBI—a figure perhaps more impressive than his 66 homers. Sosa had driven in more runs than any player since Ted Williams in 1949. Nice linkage.

What we all have from 1998 is simply a good feeling by players who seemed throwbacks to some past eras, when the game was played for its sheer enjoyment. Even folks who could have taken a negative stance toward the record-breaking feats were buoyed.

One was Steve Trachsel. Nearly a week prior to his date with McGwire, he loathed not the idea of serving up magic No. 62, but the spectacle of having to stand out on the mound for 15 minutes while the celebration whirled about. Well, that turned out to be exactly Trachsel's fate. But his memories of his involvement will remain warm for decades to come.

"Everyone seems to think that I got upset over giving up No. 62," he said. "I think it's a great thing. I was upset because I lost the game. We were in the pennant race. At that point we were still winning the game 2-1. At that point, my job was to get us a victory. That was what my focus was.

"The home run was hit. OK, that's no big deal. Everyone knows I've given up a million home runs. I wasn't pleased I gave up four runs in the fifth inning. I'd have been happy afterwards if I could have said, 'Con-gratulations, you hit the home run, we won the game.'

"It's another feather in my cap. I'm trying to put as many feathers in. I've got a few—(National League) rookie pitcher of the year (1994),

All-Star (1996), give up McGwire's homer, and got the Cubs into the playoffs for the first time in 10 years. I want to get a few more.

"I'm a quality major league starter. He's probably happier he hit it off a good pitcher rather than someone else."

Trachsel and all of us should savor those memories, freeze the moment well into a new millennium. Sixty-one was off in the stratosphere. Seventy is light years away. How can anyone, McGwire included, possibly do any better?

"Anything's possible," he said, scoffing at suggestions he could break his own record. "What I did (in 1998), a ballplayer was trying to do for 38 years. I sat back and thought about it. In order to break 70 home runs, I would have to think you'd have to be at the 40 plateau in home runs by the All-Star break to break it.

"I can only imagine the amount of pressure. I know what it entailed to reach 60, 61, 62. Try going 10 more. It's hard to fathom. Seventy's a really big number. I was in awe of myself, and I'm still in awe thinking about it."

So is everyone else. But put it in perspective. With everything else that's ever happened in the Cubs-Cardinals rivalry, it's entirely fitting that the all-time home-run record should have been set with the blue and red hook up. No two cities in the baseball universe deserved the moment more.

# 12

## Brock for Broglio

**UNLIKE the rest of society,** Monday was usually the day of rest in baseball in 1964. So instead of their blue pinstriped flannel uniforms, a large contingent of Cubs donned suits and ties to meet and greet the fans at "Cub Day" at lunch on June 15, 1964 at Wieboldt's department store on State Street in downtown Chicago.

A gaggle of kids and their moms—and a few dads stretching their lunch hours—showed up with autograph grist in hand. Flocking downtown in the manner of following the spokes of a wheel to the hub, they came from city and suburbs alike to the big State Street stores like Wieboldt's, Marshall Field's, Carson Pirie Scott and Co., and Goldblatt's for shopping and special events. No way would the Cubs or any other famous institution think of staging an event 30 miles away at one of the few suburban malls, like Old Orchard or Randhurst, already open at the start of the Great Society era. Between the huge stores and big-marquee theaters, State Street was still the center of retail for the Midwest's biggest metropolis in 1964.

But that would change in the near future—long after both the roster and the direction of the team represented at Wieboldt's.

Emceed by WGN-Radio baseball announcers Jack Quinlan and Lou Boudreau, Cub Day featured the team's hottest hitter meeting the autograph hounds. Right fielder Lou Brock, who had a nine-game hitting streak and homered in his final at-bat of Sunday's 5-2 victory over the Pittsburgh Pirates at Wrigley Field, got into the flow of publicizing a team that had won 13 of its last 19 games to finally reach the .500 mark at 27-27.

Suddenly an urgent phone call was announced for "Lou."

"Well, Lou Bourdreau went back to get it, but it wasn't for him," Brock recalled. "Then (coach) Lou Klein went to get it. I was the last Lou on the stage. Those guys knew it was John Holland (Cubs general manager).

"I was called to the phone. I just thought at first it was my wife. Then I was saddened when they told me it was Holland. I thought I was either going to the minors or being traded. I give Holland credit because he did it gently. He said he had made an 'arrangement.' He said he had 'transferred my contract.'

"I thought it was to Wenatchee (Washington), way down in the minors. Remember, I had only played Class C ball for one year. Finally, he said my contract had been transferred to the St. Louis Cardinals. I was consumed and overwhelmed with the reality I was still in the big leagues."

It took time to digest the details of the trade, completed by Cubs general manager John Holland and his Cardinals counterpart, Bing Devine, when the Cardinals arrived the night previously to begin a road series in Houston. Brock and Cubs pitchers Paul Toth and Jack Spring were dispatched 300 miles south in exchange for starting pitcher Ernie Broglio, left-handed reliever Bobby Shantz and outfielder Doug Clemens, once thought to be Stan Musial's own favorite to succeed him the preceding spring in the Cardinals' outfield.

Broadcaster Quinlan announced the trade to the Wieboldt's crowd. They booed when informed that Brock was departing. But, in the next breath, the fans cheered the news that Broglio, the Cardinals' leading pitcher at 18-8 in 1963, was coming to town.

Cheers was the predominant reaction of Cubs officials and players when Brock-for-Broglio was announced. The trade, made with a surfeit of logic on the part of both teams, seemed like one of those deals that could help both clubs. Yet in the hubbub of excitement over the transaction, none could forecast how the trade would, within months, go so horribly wrong for the Cubs. Beyond that, none could imagine how the fortunes of the Cubs and Cardinals would be forever changed with the trading of a player crossing the cusp of superstardom at high noon on Monday, June 15, 1964.

Brock-for-Broglio is the family ghost of the Cubs-Cardinals rivalry. The domino effect of its outcome drags its psychic ball and chain through the decades, having become the measuring stick of both the bad luck that has dogged the Cubs since 1945 and the quality management decisions that netted the Cardinals three World Series berths in 1964, 1967 and 1968, including two Fall Classic victories. Brock-for-Broglio is symbolic of the fortunes of the Cubs, almost always beset by a woefully unproductive farm system, finally develop a world-class player. But be it Brock, Greg Maddux, Bruce Sutter, whoever, they let him get away to achieve greater glory elsewhere while the 206-1 odds against the Cubs avoiding a World Series appearance since 1945 simply grow by the year.

Brock became the second leading base stealer in history with 938 thefts while collecting 3,023 hits and earning Hall of Fame enshrinement in 1985, five years after his career ended. Broglio only enriched the orthopedic surgeon's billfold with the removal of wayward bone chips in the elbow, not only in 1964, but almost three decades later as a high school baseball coach. He eventually was released by the Cubs on July 5, 1966, his major league career over. The trade possessed everything that brings sorrow and joy to fans in baseball's far-flung outposts-bad timing, bad luck, talent misjudgments and memories that became skewed with the passage of time.

"I don't think anything will ever take me off the hook for that deal," Broglio said. "As long as Lou and myself are alive, they'll always make that comparison.

"It never ceases to amaze me that whenever trades that don't look good are made, they're always using this trade as an example of the worst. Never any other trade."

Ol' Caleb "Chet" Chestnut, preacher man of Wrigley Field's right-field bleachers, used to bellow out that "if" is not a word, at least not in baseball. But, Chet, it's too tempting to not use. If only Brock had not come up with just one year of low-minors experience amid the chaotic atmosphere of the Cubs' "College of Coaches" regime. If only Brock had started hitting and stealing bases in May 1964 instead of just two weeks prior to the deal—after the Cubs began to put the wheels in motion to deal him. If only Broglio's elbow problems had become more noticeable, sooner. If only Broglio's sterling pitching during Cubs' spring training of 1966-seemingly starting a great comeback—had continued throughout the regular season.

You could wrack your brain and get frustrated thinking about all the angles of the trade.

Making it worse is the confusing stories told from the vantage point of three-plus decades later—memories become foggy, facts merge and recollections sometimes conflict with published statements at the time of the trade

Actually, by trading for Brock, the Cardinals rectified their own, original mistake. Growing up a fan of the Redbirds in rural El Dorado, Arkansas, Brock thought he had the chance of lifetime in 1960 when the Cardinals spotted him as he displayed his raw talents of speed and power on the Southern University baseball team. The Cardinals' initial mistake turned into a blessing when Brock first signed with an organization that mishandled him—but delivered to St. Louis virtually a finished product who had learned on the job in the majors.

"Yes, I had been mad at the Cardinals," he said. "A Cardinals scout (Charley Frey) invited me to St. Louis for a tryout. I borrowed $10, caught a bus, called the scout when I got to St. Louis and found he wasn't there. He was in Washington signing (pitcher) Ray Washburn.

"I didn't know anybody in St. Louis, so I headed for Chicago where I had a friend, Noah Pates, from high school. He got me work at a YMCA washing walls because I needed money for bus fare back home. I called the Cubs and asked to try out."

With the Cardinals out of the picture for now, Brock impressed a gaggle of baseball men when he flashed his quick bat in tryouts at both Wrigley Field and Comiskey Park.

"Everything they threw I hit off the wall or into the bleachers," Brock said of his first Friendly Confines appearance. "Every scout there had me in the batting cage. Gene Mauch (Phillies manager) said not to let me out of the ballpark without signing me. The Braves and Yankees also saw me." On the South Side, Brock was scouted by both the White Sox and Tigers. The Cubs eventually won out with a $12,000 bonus, partially due to the presence of famed scout Buck O'Neil, an former Negro League player and manager who had scoured the South for African-American talent for the Cubs since 1955. O'Neil had kept close tabs on Brock on the Southern U. campus and tried to throw off the trail of other scouts to the diamond in the rough.

Assigned to the Class C St. Cloud (Minnesota) Rox, Brock performed well in the bushes in 1961. But instead of advancing him to Class A or AA, the Cubs promoted him to Wrigley Field in September of that season, then installed him as a regular in center field, between Billy Williams in left and George Altman in right, for 1962.

Moving Brock up to the majors without an intermediate stop or two in the high minors might not have been that bad of an idea. Some great natural talents simply have to make their mistakes in the majors; they have little to prove by spending the requisite amount of time in the minors. Look at Kerry Wood with the Cubs in 1998. But Brock's quick advancement was being done with the wrong organization. In 1962, the Cubs were smack dab in the middle of their wacky "College of Coaches" system. Apparently tired of firing managers, Cubs owner Philip K. Wrigley instituted the rotating coaches for 1961 with the noble goal of having one kind of instructional style from top to bottom in the Cubs organization. The coaches would be shuffled from the parent team all the way through the minors throughout the season, and one "head coach" would run the Cubs for a short period of time. Wrigley's club would be the first in history to not be piloted by an official manager.

"The manager set-up has meant constant turnover both in personnel and style of play," was the description of the 'College of Coaches' in the 1961 Cubs media guide. "In the last 14 years in the two major leagues, 103 changes in managers have been made. And each new manager generally meant a new style of play and a new set of coaches who, for the most part, were special friends of the manager.

"The core of the new Cubs program is a standard system of play, administered by a stable, good-sized group of coaches. The coaches are selected on the basis of merit, knowledge of the game and ability to teach, rather than personal favoritism.

"The Cubs' system of play has been developed and put in writing by the coaches and other members of the management team as a group. While it is naturally subject to improvements to keep up with changes in the game, it is followed uniformly throughout the organization—from bottom to top.

"From the time a young player comes into the Cubs organization, he is trained consistently in the same system of executing baseball fundamentals. He does not have to adapt himself to a succession of different types of play. When he reaches Wrigley Field in Chicago he will know the fundamentals, and know them right.

"Furthermore, he will not come to the major league club as a stranger in strange surroundings. When he arrives on the Cubs roster, he will know personally—and be known by—the coaches who have worked with him on his way up."

Three former Cardinals were part of the coaching rotation: ex-first baseman Ripper Collins, former minor league pitcher Fred Martin and longtime farm-system functionary Vedie Himsl. Other coaches were Cubs legend Charlie Grimm, Harry Craft, Bobby Adams, Elvin Tappe, Goldie Holt, Rube Walker and Dick Cole.

The scheme may have evoked some logic on paper. But the game isn't played that way. Too many cooks did spoil the broth. The vast number of coaches did not mean a standardized system of teaching fundamentals. Brock found one coach suggesting he use his power to swing for the fences, while another coach urged him to slap at the ball and bunt. Some of the coaches realized the system was doomed and began lobbying for the eventual manager's job. Backbiting increased. Infielder Don Zimmer ripped the "College of Coaches" on Lou Boudreau's pre-game radio show late in 1961; his punishment was being made available to the expansion Mets in the following winter's draft. Ron Santo still gets irritated a generation-plus later when the politics of the "College of Coaches" is discussed in his presence.

"I was a (power) hitter who could run," Brock recalled. "There already were big hitters in the middle of the Cubs' lineup. They had me lead off, but I didn't swing like a leadoff hitter. I had no experience hitting like that.

"The instability of the College of Coaches did not help the younger players. I would have responded to one man. In a team game, you learn to follow the leader. I probably came along at the wrong time in the Cub organization.

"Players are great followers of rules and regulations of one manager or coach. When you have 14 coaches, who do you follow? All were competing for the job of head coach. Those kinds of things hurt a first-year player."

A martinet-style "head coach," Charlie Metro, took over for much of the second half of the 1962 season. Unpopular with many players, he somehow won the allegiance of Brock.

"If Charlie Metro had been the manager, not just one of the rotating coaches, I would have responded to him," Brock said. "He was a perfectionist. We got along and he started to work with me to hit like a leadoff hitter."

With all the insecurities of a raw young player and amid the confused losing atmosphere—the Cubs set a team record, equalled only once, of 103 losses in 1962—Brock needed stability of leadership and some guidance. He got little of either.

"I was a shooting star in the Cubs organization," he said. "To shoot from Class C to the majors in one year had to do with the lack of talent in the organization. I didn't start to learn to play the game until I got there. And when you're learning like that, you're going to tee off somebody."

Brock's biggest troubles were in the outfield. Between the unpredictable winds and bright sun of the daytime schedule, Wrigley Field offers a challenge for even the most adept outfielder. Imagine the mental load on Brock being placed in the traffic-cop role of center fielder as a result of his sheer speed, then being shifted to the brutal right field in 1963 after Altman was traded to the Cardinals.

"I was ready to play center and all of a sudden I had to learn to play right, which is the difficult sun field at Wrigley Field," Brock said. "I guess they felt a guy like Billy Cowan (rookie regular in center in 1964) was coming up and they wanted to make room for him.

"I was not trained on how to flip the sunglasses at the right time. We had played practically all night games in the minors and it wasn't an issue there. Then I was in the greatest sun field in the majors. It was trial and error."

He also had to learn by trial and error on the basepaths. Former Cubs farmhand John Felske, who served a term as Phillies manager in the late 1980s, remembered an instructional league game managed by Bob Kennedy. Brock got on three straight times; he was picked off base on each occasion. Miffed, Kennedy pulled Brock from the game.

Kennedy, a native Chicagoan, took over as "head coach" for the 1963 season and did not have to share time with other coaches as Wrigley started to back away ever-so-slightly from his hairbrained idea. He may not have had exactly a love-hate relationship with Brock. A stickler for fundamentals, Kennedy wasn't enamored of Brock's mistakes.

"Kennedy was irritated at times, however, by Brock's erratic outfield play and occasionally by his unsound baserunning," wrote the *Chicago Tribune*'s Richard Dozer in the story announcing Brock's trade. But for the previous 1 1/2 seasons, Kennedy had stuck with Brock as a rightfield regular through 1963, benching him only against tough left-handed pitchers. Steve Boros, later manager of the Athletics, took Brock's place in right against the top southpaws. Brock batted either leadoff or No. 2, but sometimes was dropped down to No. 6.

"Everybody makes mistakes," Kennedy, now 79 and retired in Mesa, Arizona, said. "He was a young player and you could see the potential. The thing that I used get on him is I didn't want him to continue to make mistakes. I told him that with the ability you got, to keep making mistakes is wrong. Just keep hustling, just keep trying.

"One thing I didn't do that I probably should have done was turn him loose on the bases. I wanted to control it at the time because of (Ernie) Banks, (Billy) Williams and (Ron) Santo hitting behind him."

Keeping Brock in the lineup was his exciting offensive potential. His season-ending numbers-nine homers each in 1962 and 1963, successive .263 and .258 averages-bordered on below-average for a big-league right fielder. But he had his great individual moments.

Most famous was a near 500-foot homer Brock bashed into the old Polo Grounds center field bleachers off Mets lefty Al Jackson on June 17, 1962. Only Henry Aaron and Joe Adcock had ever reached those faraway seats previously.

Then, in a performance that no doubt cemented Cardinals manager Johnny Keane's growing admiration for Brock, the young Cub almost personally took apart the Redbirds in the second game of a doubleheader on July 28, 1963, at Wrigley Field. Before 40,222—the second-largest Cubs home crowd between the years 1952 and 1967—Brock belted two homers and a triple, driving in five runs, as the Cubs roared back from an 11-6 sixth-inning deficit to win 16-11 after capturing the opener 5-1.

The Cardinals, always oriented more toward running since their "Gashouse Gang" days, believed Brock's speed was being hamstrung in cozy Wrigley Field. But by the standards of the day, Brock ran well. Maury Wills was out alone as a world-class thief, and if you stole 24 bases, as Brock did in 1963, you were doing well.

Contrary to published accounts in the 1980s and 1990s that would make you think that Brock was virtually unknown and unregarded as a Cub, he was considered an up-and-comer.

One right-field bleacher fan held up a "Go-Go Brock" sign during a game with the Dodgers in 1963. Humble Oil Co. ran an ad in the *Chicago Sun-Times* at the time, complete with a caricature of Brock, touting his services as a salesman for the company. Brock actually sold heating oil door to door; he remembers a tough job doing it "cold turkey," but making lasting friends from his off-season sales pitches.

On January 5, 1964, *Sun-Times* baseball writer Jerome Holtzman wrote a hot-stove league piece in which he described the Cubs outfield as being "settled in left field with Billy Williams and in right with Lou Brock, both of whom are excellent ballplayers." Cardinals ace Bob Gibson later said he never remembered facing Brock as a Cub. But, surely, as he looked for a competitive edge, Gibby had to notice Brock's batting spree under the late-afternoon summer sun in the 1963 doubleheader.

"I remember as a kid, my parents telling me what a great player this young kid Lou Brock was," Bruce Miles, Cubs beat writer for the Arlington Heights, Illinois-based *Daily Herald*, said of his roots on Chicago's South Side. "My mother (Bette) was a big Cubs fan in 1962, and she said this is a rookie, he's a player to watch, he's exciting."

All along, though, Brock put too much pressure on himself. Mr. Cub, Ernie Banks, remembers a conversation the two had in the dugout in New York one day. Young player Brock looked for wisdom from wise veteran Banks. "How do I succeed? I want to make it now!" Brock told Banks, the former worried about being sent back down to the minors. Banks counseled patience.

But that quality often was in short supply in a grasping-for-straws Cubs management. Worse set, expectations were raised for the team coming off the 1963 season. Kennedy was praised for guiding the team to an 82-80 record, fated to be the Cubs' only above-.500 finish between 1952 and 1967. The improved season, in which the Cubs flirted with contention until mid-August, was accomplished despite below-average offensive seasons from all regulars except Billy Williams and Ron Santo. But ex-Cardinals Lindy McDaniel and Larry Jackson had become mainstays of a surprising pitching staff that finished 1963 with a collective ERA of 3.08, second only to the Dodgers of Sandy Koufax and Don Drysdale. Lefty Dick Ellsworth was 22-10 with an ERA of just 2.11, lower even than Greg Maddux's 2.18 in 1992. Such stingy pitching has rarely been duplicated in modern Cubs annals.

Kennedy and general manager Holland still expected improvement in 1964 even after enduring the emotional jolt of young second baseman Kenny Hubbs' death in the crash of a light plane he was piloting a few weeks prior to spring training. But the team was inconsistent through the first two months, with Billy Williams, whose .400 average in May earned him National League player of the month honors, by far the hottest hitter. Brock got off to a slow start.

Even worse off were the Cardinals. Johnny Keane and general manager Bing Devine had not found a successor to Stan Musial in the outfield. The likes of Charlie James, Doug Clemens, Carl Warwick and Johnny Lewis were found wanting. With St. Louis native Mike Shannon still getting his feet wet in right field, the Cardinals outfield had little offensive production other than center fielder Curt Flood. Slowing being frittered away was the momentum of the September, 1963 surge in Musial's swan-song month that had the Cardinals challenging the Dodgers for the NL pennant—an event that even inspired Chicago newspapers to send their top baseball writers to cover St. Louis at the expense of the Windy City teams. The '63 Cards finished 93-69, inspiring hope for the following season. But on June 15, 1964, St. Louis had lost 16 of its last 22 games to fall below the Cubs at 28-30.

Knowing he had a farm system that kept producing quality pitchers, Devine believed he could spare an arm to get a bat for the outfield. Keane liked Brock's combination of speed and power. And Ernie Broglio, the Cardinals' best starter in 1963, had somehow found a home in Keane's doghouse.

"I was fit to pitch," Broglio said of his physical condition at the time of the June 15, 1964 deal. To be sure, Broglio had fought off pain previously, taking 21 cortisone shots for a sore shoulder throughout the 1962 season. He experienced some pain in his elbow near the end of the 1963 season, but said his arm was fine as 1964 progressed.

"When we sent him to the Cubs, we didn't think there was anything wrong with him," Devine recalled. But Bob Kennedy said pitcher Lew Burdette, traded to the Cubs two weeks prior to the Brock deal, told the Cubs Broglio was being administered shots in his arm. It's unclear whether Burdette meant at that time or was referring back to the cortisone injections two years previously. Meanwhile, Lindy McDaniel said he recalled rumors that Broglio had a sore arm.

"The whole problem of why I was traded was because of a conflict between Johnny Keane and myself," Broglio said. "He had something against me, which I didn't understand."

Broglio also believed management didn't like his personal living arrangements and one appearance at a then-risque nightspot. He lived during the season in Gaslight Square, a small avant-garde area of restaurants and clubs near the center of town. Management didn't like ballplayers residing in such a "bohemian" district. And the brass raised its eyebrows when Broglio was spotted the night prior to a start watching Henny Youngman's appearance at the local Playboy Club. "I didn't stay out all night. I was out of there by midnight," Broglio recalled. Gussie Busch and Harry Caray could have an active social life, but the rank-and-file players apparently had to toe the early-to-bed, early-to-rise routine in the early 1960s.

*St. Louis Globe-Democrat* beat writer Jack Herman wrote of another aspect of the Broglio-Keane conflict at the time of the trade

"Broglio did not endear himself with club brass while sidelined recently for two weeks by a minor ailment," Herman wrote of what Broglio himself called a "groin injury." "It is rumored that Broglio was unhappy in St. Louis," added the *Chicago Tribune*'s Richard Dozer in his story detailing the trade.

McDaniel, a former Cardinal who was the Cubs' relief ace in 1964, confirmed that Keane had conflicts with some of his veteran pitchers. He said he and Larry Jackson, traded with him to the Cubs after the 1962 season, both verbally sparred with Keane over the manager's desire to call pitches for them.

"A lot of people had conflicts with Johnny Keane," McDaniel recalled. "It got to the point where you couldn't throw pitches with him calling them from the bench. What made it worse is Keane dealt with it publicly, openly in front of everyone else in the clubhouse."

Broglio's record had been stellar through much of his St. Louis career. He had been the product of a good trade by Bing Devine back on October 8, 1958, when the Cardinals landed him and veteran pitcher Marv Grissom from the Giants in exchange for catcher Hobie Landrith and pitchers Billy Muffett and Benny Valenzuela. His fastball earned raves; a Cardinals season preview section in the April 5, 1959 *St. Louis Post-Dispatch* took note of Broglio's potential.

He got off to a slow start in the rotation with a 7-12 record in '59. But in 1960, Broglio became one of the game's best performers with a 21-9 record—his victory total leading the NL—along with a 2.74 ERA and 188 strikeouts in 226 1/3 innings. He had actually split his time between the bullpen and the rotation, with a 7-2 record in relief. Broglio then slumped to 9-12 in 1961, was 12-9 with a 3.00 ERA in 1962 and then regained his 1960 form with 18-8 in 1963 to go with a 2.99 ERA. He allowed just 202 hits in 250 innings.

"When I was a teen-ager (growing up in suburban University City, Mo.), I used to watch him pitch," former star Cubs pitcher Ken Holtzman said. "He was one of the best pitchers in the National League."

That was the near-unanimous opinion of Chicagoans after Devine called up John Holland, his favorite trading partner, to propose a deal involving Brock. The *Tribune's* Dozer caught wind of the Cubs' initial willingness to peddle Brock and reported the trade talks on May 26. Soon reports surfaced that the Cubs sought left-hander Ray Sadecki for Brock.

"We them a list of pitchers with three names on it," remembered Devine, now retired and still a St. Louis-area resident. "Broglio was one of them, but I don't recall the other two." Bob Gibson wasn't one of the others, he said, adding that the Cardinals wouldn't have traded Gibson. But he said the two clubs couldn't agree on the other players to be part of the package. As the 1964 season neared the trading deadline, the Cardinals needed a sparkplug for their sputtering offense.

Bob Kennedy claimed he caught wind of the trade talks and tried to dissuade Holland from going forward.

"All the coaches—Fred Martin, Lou Klein, Rube Walker and myself—were dead-set against it," he said. "We did not want to make the trade regardless of who it was for. We knew Louie was just coming on. It was just going to take a little patience.

"It was a long story."

Kennedy stopped abruptly; end of conversation. That was like a dangling participle. Was Brock traded due to impatience on the part of Holland, a desire for a veteran pitcher to vault the Cubs into contention, or some off-the-field, personal-life reason-the latter proven to be sometimes a factor in Cubs trades of the Wrigley ownership era? If Kennedy knows the absolute truth, he falls short of revealing it, adopting the stance of a good baseball man of his era.

Despite the apparent behind-the-scenes opposition, the Holland-Devine talks moved forward as the June 15 trade deadline neared.

"We were playing in Los Angeles and Holland called me and left a message," Devine said. "I had to call him back from a pay phone at Dodger Stadium. He said they needed a pitcher and were ready to deal Brock. I said, 'Who do you want?' He said, 'Broglio.' I said let me talk to my manager. When I did, Keane said, 'What are we waiting for?' It was nice to get that stamp of approval."

The club honchos finally cut the deal. Despite the previous rumors, when Brock was informed at Wieboldt's and Broglio was called to Keane's hotel room in Houston on the morning of June 15, the trade still hit like a ton of bricks. In his last weeks as a Cub, Brock finally felt confident, hitting naturally and becoming more aggressive on the basepaths. Broglio hadn't pitched all that badly despite a 3-5 record. In 11 starts he allowed 65 hits in 69 1/3 innings and had hurled one shutout.

"Being traded for a class pitcher like Ernie Broglio is a high compliment for a young player who has never hit over .263 in the majors," Brock said at the time. "When they told me I was traded, I was very anxious to know who the pitcher was they got for me. When they said 'Broglio,' I was surprised. He's been one of the mainstays of the Cardinals staff for a long time."

Although Broglio preferred to stay a Cardinal despite his tiff with management, he professed pleasure at not having to face one particular Cubs hitter. "I have the pleasure of getting away from a .400 hitter," he said. "It'll be nice to be on Billy's side for a change."

The Chicago media acted like cheerleaders, almost counting a World Series berth for the Cubs 3 1/2 months in advance.

"Cards Deal Cubs In Race; Send Broglio!" was the *Chicago Tribune's* headline. "This gives us as good a pitching staff as there is in the league," Dozer quoted Kennedy as saying when informed of the trade at the Wheeling golf outing.

*Chicago Daily News* Cubs beat writer Bob Smith was hardly objective in his lead: "Thank you, thank you, oh you lovely St. Louis Cardinals. Nice doing business with you. Please call again any time." Smith would add later: "Getting Broglio and (Bobby) Shantz gives the Cubs the strongest pitching staff in the league to go with a pesky, consistent offense and hustling, reliable defense."

Destined for an even bigger audience years later in another medium, Chicago's *American* beat writer Brent Musburger waved the pompons, too.

"It was a wet, miserable day in our town Monday, but the Cub fans couldn't have cared less," Musburger wrote. "In fact, most of the long-suffering loyalists felt like running into the streets and dancing in the rain . . . Jubulant Cub fans called the deal 'tremendous . . . a steal . . . great." Musburger also called Broglio a "handsome Italian who can make a baseball bend more than a piece of spaghetti."

Top Cubs officials were ecstatic in media accounts.

"If you want to hit the bull's eye, you have to take a shot at it," Cubs owner P.K. Wrigley said. "We're taking more than a shot at the flag. We're cutting loose with both barrels," GM Holland proclaimed. Mr. Wrigley and the rest of us believe we owe it to the fans, the players and the coaches to make that bold move that might win for us . . . It's obvious we need more pitching to jump into the thick of the pennant race. We're confident this deal will do it for us."

Frequent Holland critic Bill Gleason, then a columnist for *Chicago's American*, praised the exec.

"There have been afternoons when John Holland of the Cubs seemed as indecisive as Bill Scranton of Pennsylvania," Gleason wrote. "But I take off my tulip-festooned red beret to the gentleman this day. John has made himself a heck of a trade . . . This is the greatest thing that has happened to Holland since that kid put his finger in the dike."

The trade seemed so one-sided that Cubs fans, according to Gleason's column, called the *American's* sports desk to wonder "whether Broglio had a sore arm. That's how Cub fans are. If their team gives them a pitcher who was 18-8 the year before, they assume the guy has something wrong with his arm or his head or his liver. A lot of Cub fans remember the $185,000 that P.K. (Wrigley) paid for Dizzy Dean."

Gleason continued to raise the issue of Broglio's health without knowing how accurate either he or the fans would end up being:

"Let's say, just for argument, that Broglio should have a sore arm. He'd still be more of a pitcher than a lot of guys who have rubber arms and gelatin hearts. All Ernie has to do is stand there and stare. That alone is worth the price of admission."

And Gleason was truly a seer when he added: "Sure, I realize that Lou Brock may become one of the most exciting players in the game. Let's hope he does. Baseball needs young guys like Lou to keep the executives from falling asleep."

Among the few dissenters in Chicago—other than the private thoughts of the Cubs coaches, Banks and O'Neil, was the Miles family, who saw the same angle as fellow South Sider Gleason.

"I remember first grade had gotten out that day in 1964," Bruce Miles said. "My dad came home and told me the news that Brock had been traded. Even at that age—seven—I was devastated. My mom had the prescience to know this was a bad thing. She said, 'You watch the Cardinals now that they've got Brock.' Sure enough, she was right. My mom was an old-time Cubs fan, and she liked the young kids."

While the Chicago media ate up hundreds of inches with celebratory prose, the St. Louis newspapers were more even-handed in their treatment of the deal.

*Post-Dispatch* beat writer Neal Russo played it right down the middle in his lead: "The Cardinals traded starting pitcher Ernie Broglio to the Chicago Cubs today for promising left-handed hitting outfielder Lou Brock in a six-player deal." He re-affirmed Devine's dealing from a position of strength with his starting pitching: "For the Cardinals, whose hurling has held up even in the discouraging offensive outlook, the aspect of the deal that is most significant—next to the acquisition of the sturdy Brock—was the decision to bring up (lefty pitcher Mike) Cuellar."

Wrote the *Globe-Democrat*'s Jack Herman: "While in Chicago, Der Bingle traded off Lou Burdette for Glen Hobbie. The latter has pitched superbly in his first two starts and on that basis, (Johnny) Keane indicated Broglio became expendable."

The Cardinals had to act quickly to accomplish something before the trading deadline," opined columnist Bob Burnes of the *Globe-Democrat*.

But in a second-day analysis of the deal, Russo was more cautionary, writing that the trade "is expected to be X-rayed by fans and observers more than most of Bing Devine's many trades.

"The first question raised by many is: Why didn't the Cardinals get more than Brock, a flashy outfielder who cold become a star, for Broglio, an 18-game winner last season and still regarded as a top pitcher?

"For one thing, the market for Broglio was surprisingly lukewarm in a league that has a bumper crop of pitching talent, if little else in the way of a surplus."

Devine said from the hindsight of history that the media and fans were right to question him.

"Giving up a No. 1 pitcher (from 1963), that was something you just didn't do," he said.

Keane was virtually in a majority of one among field personnel and players in praising Brock.

"Brock adds youth and great running speed, and he is a boy that is on the upgrade," the Cardinals manager said. "He is a fine young ballplayer."

Most of the Cardinals players thought they didn't get enough for Broglio. Cubs players were delighted.

"I just couldn't believe it," said Ron Santo, the newly minted team captain. "I've been with this club four years now, and I never had the feeling before that we could go all the way. With our pitching staff now we can win the pennant."

Memories become foggy, though. Now a Cubs radio announcer, Santo said he did not make that statement, that in fact he was sure Brock was going to blossom into a star that season.

Even from hindsight, other major leaguers saw the logic of the trade

"The importance of an every-fourth-day, 20-game winning pitcher is paramount in our game," Ken Holtzman said. "As great as Lou Brock became, I still think if you asked every man on that (1964 Cubs) team, they were certainly glad to have Ernie Broglio on that club."

Two notable, but quiet, dissenters to the prevailing mood were Ernie Banks—"Mr. Cub" himself—and scout Buck O'Neil. Both knew that Brock's enormous potential was about to be fulfilled.

In the first moments of his new life, Brock headed from Wieboldt's to the Cubs' clubhouse at Wrigley Field. There, he penned a farewell note to his now-former Cubs teammates. "To the fellows: It's sort of hard to say farewell to a nice bunch of guys . . . I enjoyed every moment of it . . . even being called 'X' (after Brock picked Muhammad Ali to beat Sonny Liston). But as you and I know, that's part of the game called baseball. So, fellows, take care and the best of luck to each one of you . . . Brock. P.S. Don't try to take that extra base. I'll gun you down."

Broglio flew to St. Louis, where he picked up his car and drove Bobby Shantz to Chicago on Tuesday, June 16. By the time he arrived in town, Broglio could have read a *Chicago's American* headline: "Ex-Cubs Now Part of St. Louis Sag." The story described the Cardinals' 9-3 loss on Monday night, June 15, in Houston. "The St. Louis Sag apparently is contagious," the story lead. "Ex-Cubs Jack Spring and Lou Brock caught it only a few innings after they joined their new Cardinal teammates Monday night." Brock batted for pitcher Jack Spring, who had come over in the trade with him, in the eighth inning after arriving in mid-game at Colt Stadium. Brock fanned. Spring had allowed four runs in the seventh inning.

Devine and assistant Art Routzong were leaving the Houston ballpark when a fan who didn't recognize him said to a seatmate: "Brock for Broglio? Who made such a deal?" The GM thought of the humor in the situation, telling Routzong: "Who could have made such a deal?"

But the last laugh ended up on Holland and the Cubs.

Settled into a regular lineup spot by Keane, Brock's hitting continued, and even picked up. Brock also remembered a team meeting called by Keane in which he was drafted to match Maury Wills' base-stealing prowess. On June 15, 1964, Brock had 10 steals for the Cubs; the entire Cardinals team had 14 thefts.

The Cubs hoped to replace Brock in right field with a combination of Doug Clemens, hulking Len Gabrielson and switch-hitting rookie Billy Ott, recalled on June 15. None were up to the task. The highly touted Ott went 7-for-39 before disappearing forever from the big leagues.

Brock thrived, Broglio struggled, and the two finally met for the first time in their new uniforms when the Cards came to Wrigley Field for a three-game series on Tuesday, July 28, 1964 before a paid crowd of 16,052. On a blazing hot day that knocked out plate umpire Doug Harvey from heat exhaustion in the eighth inning, Brock went 2-for-6 with a run scored as the Cards rallied from 4-1 and 6-4 deficits against Broglio. Ken Boyer tripled and Bill White homered in a three-run sixth, then Broglio was knocked out in the seventh, yielding six runs and eight hits in six-plus innings. St. Louis finally won 12-7 on a five-run 10th keyed by Curt Flood's two-run triple. The Cubs fell to 48-49 with the loss; they would never see the .500 mark again in 1964.

The next day, Brock showed how his legs could prevail. During a seven-run Cards seventh that blew open a 1-0 game, Brock collected an RBI single, stole second, went to third on a throwing error by Cubs catcher Dick Bertell and scored in the eventual 9-1 victory. He was 4-for-5 with a double.

The Cardinals completed the three-game sweep on Thursday, July 30, with a 5-2 victory. White was the batting star with four RBI, while Brock legged out a fifth-inning double. He was 7-for-16 in his return to Chicago, batting .348 overall as a Cardinal—the exact same average he would sport for all of his 419 St. Louis at-bats in 1964.

Broglio would soon find his season and career unraveling. He won four games in late July and August, but he wasn't the same pitcher. Watching from the Cubs bullpen, Lindy McDaniel noted that Broglio's fastball had lost a lot of steam, even though he still possessed that tricky curve. "He had a great fastball that set up the curve, but I thought he didn't have enough speed," he said. On Sunday morning, August 23, 1964 in New

York, Broglio—due to pitch one of the games of that day's doubleheader at Shea Stadium—awakened in his hotel room to prepare to go to church with roommate Joey Amalfitano. He found his right elbow swollen the size of a cantaloupe and in a locked position; he couldn't even comb his hair. Broglio told Amalfitano the elbow was locked. "He throws the hotel room key to me and says, 'Here, unlock it,'" Broglio recalled. Amalfitano confirmed that story.

Reporting his swollen elbow to Kennedy, Broglio was sent back to Chicago that day as lefty John Flavin was called up to take his place on the roster. Broglio lost two more games the remainder of the 1964 season, but then underwent surgery to remove the bone chips and a damaged ulnar nerve after the season.

Broglio keeps insisting he was not damaged goods when the Cubs traded for him. But the injury could have been a cumulative affair, common in an era when pitchers did not advertise that their arms ached due to fears over job security. Dick Ellsworth, for one, suffered through tendinitis in 1964 and could not throw a biting slider that had helped him win 22 games the previous season. But Ellsworth still made 36 starts while his record dipped to 14-18 and his ERA inflated more than 1 1/2 runs to 3.75.

"You always tried to hide everything you could, because you never knew who was waiting to take your position," Broglio said. "You didn't do it to jeopardize your career. You did it to get that ball every fourth day as a starting pitcher."

Brock's contributions to the Cards' last-ditch pennant-race rally over the Phillies—they had trailed by 6 1/2 games with two weeks to go—and the World Series victory over the Yankees are well-documented. But Broglio wants to stick up for his contribution, too.

"I won three games for the Cardinals before the trade," he said. "That helped them get into the World Series; they only won the pennant by one game."

His old Cardinals teammates did not forget him.

"The whole ballclub called me from a pay phone in Stan Musial's restaurant after they won in '64," Broglio said. "That showed me what they thought of me."

Brock didn't forget his ol' Cubs teammates, either. After the Cards opened the season at Wrigley Field in 1965, he sent Billy Williams a "gift."

"He sent me a box . . . like what the World Series rings come in," Williams said. "Only this box was empty. Yeah, he had a sense of humor."

And a sense of timing against the Cubs. Starting with key three-run homers that won games in Wrigley Field in both 1966 and 1967, Brock, would bedevil the Cubs for the next 15 years, all the way through his 3,000th hit against Dennis Lamp at Busch Stadium in 1979.

Kennedy could only admire the kid that got away. Brock collected hit No. 3,000 against Dennis Lamp and a Cubs team for whom Kennedy served as general manager in 1979.

"The amazing thing about Brock is that Louie stole so many bases as a low bases-on-balls hitter," he said. "He hardly ever bunted. He was a good extra-base hitter because he was so strong. I thought Louie was the most perfect runner I ever saw. He would run to first base, you could put a cup of tea on his head and he wouldn't spill any."

Broglio simply struggled to take the mound. He finished 4-7 with a 4.04 ERA as a Cub in '64. As a surgery-rehabbed case in 1965, he was batting-practice fodder at 1-6 with a 6.93 ERA in 26 games, but only six starts.

But Broglio seemed to revive and try to salvage the trade in spring training 1966 at Long Beach, California, the first under new manager Leo Durocher. Describing his season as a "do or die year," Broglio spun one good performance after another in spring games. On March 20, 1966, he hurled five shutout innings with six strikeouts against the Indians.

"This isn't the same fellow I umpired behind last spring. His ball is really moving," AL umpire John Rice said after the game.

"Last year it was curve, curve, curve and he'd get behind, come in with a fastball and get murdered," Durocher said. "But he's a pitcher again now. He's breaking off a fast curve, a slider, mixing in that big downer and busting that hard one in there with some mustard on it."

Ron Santo theorized at the time that Durocher re-instilled confidence in Broglio. "Leo gives him all the support in the world," he said.

On March 25, 1966, Broglio amassed six more shutout innings against the Angels, bringing his spring yield to just two runs in 18 innings. Then, on March 30, he extended a scoreless-innings streak to 16 innings before Fred Whitfield touched him for a homer. Broglio yielded just one earned run in six innings in the 8-5 victory. The Cubs were sure the old Broglio had returned.

That proved to be a desert mirage in California and Arizona. He had a poor final spring outing that carried over into his second start of the season on April 13 against the Giants in San Francisco. Broglio was wild, throwing 80 pitches in the first four innings and walking seven in his seven-inning stint in the 4-0 loss. He went downhill from there as the entire Cubs staff collapsed. Durocher began shuttling in new pitchers almost weekly; he used 23 hurlers during the 10th-place, 103-defeat season.

Broglio walked 38 and fanned just 34 in 62 1/3 innings in 1966 as he compiled a 2-6 record and 6.35 ERA. Durocher, as was his custom, had little patience for non-producers and loved to "back up the truck." The reverse-gear came for Broglio on a holiday Monday, July 5, at Wrigley Field, as he was released outright to Triple-A Tacoma. The *Chicago Sun-Times* headlined: "Broglio Released; Remember Brock?" "Broglio's departure closes the books on one of the worst deals the Cubs ever made," the accompanying story said.

Despite the disastrous outcome of the trade, the Cubs did salvage something from Brock for Broglio. A little bit of the sore-elbowed pitcher's knowledge went along with Ken Holtzman as he hurled two no-hitters for the Cubs, with Fergie Jenkins as he won 20 games six seasons in a row in Wrigley Field, and with Bill Hands as he became a tough pitcher, winning 20 with a 2.49 ERA in 1969.

"When I finally made the major leagues in 1965, I purposely went up to him," Holtzman said of Broglio. "It was a big thrill for me when I got to meet Ernie Broglio, Larry Jackson and Lindy McDaniel.

"I know three guys who are especially thankful that Ernie Broglio was with the Cubs: Fergie Jenkins, Bill Hands and myself. I remember when Fergie, Bill and myself were in our first and second years. The guys we looked to in order to learn how to play this game were veterans like Ernie Broglio. You just can't measure what a guy like that means to his career, to be able to talk to him about the game. I learned more in the first three weeks from these guys like Ernie than I did all my previous playing career. Certainly, Ernie made a difference in all three of our careers."

Brock and Broglio were reunited twice in the 1990s—at an old-timers game at Wrigley Field and at the 1995 Cubs Convention. Brock asked for Broglio to be at his side.

"They told me if you don't come, Lou Brock won't show," Broglio said of the old-timers game. The fans didn't forget Brock for Broglio.

"They introduced me next-to-last, and Lou Brock was last," he said. "As I was introduced, I came out and took my hat off. Everyone stood up and gave me a great ovation of boos. I started laughing and took a bow. Then they introduced Lou Brock and, my God, I thought Wrigley Field was going to collapse the way they cheered him.

"I'm so happy Lou made the Hall of Fame."

In addition to catcalls at the ballpark, Broglio became material for the most popular modern-day play about baseball.

"I saw the play *Bleacher Bums* on TV," he said. "After Brock's name was announced in the lineup (based on a 1977 Cubs-Cards game), one of the characters says, 'I wonder where that bum Broglio is?'"

Where he ended up was first working in a warehouse, then helping out as an assistant baseball coach at Saratoga (California) High School, near his home in San Jose. Meanwhile, Brock marketed his Broccabrella, a self-attached umbrella on the top of the head, while also owning a variety of businesses in St. Louis. He is busy these days on the card-show circuit.

What "if?" What would have happened to Brock's career had he not been traded? What would have been the Cubs' fate had he blossomed along with Billy Williams, Ernie Banks, Ron Santo, Don Kessinger, Glenn Beckert, Randy Hundley and Fergie Jenkins in the same lineup?

After all, Brock by himself often doubled the stolen-base total of the Durocher-led Cubs contenders of the late 1960s and early 1970s. In 1968, the Cubs stole just 30 bases; Brock swiped 64. And, up to the present day, Ryne Sandberg's 54 steals in 1985 remains the Cubs' highest season total since the dead-ball era after the turn of the century. Baserunning never became a Wrigley Field speciality; only two other Cubs, Ivan DeJesus and Davey Lopes, even stole as many as 40 bases in a season since World War I.

"I think it would have been the same," Brock said of his career outcome had John Holland suddenly gotten cold feet in mid-June, 1964. "I thought the Cubs would have won (in the late 1960s) if they had a leadoff man with my numbers.

"I still think Cubs fans have a lot to be thankful for. They have traded for great players from other teams. You win a few, you lose a few. It's all in the mind of the beholder."

# 13

## The Trading Market

**THE Cubs and Cardinals may have been arch-rivals** in head-to-head action. But in the private conclaves of the front office, they often were business partners.

Since the rivalry began, both teams have transacted lot of business in the form of flesh-peddling. Players, big reputations or not, have traded uniforms. Traffic first down the railroad line, then Route 66, then Interstate 55 became heavy at times—particularly during the tenure of Cubs general manager John Holland from 1956 to 1975.

Lou Brock was only one of a number of stars who have worked both cities, moving via trades. Mention the big name, and he's probably worn both a Cubs-Cardinals uniform: Mordecai "Three Finger" Brown, Dizzy Dean, Lon Warneke, Hank Sauer, Larry Jackson, Lindy McDaniel, Bruce Sutter.

Despite the high level of traffic up and down Illinois, the player pipeline was cut off for 14 1/2 years recently. No Cubs-Cardinals trade was consummated between December 9, 1980, when Bruce Sutter was dispatched from Chicago in exchange for Leon Durham and Ken Reitz, and June 16, 1995, when the Cardinals finally gave up on golden boy

Todd Zeile, sending him north for pitcher Mike Morgan and two minor leaguers. Through the start of the 1999 season, no other Cubs-Cardinals deal has been completed.

General managers Ed Lynch of the Cubs and Walt Jocketty of the Cardinals both were surprised when informed the Zeile deal had been the first since then-Cubs GM Bob Kennedy, following orders to dump salary, pulled the trigger on Sutter. Four other Chicago GM's—Herman Franks, Dallas Green, Jim Frey and Larry Himes—had served in the interim without conducting business with their Cardinals counterparts.

"Walt Jocketty and I were rookie general managers then," Lynch said. "Each of us would probably be less likely to deal with each other than we were four years ago. It's more of a division rivalry thing-we don't want to do anything that will help anybody in our division who will be our competition.

"But if I was absolutely convinced it (a trade) with the Cardinals would make us a better club, sure I would do it."

Jocketty also confirms he gives pause to dealing with Chicago.

"There's always some hesitancy to deal with teams in your division. You don't want to strengthen them more than you strengthen your own club.

"Ed and I have a good relationship. But we'd always be very careful about making a deal. There's more fan and media scrutiny."

While we all wait for the next Cubs-Cardinals deal—whenever—we have plenty of time to look back at many of the trades made and the players involved:

## Mordecai "Three Finger" Brown for Jack Taylor and Larry McLean
### December 12, 1903

In all the long history of the Cubs-Cardinals deals, St. Louis more often than not came out on top. But the Cardinals got off to a bad start in this trade, made just as man took the air in powered flight for the first time via the Wright brothers.

A 27-year-old rookie in 1903, Mordecai Peter Centennial Brown had pitched well for St. Louis despite a 9-13 record. In contrast, Taylor was an established pitcher with 22- and 21-win seasons for the Cubs in 1902 and 1903, respectively. McLean was a little-used backup.

At the National League meeting in New York, the Cubs and Cardinals completed the deal, and the *Chicago Tribune* reported it in the florid newspaper prose of the era:

"On the basis of last year's performances the trade looks like an excellent one from a Chicago standpoint . . . Taylor desired to get away from Chicago, where he has played himself so long that he does not feel able to do himself justice in the face of some of the inevitable 'knocking' that comes to a veteran player. He will never be any better pitcher than he has been in Chicago, while Brown is a comparative youngster and is believed to have a future."

The *Trib* turned out to be an accurate forecaster of the future.

### Outcome of the trade

Brown was one of the great finds of the dead-ball era. After 15-10 and 18-12 marks in 1904 and 1905, Brown became a top contributor to the record-breaking 116-win Cubs team of 1906 with a 26-6 record and NL-leading 1.04 ERA. He would go on to win 20 or more games five more consecutive seasons, including 29-9 and 27-9 record in 1908 and 1909. Only Fergie Jenkins, a fellow Hall of Famer, matched Brown in Cubs annals with six consecutive 20-win seasons six decades later. Brown later had a short stint with St. Louis Federal League team, but the Cardinals had to watch helplessly as Brown mowed down an entire league with ease.

This had to rank with the Cardinals' all-time worst deals, especially since Taylor pitched just 2 1/2 seasons in St. Louis. He had 39 complete games in 40 starts in 1904, going 21-19 with a 2.22 ERA. But he declined to 15-21 in 1905. After an 8-9 record in the first part of the 1906 season, he was traded back to Chicago for Fred Beebe, Pete Noonan and cash on July 1, 1906. He pitched only one more season in 1907, finishing his career with a 151-139 record.

# Cliff Heathcote for Max Flack
## May 30, 1922

General managers have often made deals between games of a double-header. But only once in modern major league history have players on opposing teams switched uniforms between contests and competed against each other in the second game.

That happened in the Memorial Day 1922 double-header between the Cubs and Cardinals in Chicago. Between games the teams traded outfielders, Cliff Heathcote of the Cardinals going to the Cubs for Max Flack.

Both men played both games. In the opener, Heathcote, 22, a Cardinal for four seasons, started in center field, batted seventh, and went 0-for-3; Flack, 32, a Cub for the previous six years, started in right field, batted fifth and went hitless in four plate appearances. Chicago won 4-1.

Teams hadn't yet begun to put numbers on uniforms.

In the nightcap, Flack led off in right field for the Cardinals and went 1-for-4. Heathcote started in center for the Cubs and batted fifth, going 2-for-4. The Cubs pushed across two runs in the bottom of the eighth that were the difference in a 3-1 Cubs win.

The sweep brought the fifth-place Cubs to 20-20 on the season and dropped the Cardinals one notch to third at 23-20.

## Outcome of the trade

Both players improved that season after the trade. Flack had been hitting .222 for the Cubs and batted .292 for the Cards. Heathcote went from .245 with the Cardinals to .280 with Chicago. The Cardinals finished fourth and the Cubs fifth.

Flack finished his 12-year career as a reserve outfielder for the Cardinals in 1925, retiring with a .278 lifetime average. Heathcote played eight more seasons for the Cubs and completed a 15-year career in 1932; his lifetime mark was .275.

# Hack Wilson and Bud Teachout for Burleigh Grimes
# December 9, 1931

Hack Wilson was just about the second biggest-name in baseball after Babe Ruth in 1931. The Cardinals landed Wilson from their arch-rivals—but he never suited up as a Redbird.

The Cardinals can lay claim to having had in uniform two of the four players who set single-season records for homers. Mark McGwire walloped 70 for the Redbirds in 1998; Roger Maris came to St. Louis six seasons after hitting 61 for the 1961 New York Yankees.

But the Cardinals also possessed, for a little more than a month, the contract of Wilson, who set the NL record of 56 homers while playing for the Cubs in 1930. Just one season later, he plummeted to 13 and was traded to St. Louis on December 9, 1931. It was popularly believed the deal was made because of friction with Cubs manager Rogers Hornsby.

"Why should I be shocked?" Wilson said when informed of the trade.

"The treatment I received in Chicago was terrible, especially from the officials of the club.

"You can say for me—and make it as strong as you like—that they took that bat right out of my hands in Chicago. How is a fellow going to live up to his reputation as a hitter if he is not allowed to hit? When I made a home-run record in the National League, I was not under any big handicap at the plate as was the case last year (1931)."

Wilson claimed Hornsby ordered him to "take a lot of sweet strikes I might have hammered out of the lot."

Hornsby responded Wilson was allowed to hit pitches in favorable hitters' counts. "I am not bothered by anything Wilson says, as he now is the property of another club," the irascible manager said.

Packaged with Wilson was pitcher Bud Teachout. In return, the Cubs got pitcher Burleigh Grimes, last of the legal spitballers.

Then, on Jan. 23, 1932, the Cardinals sold Wilson to the Brooklyn Dodgers for $45,000—great money in those days—and a minor league pitcher.

Contemporary newspapers speculated the Cardinals had acquired Wilson as security if contract negotiations with their sparkplug center fielder, Pepper Martin, fell through. Martin, fresh from helping the Cardinals win the World Series, had in the off-season had gone on the vaudeville circuit as part of the spoils. In three months on stage he'd reportedly earned $12,600, nearly tripling his $4,500 Cardinals salary.

That newspaper explanation, however, seems curious since players then didn't have free agency, and Martin would have had to play in St. Louis no matter how unhappy he might have been with any contract offered. More likely, the Cardinals had unloaded Grimes because of his high salary and hoped to use Wilson as trade bait elsewhere.

St. Louis fans, however, had looked forward to seeing the stocky Wilson playing in Cardinal red.

One stumbling block stood in the way of that: Branch Rickey, the Cardinals' general manager and the man who'd started its bountiful farm system, wanted Wilson to take a pay cut, from $33,500 to $7,500. Wilson said he was willing to play for less—but not that much less.

When the Cardinals signed Martin to a $7,500 contact in January, they almost immediately dealt Wilson. Hack said after the deal to Brooklyn he'd never expected to play in St. Louis, that it was just "a stopover." Right after the trade to St. Louis, Hornsby had bet Rickey that Wilson would never play a game for the Cardinals.

Martin, meanwhile, said after the trade of Wilson to Brooklyn that he expected the Cardinals to again win the pennant. Martin pointed to two young hurlers, Dizzy Dean and Tex Carleton, and said they should be able to combine for 35 wins together.

### Outcome of the trade

Martin broke a finger and played only 85 games in 1932, hitting .238. Dean won 18 games, Carleton 10, Teachout none, and the world champs fell to seventh place.

Wilson came back with 23 homers, 123 RBI and a .297 average for the Dodgers, who finished third.

Johnny Moore took Wilson's place in the Cubs outfield and hit .305 with 13 homers. Grimes won six games. The Cubs hit only 69 homers, fired Hornsby two-thirds of the way through the season, and won the pennant, only to lose the World Series to the Yankees and Babe Ruth's famed "called shot" homer.

# Tex Carleton for Bud Tinning, Dick Ward and cash
# November 21, 1934

Here was another deal that turned out poorly for the Cardinals.

Right-hander Carleton provided some nice depth in the Redbird rotation behind Dizzy Dean in 1933-34, winning 17 and 16 games, respectively.

Pitchers Tinning and Ward, the latter a former minor league sensation, were lesser contributors to the Cubs.

In analyzing the trade, the *Chicago Tribune* focused oddly enough on the players' weight.

"He is expected to weigh for now that he will not have to play 77 games in torrid St. Louis," the paper wrote of the 176-pound Carlton. Of Tinning, it said: "Bud, a pleasant, earnest fellow, found great difficulty in battling his tendency to obesity and to this was attributed the fact that he won only four games this year (1934) as compared to 13 in 1933.

### Outcome of the trade

Carleton did pitch longer and gained a couple of pounds (up to 180) with the cooling Lake Michigan winds at his back often in Chicago. He was a back-of-the-rotation starter with 11-8 and 10-9 records, respectively, for the 1935 and 1938 Cubs pennant winners. In between, he was 14-10 in 1936 and 16-8 in 1937.

Tinning and Ward won exactly zero games in five contests combined for the Cardinals.

## Lon Warneke for Ripper Collins and Roy Parmelee October 8, 1936

The Cardinals finally obtained a first-class pitcher from the Cubs in Warneke. The Cubs desired desperately-needed power in Collins. The World Series between the Giants and Yankees was hardly over when the teams cut the deal.

Warneke, a good ol' country boy from Arkansas, caused sportswriter Edward Burns to say that in admiration of the pitcher, he was a member of the "Squirrel Shooting, Hound Dog Fancying and Arkansas Wisecracking Guild." But Warneke's first specialty was pitching, including the clutch effort in the 1-0 victory over the Cardinals in St. Louis that clinched at least a tie for the 1935 NL pennant for the Cubs.

Warneke had burst on the scene in 1932 to spark the Cubs to their previous pennant. He was 22-6 with an NL-leading 2.37 ERA. In successive years, Warneke was 18-13, 22-10, 20-13 and 16-13.

The switch-hitting Collins packed a lot of power into a 5-foot-9, 165-pound frame. He was the regular first baseman during the "Gashouse Gang" peak days, with his best season during the pennant campaign of 1934. Collins had an NL-leading 35 homers and drove in 128 runs, batting .333. He followed that up with 23 homers and 122 RBI in 1935, but his salary inflated a little too much for the Cardinals' tastes in 1936 as he gave way to promising rookie Johnny Mize at first base.

Parmelee, originally a mid-rotation Giants starter, had been 11-11 in his only St. Louis season in 1936.

### Outcome of the trade

The Cardinals finally got the better of a deal with the Cubs. Warneke was 18-11 in his first season in 1937, then was 13-8, 13-7, 16-10 and 17-9 through 1941.

On July 8, 1942, Warneke followed the path of Jack Taylor some 36 years previously, getting traded back to the Cubs for $75,000 in cash and missing the first of three Cardinals pennants. He was only a part-time starter, though, in Chicago in 1942-43. Warneke came back briefly to pitch for the Cubs in 1945, going 1-1, but, again, missing out on the World Series that fall in Chicago.

After trying out Babe Herman and Chuck Klein, the Cubs struck out again in their search for a true slugger to replace Hack Wilson. Collins had just 16 homes in 1937. He fell to 13 homers in 143 games in 1938 before departing the majors, re-surfacing for only a 49-game stint in Pittsburgh in 1941.

Parmelee was 7-8 in one Cubs season before finishing up with the Philadelphia Athletics in 1939.

## Dizzy Dean for Curt Davis, Clyde Shoun, Tuck Stainback and $185,000
### April 16, 1938

Jay Hanna Dean needs no introduction to any baseball aficionado.

One of the most colorful players of all time, Dean was bombastic, boastful and a bearer of fractured syntax. He had two baseball lifetimes— as the second-to-last pitcher ever to win 30 games, and as the grammar-mangling announcer on CBS-TV's Saturday "Game of the Week" in the 1950s and early 1960s.

Dean symbolized the spirit of the Cardinals' Gashouse Gang. Only 21, he went 18-15 as a rookie in 1932. He then went 20-18, and astounded baseball with his 30-7 mark (26-5 as a starter) and 2.66 ERA in 1934 as the Cardinals won it all. He was "Dizzy," younger brother Paul was "Daffy," and you just didn't outpitch the Cardinals when the Deans took the mound.

But Dean's ever-growing achievements came at a price. He demanded fair payment for his achievements, holding out almost every spring. That was like waving a red flag at a bull. Under owner Sam Breadon and general manager Branch Rickey, the Cardinals were penny pinchers. So even though Dean was 28-12 in 1935 and 24-13 in 1936, he was on the trading block by the fall of the latter year.

"I'd trade Dizzy, but the deal would have to be such that it would bolster the Cardinals," Breadon said on October 8, 1936, the same day he traded for Lon Warneke from the Cubs.

Two events finally gave the Cardinals the out they needed. On July 7, 1937, Dean's toe was broken by a line drive off the bat of Earl Averill, Sr. during the All-Star Game in Washington, D.C. The stubborn Dean tried to come back too soon from the injury, hurting his arm as he favored the bad foot. He dropped to 13-10 for 1937, pitching in just 27 games.

Then, in spring training 1938, Dean held out again. The Cardinals wanted to cut his salary by $5,000. Without free agency, Dean had to cave in to accept $17,500. But the die was cast. Breadon and Rickey found a willing buyer in Cubs owner P.K. Wrigley, who had spent the previous six years mimicking his late father, William Wrigley, Jr., in using the family gum fortune to acquire big-name players to bolster the Cubs. The elder Wrigley had been successful with Rogers Hornsby, but junior had been less successful with Ripper Collins, Babe Herman and Chuck Klein.

Dean opponents in spring training in Florida spoke out about how Dean had changed his motion and lost steam off his fastball.

"Dean is throwing side-arm all spring and with a stiffness unusual for him," Tigers manager Mickey Cochrane said. "He wasn't a bit loose or easy the day we faced him. Never threw overhand at all."

"He was throwing crooked-arm to any way of looking," said Tigers second baseman Charlie Gehringer. He was seconded by slugger Hank Greenberg.

When Wrigley finally completed the deal, Giants manager Bill Terry said Rickey knew what he was doing.

"I do not believe that Branch Rickey would get rid of the pitcher that Dean was two years ago," Terry said. "If he were still a man who could win 20 to 30 games, I think he would have stayed with the Cardinals. Rickey must know that he is through as a great pitcher and has got what he can for him."

Cubs players themselves knew they were not getting the Dean of 1934.

"We knew he had a sore arm," Phil Cavarretta said from the hindsight of six decades later. "But Dizzy was great in the clubhouse. He loved everybody. The greatest thing I saw in him was his determination. Even with his bad arm, he felt he could beat everybody."

Wrigley dealt right-hander Curt Davis, a part-time starter who was 10-5 in 1937; lefty reliever Clyde Shoun, and outfielder Tuck Stainback, who had hit .306 as a rookie in 1934 but had done little else ever since. Most astounding was Wrigley writing a check for $185,000 to the Cardinals, an astounding sum in the latter stages of the Depression. Breadon and Rickey could have paid most of their big-league roster from Wrigley's largesse.

Despite the negative reports about his arm, Dean was as optimistic as ever as he set out for Chicago.

"Yes, sir, I'll win 20 games," Dean proclaimed. "Might do better than that with that great Cub infield behind me. My arm feels fine. I'm more enthusiastic than I've been in a long while, and I'm getting more and more like that every minute."

Dean compared moving from the Cardinals to the wealthy Cubs as akin to trading hamburger for steak.

"Them Cubs is sure a great outfit," he said. "They really treat a fellow right. Six uniforms they give a feller—three home and three road. Them Cards just give you one of each."

Even though they knew he was not the ace of old, Dean's Cardinals teammates were sad to see him go.

"There goes our pennant and World Series money," third baseman Pepper Martin said. "You can't play cash on the baseball field."

"Yeah, we'd have been a cinch with Diz," center fielder Terry Moore said.

Manager Frankie Frisch was too upset to talk. "I haven't anything to say," he said, sourly.

While the Cardinals appeared hungry for cash, Wrigley apparently attempted to buy even more talent. Immediately after the Dean trade, the *St. Louis Globe-Democrat* reported that the Cardinals rejected a cash offer of $100,000 for young outfielder Enos Slaughter.

## Outcome of the trade

Dean never had a chance to win 20 for the Cubs. His balky arm limited him to a role as a "Sunday pitcher"—a gate attraction whom Chicago would use to boost the crowd on Sundays. Dean pitched in just 13 regular-season games, including 10 starts, for the NL champion 1938 Cubs. But he made the most of his off-speed stuff, compiling a 7-1 record and 1.81 ERA while issuing just eight walks in 74 2/3 innings.

Dean was entrusted with the start in Game 2 of the World Series against the powerful Yankees. With his guile, he held the Bronx Bombers to just five hits while nursing a 3-2 lead through seven innings. True to form, the Yankees tallied two each in the eighth and ninth for a 6-3 victory on their way to a Series sweep.

"That was the greatest game I saw him pitch for us," Cavarretta said. "He was dazzling them with slow stuff. He got the Yankees to pop the ball up. They finally got to him in the eighth."

Dean had a similar role in 1939 with a 6-4 record and 3.36 ERA in 19 games, including 13 starts. He was 3-3 in 10 games (nine starts) in 1940 before calling it quits after one game in 1941—until making a one-game, four-inning return for the St. Louis Browns in 1947 as his broadcasting career began. Within the next decade, Dean would be a household name in all non big-league cities allowed to carry CBS' "Game of the Week," famed for using "slud" instead of "slid" and a variety of other Dean-isms. Buddy Blattner and Pee Wee Reese served as his broadcast partners as Dean became better known for his on-air work than his too-short pitching career.

Branch Rickey indeed knew what he was doing. Curt Davis was 13-8 in 1939 for St. Louis, then was 22-16 in 1940. On June 12, 1940, he was packaged with Ducky Medwick in a trade to the Brooklyn Dodgers for Ernie Koy, Carl Doyle, Sam Nahem, Bert Haas and, as always, cash —$125,000.

Shoun turned in some decent work out of both the starting rotation and bullpen as a Cardinal, then was sent packing to the Reds early in the 1942 season. Stainback had a six-game cup of coffee in St. Louis before moving on to a journeyman's career with five other teams through 1946.

## Hank Sauer for Pete Whisenant and cash
## March 30, 1956

Hank Sauer was synonymous with the Cubs of the post-war era. He was the biggest star in between the 1945 pennant winners and the arrival of Ernie Banks in 1953. His slugging feats earned him the nickname, "The Mayor of Wrigley Field," and showers of his favorite chewing tobacco from adoring bleacher fans after one of his homers.

Product of a great trade that also landed center fielder Frankie Baumholtz early in the 1949 season from the Reds, Sauer won the National League's MVP award in 1952 for a league-leading 37 homers and 121 RBI. Injured much of 1953, he rebounded with 41 homers and 103 RBI in 1954. But Sauer was 38 in 1955 when he was hurt again, belting just 12 homers as Banks emerged as the new top Cubs gun with 44 homers, including five grand slams.

Whisenant was a light-hitting, little-used outfielder for the Cardinals. He batted just .191 with two homers and nine RBI in 58 at-bats.

Sauer was shocked by the trade.

"P.K. Wrigley told Wid Matthews (the Cubs' general manager prior to John Holland) not to trade me," he recalled decades later. "I was playing golf on Good Friday (1956) with Paul Richards, who was managing the Orioles. I had a feeling I was going to be traded. Richards said no way.

"I got a letter in my box to see Matthews. He wanted me to play at Los Angeles (the Cubs' Triple-A affiliate), then manage there later. The alternative was St. Louis. I didn't trust him about the Los Angeles deal. If Wrigley would have talked to me, I would have done it. I don't even think he knew the trade to St. Louis was going on. Matthews got fired after that season."

Matthews' explanation at the time of the deal: "We feel we have made a step for the future and a step for depth in the Cub outfield picture."

Frank Lane, who had just taken over as Cardinals general manager, was overjoyed to land the slugger. "Sauer is just what we've been looking for," Lane said. "He'll help us against the 'softball' left handers those other teams threw against us last year."

## Outcome of the trade

The deal was a virtual bust for both sides. Sauer played only part-time as a Cardinal, batting .298 with just five homers in 75. Let go after the season, Sauer hooked on with the Giants, for whom he slugged 26 homers in 1957. Sauer followed the Giants out to San Francisco, played for two more seasons through 1959, and ended up as a scout for the team. He is retired and lives near the San Francisco airport.

Whisenant was not the solution to the Cubs' center-field hole with a .239 average, 11 homers and 46 RBI in 1956. He moved on to the Reds, Indians, Washington Senators/Minnesota Twins in a career that lasted through 1961.

# 14

## Mr. Holland's Opus, 1956-1975

**JOHN Holland was the epitome** of the old-fashioned baseball front-office man. The Cubs' longtime general manager often could be found amid billowing cigarette smoke. He imbibed, too—"John liked his Scotches," said longtime front office associate E.R. "Salty" Saltwell—and Wrigley Field's "Pink Poodle" lunchroom, with its open bar that served the hard stuff all the way through the early 1980s, was a perfect postgame stop.

Holland, of course, is most infamous for trading Lou Brock. He also made some equivalent good deals, such as trading for Fergie Jenkins in 1966. But the overriding theme of Holland's stewardship, by far the longest for a Cubs general manager in modern times, was his transactions with the Cardinals.

The Brock deal was just one of an assembly line of transactions—17 that can be tracked down through research—that Holland completed with not only favorite trading partner Bing Devine, but also other Cardinals GM's such as Frank Lane and Bob Howsam. Just appointed GM in the fall of 1956 as part of a front-office housecleaning ordered by P.K. Wrigley, Holland made his first deal with St. Louis the biggest in terms of numbers—a 10-player swap that dispatched wild, curve-balling Sam "Toothpick" Jones in exchange for a whole bunch of players who didn't work out. His last deal came almost 19 years later, when he traded long-time favorite Don Kessinger for reliever Mike Garman. In between, he seemed to try to trade anybody and everybody to the Cardinals.

His motivation for dealing with the neighbor 300 miles down the highway is unclear. Maybe he liked Devine and the other Cardinals execs, as hinted at in a comment on May 26, 1964, when the first rumors of Holland trying to peddle Brock to the Cardinals surfaced. "We've helped each other in the past and we may do it again," he said.

More than a generation later, Devine confirms a good relationship between the two GM's. "We understood each other," he said.

Saltwell, the Cubs' concessions manager who actually succeeded Holland for one season as GM in 1976, said Holland and Devine "had mutual affection" for each other. But even he was surprised when informed that Holland had made at least 17 trades with the Cardinals in a 19-year span.

St. Louis wasn't the only frequent destination for traded Cubs. Holland and Oakland Athletics owner Charles O. Finley, who lived and worked in the Chicago area, practically ran a shuttle between the two teams in the early and mid-1970s. Prime players like Ken Holtzman and Bill North found their way into A's uniforms just in time to contribute to the string of World Series championships of the era. Finley usually ended up with the best of the deals; Rick Monday was the only former Athletics player who produced as a Cub.

Favored trading partners was just a part of the collegial front-office atmosphere of those pre-free agency days. "General managers were more forthright with each other on players' physical conditions," Saltwell recalled. They also took writers into their confidences more, and sometimes got an embargo on advance news of a trade in return.

"Holland would call the Chicago beat writers together in the hotel lobby in spring training and let them know the details of a trade beforehand," Saltwell said. "That way, they could prepare their background information ahead of time, and be ready to write the story. For the most part, they honored the embargo and sat on the news of the trade until it was announced."

Not anymore. Give a baseball writer a crumb, a rumor, and he'll run with it. They are no longer so chummy with the front office. Why, a GM like the beleaguered Dan Duquette of the Boston Red Sox isolates himself behind a palace guard, available to the media only in controlled situations.

Ah, for the good ol' days. The following is a look at Holland's deals with the Cardinals—other than Brock-for-Broglio—and how they turned out:

# 10-player swap
# December 10, 1956

Holland made a big splash at the 1956 winter meetings at Chicago's Palmer House Hotel on the same day White Sox owner Grace Comiskey died a few miles away at her Lake Shore Drive apartment. Players took the first steps to forming their own union, electing Bob Feller as president in New Orleans.

Sam Jones, who with toothpick firmly planted between his lips had no-hit the Pirates in 1955, was dispatched along with left-hander Jim Davis, catcher Hobie Landrith and utility player Eddie Miksis. Coming to Chicago were pitchers Tom Poholsky and Jackie Collum, catcher Ray Katt and minor league infielder Wally Lammers. Two other Cardinals minor leaguers were later sent to the Cubs.

Jones possessed some of the best stuff in baseball, but he was exceptionally wild. The Cubs tired of waiting for Jones to harness his control. Although Poholsky matched Jones' 1956 record at 9-14, new Cubs manager Bob Scheffing, a St. Louis native, expected the right-hander to have a good influence on a coming crop of young pitchers that included Moe Drabowsky and Dick Drott.

"Maybe this is no more than an even deal," said Scheffing, "but we think, of course, we profited."

That did not turn out to be the case.

## Outcome of the trade

None of the Cardinals traded to Chicago made any impact at all. They were gone within a year, Collum and Katt being dispatched again by Holland by early season 1957. But St. Louis also got some interesting mileage out of Jones and Landrith.

Jones was 12-9 and 14-13 in 1957 and 1958, respectively, leading the NL in strikeouts with 225 in '58. Then, just before the 1959 season, he was traded to the Giants in a deal that was unpopular at first. But the Cardinals got an up-and-coming young hitter named Bill White in return. So Jones' league-leading 21 wins, followed by 18 in 1960, didn't hurt in the long run after all. Bing Devine was a busy man trading with the Giants at that time. Landrith had been dealt along with Billy Muffett immediately after the 1958 season for a promising young pitcher, Ernie Broglio, who, as you know, Devine eventually turned into Lou Brock. So an interesting circle was completed with the Cubs.

## Jim Brosnan for Alvin Dark
## May 20, 1958

Brosnan, baseball's first author-pitcher, had finally made the Cubs' starting rotation coming out of spring training in 1958. Owner P.K. Wrigley decided all starting pitchers should be paid a minimum of $15,000. So when Brosnan was traded to the Cardinals, Devine was shocked at his salary, wondering who was Brosnan's sugar daddy.

"But Bing said a contract was a contract," Brosnan recalled. "He gave me a nice raise for the following season."

With younger infielders coming up, the Cardinals could spare the veteran Dark, who had hit .290 with 64 RBI in his only full St. Louis season in 1957.

### Outcome of the trade

Dark plugged a hole at third for the next 1 1/2 seasons in Wrigley Field, then was traded in the winter of 1959-60 for center fielder Richie Ashburn, who had his last good season for the Cubs.

Brosnan's stay in St. Louis was relatively short. He was 8-4 the rest of the 1958 season. He was earmarked as the Cardinals' closer for 1959. "But I didn't get along with Solly Hemus (then rookie Cardinals manager)," he said.

Devine soon traded Brosnan to the Reds for ex-Cub Hal Jeffcoat. The Cardinals got the short end of the stick when Brosnan became a dependable reliever for the next few seasons, including a 10-4 record with 16 saves for Cincinnati's 1961 NL pennant.

"Bing had me on his talk show some years ago," Brosnan said. "He told me the worst deal of his life was when he traded me."

When Brosnan went to Cincinnati, he published *The Long Season*, the first realistic, honest book looking at everyday baseball life. That was followed up by *Pennant Race*.

## Irv Noren for Charlie King
## May 19, 1959

Noren had been a longtime platoon-outfielder type who saw service on four World Series-bound Yankees teams in the early and mid-1950s, before arriving in St. Louis. The left-handed hitter batted .264 as a part-timer with the Cardinals in 1958.

King was a cup-of-coffee outfielder with the Tigers before briefly appearing with the Cubs in 1958 and 1959.

### Outcome of the trade

Noren did little with the Cubs and finished out his career in Chicago and Los Angeles in 1960. King played in only five games for the Cardinals.

## Moose Moryn for Jim McKnight
## June 15, 1960

Lumbering outfielder Moryn was fresh from the hero's role, making a shoetop catch of Joe Cunningham's liner in left field on May 15, 1960, to end Don Cardwell's no-hitter against the Cardinals. He was coming off several productive Cubs seasons, including a 26-homer outburst in 1958.

### Outcome of the trade

Near the end of his career, Moryn slugged 11 homers in a part-time role the rest of the 1960 season in St. Louis before ending his career on the Pirates the following year. McKnight was just a little-used player for the Cubs.

## Bobby Gene Smith and Daryl Robertson for
## Don Landrum and Alex Grammas
## June 5, 1962

Outfielder Smith originally came up to the Cardinals in 1957 and played three seasons in a part-time role before moving on to the Phillies, Mets and Cubs. Landrum was a similar kind of player, only he batted left-handed. Grammas had been a longtime slap-hitting infielder for the Cardinals and Reds, while Robertson was an unknown infielder.

## Outcome of the trade

This was a wash, one slap-hitting outfielder for another. Smith hit .231 in 91 games the rest of the '62 season in St. Louis, disappearing into the minors until he re-surfaced in 1965 with the Angels. Meanwhile, Landrum split time in center field in Chicago with the likes of Lou Brock, Ellis Burton (an ex-Cardinal) and Billy Cowan. He finally became a Cubs regular in 1965, in time to serve as trade fodder along with Lindy McDaniel after that season with the Giants for two promising young players-catcher Randy Hundley and pitcher Bill Hands.

Grammas finished out his career with the Cubs in 1963, while Robertson never saw major league action again after his cup of coffee in Chicago.

# George Altman, Don Cardwell and Moe Thacker for Larry Jackson, Lindy McDaniel and Jimmie Schaffer October 17, 1962

The second-biggest trade in numbers of players after the 10-player deal in 1956, the deal was made to solve the crying problems of both teams.

Altman was one of the NL's top left-handed hitters in 1961 and 1962. He had 27 homers, 96 RBI and a .303 average in '61, following that up with 22 homers and a .318 mark in '62. The Cardinals figured that Altman would provide much-needed left-handed power with Stan Musial in the deep twilight of his career.

Cardwell had no-hit the Cubs in his first Chicago start in 1960, then was 15-14 for a lousy Cubs team in 1961. But he slumped badly to 7-16 with a 4.92 ERA in 1962. Batterymate Thacker was the epitome of the good-field, no-hit catcher.

Always realizing he had young pitchers coming up through his farm system, Devine felt he could spare Jackson and McDaniel, Cardinals pitching mainstays since the mid-1950s. Jackson had won 18, 14 and 16 games from 1960 to 1962. Former "bonus baby" McDaniel, who had begun his career as a starter, had become the Cardinals' first true modern stopper with a 12-2 record in relief and 26 saves in 1960. He possesses a steel-trap mind, recalling that Tony Curry and Smoky Burgess were the only two batters who got hits off his trademark forkball in 1960. But McDaniel declined in effectiveness the next two seasons,

## Outcome of the trade

This deal turned out disastrously in all aspects but one for the Cardinals.

Senior St. Louis advisor Branch Rickey, by then in his 80s, suggested Altman alter his inside-out stroke (originally developed to catch the inviting left-field power alley and outblowing winds at Wrigley Field). Instead, Rickey wanted Altman to pull the ball to take advantage of the short porch of old Busch Stadium's right-field pavilion.

Altman's power output slumped to just nine homers and 47 RBI in 464 at-bats. "I thought the trade hurt me after just getting settled down in Chicago," he said. "What it did was put pressure on me, to show the world the Cubs made the wrong deal. I wanted to vindicate myself. I started off well, but then you had that ill-timed advice about pulling the ball. I don't blame anybody but myself for that (1963) season. I should have ignored the advice."

Meanwhile, just as the Cardinals seemed primed to challenge the Sandy Koufax-led Dodgers, McDaniel revived his career like never before, taking pre-game whirlpool treatments to better condition his arm. He was 13-7 with 22 saves for the Cubs in 1963.

"I'm not sure the Cubs were expecting great things," McDaniel said. "I hurt my arm in spring training (1963). But as soon as we opened (the season), I came out of the injury. It was really unexplainable. Maybe (the sore arm) relaxed me. I spent time in whirlpools in the spring and that continued in the season. I got into a great rhythm."

His old team helped right his career. "The Cardinals didn't score a run off me in 1963," McDaniel recalled. "I pitched 25 innings against them, walked just one and struck out 19. They might have won the pennant in 1963 if you take away my pitching against them."

Jackson was 14-18 in 1963, but was the league's tough-luck pitcher with a 2.56 ERA. The next year, he was baseball's leading winner with a 24-11 record. And in an about-face that could only happen with the Cubs of the era, Jackson turned around and lost 21 games (winning 14) in 1965, joining teammate Dick Ellsworth as one of the few pitchers to have 20-win and 20-loss seasons in successive years.

Schaffer and Thacker were a wash as backup catchers. But the Cardinals did salvage something out of this deal. Cardwell never wore a Cardinals uniform. On November 19, 1962, Devine dealt him to the Pirates for shortstop Dick Groat, a major contributor to the 1964 world championship team. Ditto with Altman's value. He was peddled to the Mets for Roger Craig, a versatile starter-reliever for the '64 Cards who pitched five shutout innings in relief, picking up a win, against the Yankees in the World Series.

Holland eventually turned McDaniel and Jackson into his two best deals. McDaniel was packaged with Don Landrum to the Giants for soon-to-be Cubs stars Randy Hundley and Bill Hands after the 1965 season. Jackson was dealt along with fellow starter Bob Buhl early in the '66 season to the Phillies primarily for promising center fielder Adolfo Phillips, who was accompanied to Chicago by young reliever Fergie Jenkins—a future Hall of Famer, of course, and Cardinals Killer.

## Barney Schultz for Leo Burke
## June 24, 1963

Devine's constant dealings with Holland netted him another piece of the 1964 puzzle here.

An original Cardinals product, right-hander. Schultz acquitted himself well in the bullpen for bad Cubs teams in 1961-62. Burke was a backup infielder with the Orioles and Angels before his cup of coffee with the Cardinals

### Outcome of the trade
Holland must have been sincere when he said he had helped the Cardinals prior to the Brock deal. Schultz was a late-inning savior with 14 saves and a 1.64 ERA in 1964. He was less effective in the World Series, picking up just one save. Burke played little for the Cubs.

## Glen Hobbie for Lew Burdette
## June 2, 1964

Last of the strong-armed, but eventually injured stable of young pitchers the Cubs possessed in the late 1950s, Hobbie was on the way down when Devine and Holland swapped second-line pitchers. Former Braves great Burdette, 37 at that point, had not pitched well for St. Louis.

### Outcome of the trade

Hobbie had one moment of Cardinals glory—a homer for the Cardinals that got Harry Caray excited on KMOX-Radio. He soon disappeared into the minors and out of the big leagues forever, washed up at 28. Burdette went 9-9 for the Cubs the rest of '64, then went on to one last achievement, going 7-2 as a reliever for the 1966 Angels.

## Bob Humphreys for Bobby Pfeil and a minor leaguer
## April 10, 1965

Bob Howsam had replaced Devine as Cardinals GM at this point, but must have felt he owed Holland for all his past favors. Humphreys had been an effective middle-reliever for the Cardinals in '64 with a 2.53 ERA. Infielder Pfeil had not played in the majors at that point.

### Outcome of the trade

Humphreys had much the same year with the Cubs as with the Cardinals-2-0, 3.15 ERA. Pfeil went on to play briefly with the Amazing Mets of 1969 and the Phillies.

## Curt Simmons for cash
## June 22, 1966

Ex-Phillies Whiz Kid Simmons had been the Cardinals' crafty southpaw with 15-9 and 18-9 records in 1963 and 1964, respectively. But by mid-season 1966, Howsam was busy cleaning out many of the older veterans from '64 and re-tooling the Cardinals for their 1967-68 pennant runs.

### Outcome of the trade

Simmons and ex-Phillies teammate Robin Roberts were re-united as ancient mariners in the second half of the 1966 season with the Cubs as new manager Leo Durocher scrambled to find anyone to pitch on a 103-loss season. Simmons lasted long enough to see the Cubs' famed revival in 1967 before being traded to the Angels.

# Ted Savage for cash
# May 14, 1967

St. Louis-area native Savage had a journeyman's career as a corner outfielder with eight teams from 1962 to 1971. After starting out with the Phillies, hitting .266 in 1962, he found his way home with the Cardinals starting in 1965, but was used sparingly.

### Outcome of the trade

Savage ended up as more-or-less the regular Cubs right fielder, hitting .218 in their breakthrough 1967 season. Also serving time in the sun field were the likes of Lee Thomas, Clarence Jones and Al Spangler. Savage's greatest value was trade bait early in the 1968 season. Holland pulled off one of his better deals, sending Savage and lefty pitcher Jim Ellis to the Dodgers for two key contributors of the Durocher-era teams-outfielder Jim Hickman and reliever Phil Regan.

# Jack Lamabe for Pete Mikkelsen
# April 22, 1968

Lamabe had been a bullpen contributor to the '67 world champion Cardinals. Mikkelson, as a young pitcher, had hurled against the Cardinals in the '64 World Series as a Yankee.

### Outcome of the trade

Lamabe finished up his career in the '68 Cubs bullpen. Mikkelsen was let go by the Cardinals to become a decent middle-inning reliever for the Dodgers from 1969 to 1972.

# Rich Nye for Boots Day
# December 4, 1969

Left-hander Nye had been the rookie surprise for the 1967 Cubs with a 13-10 record, but then went downhill through 1969. Day was a minor leaguer.

## Outcome of the trade

Nye spent only six games as a Cardinal before moving on to the Expos in 1970. He is now a top veterinarian, specializing in exotic animals, in suburban Chicago.

Day played a little center field for the Cubs, but then also moved on to Montreal, which specialized in players with unusual names at the time: Coco Laboy, Jim Fairey and John Boccabella.

# Ted Abernathy for Phil Gagliano
# May 29, 1970

Submariner reliever Abernathy had been ignored by Leo Durocher down the stretch in 1969 while stopper Phil Regan was just plain worn to a nub. Abernathy had been in his second tour of duty with the Cubs after saving 31 games and appearing in a team-record 84 contests in 1965. Gagliano had been a utility infielder on the 1967-68 Cardinals pennant winners.

## Outcome of the trade

Holland made his second mistake with Abernathy—and Devine must have caught the disease, too. When Holland traded Abernathy to the Braves for future Phillies GM Lee Thomas early in 1966, he left a gaping hole in the bullpen he did not fill for two years, when Regan arrived. Holland let Abernathy go again just as Regan's effectiveness wore down from overwork.

Devine then turned around and traded Abernathy to the Royals for Chris Zachary on July 1, 1970. Sure enough, Abernathy was 9-3 the rest of the season in Kansas City, then saved 23 games in 1971. He had a 1.71 ERA in his final big-league season in KC in 1972. All through that time, both the Cubs and Cardinals could have used him.

Gagliano was a little-used player for the Cubs.

# Jim Hickman for Scipio Spinks
# March 23, 1974

Hickman, another original Cardinals product who made his big-league debut for Casey Stengel's Mets in 1962, found himself as a Cub.

He was a late-season hero in 1969. In 1970, he slugged 32 homers, drove in 115 runs and batted .315. But he was aging and in decline by 1973.

Spinks was a hard-throwing prospect the Cardinals had acquired from the Astros. In 1972, Spinks showed a lot of promise with a 5-5 record and 2.67 ERA in 16 starts, but was belted around the following year.

### Outcome of the trade

Hickman was a backup player and pinch-hitter for the Cardinals in his final big-league season in 1974. Chicago native Spinks never got to pitch in his hometown.

# Don Kessinger for Mike Garman
# and minor leaguer Bobby Hrapmann
# October 28, 1975

Shortstop Kessinger, one of the greatest in Cubs history, was the last of the Leo Durocher-era players still remaining with the Cubs. He completed his 11th season in Wrigley Field in 1975, slowing down a little in the field, but still a capable two-way player. However, he finished the final month playing third base in place of an injured Bill Madlock while prospective successor Davey Rosello took over at shortstop.

Right-hander Mike Garman had been the No. 2 man in the Cardinals bullpen after Al "Mad Hungarian" Hrabosky in 1974-75. He had been particularly effective in his first season with a 7-2 record and just 66 hits and 27 walks yielded in 82 innings.

Holland was about to turn over the GM reins to Saltwell—another strange move for owner P.K. Wrigley, then 80 and challenged in making baseball decisions. Saltwell was a loyal ballclub functionary as concessions manager who knew the ins and outs of daily Wrigley Field operations. But he certainly wasn't the first man you'd think to take over for Holland.

Before he officially entered semi-retirement, Holland set up the Kessinger deal, as he desperately needed pitching to shore up a horrid '75 Cubs staff. Steve Stone was the ace with a 12-8 record. Holland, who never could lift the Cubs consistently into contention other than the Durocher era, had one classy act left—giving Kessinger a choice of future employers.

"I did have a right to refuse a trade," Kessinger said of his status as a 10-year veteran with five years' seniority on the same team. "It was probably time that I moved on, though. John told me that two clubs were most interested in me-the Cardinals and Yankees. I said being from the area (Arkansas), my preference was the Cardinals. I appreciated what he did."

## Outcome of the trade

The Cardinals hoped to contend with Kessinger plugging the hole at shortstop while prospect Garry Templeton gained more experience in the minors.

"I thought they were going to have a good team in '76," Kessinger said. "I asked Ken Boyer, and he said they had one the best teams they ever had coming out of spring training. But a lot of guys had bad years. It never really worked out well for me, and never felt a part of what they were trying to do."

The Cards slumped to 72-90, fifth place behind the Cubs in 1976. Kessinger hit .239 with 51 RBI, but started moving over to second base to accommodate Templeton. He played shortstop, second and third as a backup as Templeton took over full-time in '77, and was traded to the then-contending White Sox for a minor league pitcher late in August.

Kessinger thus became the second top '60s Cub after Ron Santo to move to the South Side, playing well as a regular in 1978 before being named player-manager for 1979. Kessinger lasted on the job for the slumping Sox only until August, when Bill Veeck promoted a 34-year-old Triple-A manager to his first big-league post. Guy's name was Tony La Russa. Another great circle route years down the line for a Cubs-Cardinals transaction.

Garman was horrible as a Cub with a 2-4 record and 4.97 ERA as the Chicago staff collapsed again in 1976. But he and his teammates' failures did have some side benefits. Saltwell was forced to call up a young reliever with a baffling drop pitch-Bruce Sutter. And after Bob Kennedy took over as GM following the '76 season, he was able to package Garman and center fielder Rick Monday to the Dodgers in a great deal, acquiring first baseman Bill Buckner and shortstop Ivan DeJesus. Five years after that, DeJesus was traded to the Phillies for Ryne Sandberg.

So John Holland's last Cubs-Cardinals deal did pay off handsomely in a twice-removed manner—if you consider Sandberg an eventual worthy exchange for Kessinger.

# 15

---

# The Kennedy Administration
# 1976-1981

**BOB Kennedy, one of the central figures** in the Lou Brock deal, was fired as Cubs head coach 56 games into the 1965 season. He moved on to manage the Oakland Athletics in 1968, then joined the Cardinals organization as a scout and farm director under Bing Devine. After the 1976 season, he was summoned back to Chicago to take over as general manager.

After trading away Bill Madlock and Rick Monday, he made the first of four deals with the Cardinals in his tenure that lasted until early in the 1981 season. He transacted business with St. Louis at the same pace as Holland.

"I was familiar with the people and the players," Kennedy said of his dealings with the Cardinals.

Following is a look at Kennedy's trades with Devine, John Claiborne and Whitey Herzog:

# Buddy Schultz for minor league pitcher Mark Covert
## February 28, 1977

Left-hander Schultz was a back-of-the-bullpen type with a 6.00 ERA in 29 games for a bedraggled Cubs staff in 1976. Covert was one of Kennedy's prospects.

### Outcome of the trade

Schultz had some decent moments in the Cardinals bullpen with a 6-1 record and 2.33 ERA in 1977. He was the top lefty after Al Hrabosky left, appearing 62 games in 1978 before fading out in 1979.

Covert remained true to his name. He never pitched in the majors.

# Jerry Morales, Steve Swisher and cash for
# Dave Rader and Hector Cruz
## December 8, 1977

Julio Ruben Morales was one of the Cubs' best clutch hitters of his era. Acquired for Glenn Beckert from San Diego after the 1973 season, the team's first Puerto Rican star had 82 and 92 RBI, respectively, in '74 and '75. After dipping a bit in 1976, Morales made the NL All-Star team as a center fielder in 1977.

Swisher had been a catching prospect, obtained in the Ron Santo trade with the White Sox after the 1973 season. Strangely, he was the Cubs' lone All-Star representative in 1976, chosen over batting champ Bill Madlock. Swisher ended '76 hitting .236.

Rader had been a slap-hitting lefty-swinging catcher for the Giants. The Cardinals had acquired him after the 1976 season along with pitcher John D'Acquisto for outfielder Willie Crawford, infielder Vic Harris and pitcher John Curtis. Rader hit .266 in 66 games for the Cardinals in '76.

Cruz, nicknamed "Heity," was member of a famous ball-playing family, all of whom were signed by the Cardinals. Older brother Jose underproduced for the Cardinals in the early 1970s, then became a star outfielder with the Houston Astros. Another older brother, Tommy, played three games for St. Louis in 1973.

### Outcome of the trade

The deal was a bust for both teams. Rader hit just .203 in 116 games for the Cubs in 1978. Kennedy then re-packaged him after the season in a deal to the Phillies that netted ex-Cardinal Ted Sizemore, outfielder Barry Foote and outfielder Jerry Martin.

Morales had his worst year in six seasons as a Cardinal in '78, batting just .239 with a paltry four homers and 46 RBI. Like Rader, he was shuffled out of town after just one season. The Cardinals traded him along with pitcher Aurelio Lopez to the Detroit Tigers for pitcher Bob Sykes and a minor leaguer. But two years later, Morales returned to the sagging Cubs as a part-time outfielder.

Cruz played briefly as an outfielder and third baseman for the Cubs before being traded to the Giants for ex-Cardinals pitcher Lynn McGlothen. He moved on the Reds before finding his way back to the Cubs, where he became a teammate of Morales in 1981-82.

Swisher played three seasons in St. Louis as a little-used backup catcher to Ted Simmons before finishing his career with the Padres.

## Mike Tyson for Donnie Moore
## October 17, 1979

The stout Tyson had been the Cardinals' regular shortstop or second baseman through most of the 1970s. Early on in St. Louis, he teamed with second baseman Ted Sizemore, who went on to play for the Cubs in 1979. His best season was .266 in 1975. But he had become a spare part by 1979, playing in just 75 games and hitting .221.

Moore was a hard-throwing reliever who made his first Cubs appearance in 1975. He was a busy man in 1978, going 9-7 in 71 games. But he was bombed around in 1979 and demoted to the minors at mid-season.

### Outcome of the trade

Moore wasn't around long enough with the Cubs or the Cardinals to regret his later success, achieved two organizations' worth after he left St. Louis. Moore pitched in only 11 games (6.14) ERA as a Cardinal in 1980, then moved on for one season with the Milwaukee Brewers. Finally, he found himself with the Braves, emerging as a quality reliever in 1984 before moving on to the Anaheim Angels as their stopper in 1985.

This was one of baseball's most tragic stories. Moore was 8-8 with a 1.92 ERA in 1985 in Anaheim, but was most noted for giving up Dave Henderson's dramatic game-tying homer in the 1986 AL Championship Series that cost the Angels the pennant. He never really got over the shock of the homer. Two years later he was out of the majors. On July 18, 1989, he committed suicide.

Meanwhile, Tyson did little as the Cubs' regular second baseman in 1980. He hit .238. Pushed out of the starting lineup the following year by the immortal Joe Strain, Tyson did one last thing of note in the majors: slugging a homer off Fernando Valenzuela to beat the lefty sensation in his first-ever Wrigley Field start in 1981.

## Bruce Sutter for Ken Reitz, Leon Durham and Tye Waller
## December 9, 1980

Forget Dennis Eckersley and Big Lee Smith.

Bruce Sutter is probably the greatest reliever of all time. He certainly possessed the trickiest pitch-popularizing the use of the split-fingered fastball that came in straight like a regular fastball, then dived under the level swings of hitters like something out of the 1949 movie, "It Happens Every Spring."

His career given up for dead in the low minors in the early 1970s, Sutter was taught the splitter by veteran pitching coach Fred Martin, a former longtime Cardinals farmhand. He was an immediate hit when the Cubs called him up early in 1976. A shoulder injury was the only thing that could slow Sutter down in 1977 when he fashioned a 1.35 ERA, 31 saves and 129 strikeouts in 107 innings on the baffling pitch.

Sutter won the NL Cy Young Award for a then record-tying 37 saves and 2.23 ERA in 1979. That's when his troubles—and his road to St. Louis began. Seeking a big boost in pay, Sutter went to arbitration after the season. He wanted a then-hefty $700,000. The Cubs, represented by Kennedy's young assistant, Andy MacPhail, offered $350,000. Sutter won. Cubs owner William Wrigley, beset by the burden of inheritance taxes after the 1977 deaths of his parents, Philip K. and Helen Wrigley, was dumping payroll like ballast from a sinking balloon. After the 1980 season in which he saved 28 of the Cubs' last-place 64 victories, Sutter was earmarked for employment elsewhere.

"When you lose money, you have to cut back," Kennedy said at the time. "Sure, they (fans and press) will knock me. But what the hell else is new? They blasted me when I didn't do anything. Now, we did something and they'll blast me again."

Bombs away! "The man is worse than brainless. He is shameless," wrote *Chicago Sun-Times* columnist John Schulian at the time.

The GM did fulfill his goal of getting younger by asking for—and getting—Durham. The Cardinals' best left-handed hitting power prospect, Durham hit .271 with eight homers and 42 RBI in 96 games for the Cardinals in 1980.

Reitz was a popular third baseman for the Cardinals from 1972 to 1975 and 1977 to 1980. He was traded to the Giants for one season in 1976, but came back better than ever with his best year-17 homers and 79 RBI-in 1977. He still was in near-peak form in 1980 and established in St. Louis. The Cardinals had to pay the full cost of a $150,000 bonus, a buyout of his veteran's status to get him to agree to a trade to Chicago.

"I've been here (St. Louis) long enough to know that if we had a good reliever we would probably win the pennant," said Reitz, who turned out to be correct. "It's kind of disappointing to be the one to go for Sutter."

Reportedly, the original Sutter-to-St. Louis trade included Tommy Herr along with Durham and Reitz. That would have really made the deal worthwhile in the long run for the Cubs. But the Cardinals apparently refused to part with up-and-coming second baseman Herr, and that decision eventually paid off handsomely in St. Louis.

Instead, the Cubs got Waller, a speedy infielder-outfielder prospect.

## Outcome of the trade

Sutter paid big dividends immediately. He saved 25 games in the strike-shortened 1981 season, then came through big with 36 saves in 70 games to spark the Cardinals to their first World Series win in 14 years in 1982.

He wasn't finished, though. After an off year in 1983, Sutter rebounded to set the record for saves at the time with 45 in 1984, with only Ryne Sandberg's other-worldly two-homer game against him on June 23 spoiling a sensational season. Sutter also had a paltry 1.54 ERA and just 23 walks yielded in 122 2/3 innings.

That performance earned Sutter a rich free-agent deal from the Atlanta Braves. But he had seen his best days. Sutter saved just 23 games in 1985 as his ERA ballooned to 4.48. Beset by arm problems and the resulting surgery, he missed most of the 1986 and 1987 seasons before finishing up his career a shadow of his old self in 1988, going 1-4 with 14 saves and a 4.76 ERA for the Braves.

That arbitration case apparently still sticks in Sutter's craw. Most prominent ex-Cubs, ranging from Lou Brock to Dave Kingman (who departed the Cubs on bad terms), have found their way to make appearances at the annual mid-winter Cubs Convention in Chicago. Not Sutter.

He reportedly does not want to help out the Cubs, whose president is none other than Andy MacPhail, his old arbitration nemesis.

At least one of the players the Cubs got for Sutter produced in the short run. Durham hit .290 in his first Cubs season in 1981, then batted .312 with 22 homers and 90 RBI in 1982. Injuries marred his 1983 season. When healthy in 1984, Durham was a big bat for the NL East champs with 23 homers and 96 RBI. However, he declined after that. He hit 20 or more homers each of the next three seasons, but his RBI totals plummeted as personal problems mounted. Durham was traded to the Reds early in the 1988 season to make way for Mark Grace at first base.

A fish out of water in Chicago, Reitz hit just .215 in 82 games for the Cubs in 1981. Released in spring training 1982, he finished up with the Pirates that season.

Waller played in just 58 big-league games for the Cubs and Astros.

Under orders from Wrigley, Kennedy had stripped the Cubs down to an expansion-level outfit. The Cubs started out 6-28 in 1981. He was pushed out. Tribune Co. bought the team, Dallas Green took over as GM, and the Chicago-St. Louis player pipeline was cut off until 1995.

# 16

---

# Foibles, Fumbles and Fracases

**JOE Garagiola wrote that "baseball is a funny game."** Humor coupled with just plain weirdness is never far away from any game, and that certainly applies when the Cubs and Cardinals throw out the first pitch.

*Ripley's Believe It or Not* would find a home with some of the oddball events that have transpired between the two teams. Appropriately, two of the best pitchers in St. Louis history were nicknamed Dizzy and Daffy.

## Two balls in play at the same time
### June 30, 1959, Wrigley Field

Nobody has ever invented a way to play with two balls in one sport. But on one Thursday afternoon, while the Twilight Zone's first episodes were being filmed 2,000 miles away, the Cubs and Cardinals tried to re-invent the game with twin baseballs flying toward second base.

In an otherwise humdrum 4-1 St. Louis victory before 9,883, plate umpire Vic Delmore's brain cramp resulted in a Keystone Kops display that would be fine fodder for a "baseball bloopers" video. The episode was actually videotaped off the WGN telecast, but later disappeared. More about that later.

Stan Musial went to bat with one out in the fourth inning. Cubs starter Bob Anderson worked the count to 3-and-1 on Stan the Man. The next pitch was inside, and the ball bounced back toward the screen.

"The way Stan batted, it looked like he was peeking around a corner," Anderson, now a Tulsa resident, recalled. "It looked like he was nearly checking his swing all the time, his bat was moving so much."

What Musial actually did and the resulting confusion, was high, or low comedy, depending on your point of view.

Cubs catcher Sammy Taylor argued with Delmore that the ball had ticked Musial's bat as the latter trotted to first base. Anderson came in from the mound to join the debate. But time had not been called. The Cardinals bench yelled at Musial, and he continued to run toward second base.

Immersed in the argument, Delmore absent-mindedly lost track of the original ball, pulled a second ball from his pocket, and flipped it to Anderson. Eyeing Musial's dash to second, Anderson fired the ball over the head of Cubs second baseman Tony Taylor.

The original ball inadvertently was touched by Cubs batboy Bob Schoenfeldt, a freshman at Chicago's Foreman High School, near the screen. Public address announcer Pat Pieper also apparently touched the ball. An alert Cubs third baseman Alvin Dark tracked it down. Seconds after Anderson's errant heave, Dark threw a one-hopper to shortstop Ernie Banks. Musial had just slid in to second and, seeing the wild first throw, was getting up to continue on to third when he got the surprise of Banks tagging him out with ball No. 2.

An old-fashioned baseball rhubarb ensued as Cubs manager Bob Scheffing and his Cardinals counterpart, Solly Hemus, converged on the infield to debate with the umpiring crew headed by Al Barlick. There was plenty of wild gesturing for 20 minutes as the arbiters twice broke away to discuss the *faux pas*. Finally, Musial was ruled out. But it wasn't over. Just before Anderson prepared to throw his next pitch, Hemus charged out of the dugout to announce the game was played under protest.

Here were the postgame accounts of some of the principles involved:

**Musial:** "Taylor thought the ball was a foul. I heard our bench yelling for me to run. When I slid into second base, I saw Banks (in reality, Taylor) jump for the ball. I got up and started for third never feeling a tag. As far as I was concerned, I didn't know there was a second ball in the game. The umpires finally told me to go back to first and later that I was out."

**Hemus:** "The original ball was never out of play. When it hit the umpire, Sammy must have thought it was a foul, else he would have gone after the ball. When I saw these two balls going toward second base, I thought: 'What the hell's going on?' Pat Pieper had that first ball in his hand, but when the Cubs started yelling he dropped it like a hot potato."

**Pieper:** "I let that ball lie right there, after the boy threw it toward me. Dark yelled at me, 'Give me the ball.' I told him to pick it up. I never touched it."

**Schoenfeldt:** "I saw Dark flying toward me, but I already had thrown the ball away."

**Scheffing:** "That fourth ball either hit Musial or was a foul. If it hit him, it was a dead ball so there could be no advance. Sammy Taylor said the umpire did not announce his decision. I know this—it would have been a protest either way. I would have protested that Musial was retired on the ball which was in play."

**Barlick:** "When Dark charged in from third base, I thought he was joining in the argument. But he picked the ball up in front of Pieper. Musial was safe, but as he rounded the bag, Banks tagged him with the ball Dark had thrown. This was the ball that was in play. The other ball was not."

Barlick cited the rule covering the decision:
"No person shall be allowed on the playing field during a game except players, coaches in uniform, managers, news photographers authorized by the home team, umpires, officers of the law and watchmen or other employees of the home club.

"In case of unintentional interference with play by any person herein authorized to be on the playing field, except umpires, the ball is alive and in play. If the interference is intentional the ball shall be dead, at the moment of the interference and the umpire shall impose such penalties as, in his opinion, would nullify the act of interference."

Order was restored. The Cardinals' (and future Cub) Larry Jackson won on a four-hitter. Hemus' protest was moot. Decades later, Anderson can put the goofy play in its proper context.

"A comedy of errors," he said. "Only with the Cubs at that time could something like that happen."

Oh, one more thing. Then-WGN producer Jack Jacobson recalled that the two-baseballs blooper was taped and shown on the evening news for comic effect the next few nights. Also taped and replayed was the White Sox's pennant-clinching double play started by Luis Aparicio in Cleveland on September 22, 1959.

Now for the final blooper. The tape of both seminal events from the second Eisenhower Administration either was erased and recorded over, or tossed out completely. We only have the accounts of those remaining alive from the event and some old black-and-white photos.

"Did that really happen?" asked one incredulous present-day baseball executive.

Yes, it did—and was merely in keeping with the tradition of Cubs-Cardinals games.

## The homer in the glove
## April 30, 1949, Wrigley Field

Inside-the-park homers are exciting. Especially when the baserunner's touching 'em all while a fielder has possession of the ball—and is holding it up for the umpire.

Running out of time fast while trailing the Cubs 3-1 going into the ninth inning before a Saturday crowd of 30,775, the Cardinals tried to rally against an effective Cubs starter Bob Rush, who had held them to just four hits.

Rush got Stan Musial looking at strike three. Enos Slaughter doubled to left center, but "Round Ron" Northey tapped weakly to Rush for the second out. Eddie Kazak barely kept the rally going with a bloop single to left, scoring Slaughter. Charlie Diering pinch-ran for Kazak.

Rookie first baseman Rocky Nelson came to bat. "Rocky gnawed determinedly on that big chew of tobacco stuffed in his left cheek, looked over a strike and a ball and then swung, lashing a line drive to left center," wrote the *St. Louis Post-Dispatch*'s Bob Broeg in the May 1 account of the game.

Cubs center fielder Andy Pafko was shaded toward right for the left-handed hitting Nelson. But he recovered to converge on the ball. At the last moment, Pafko lunged to his right and tried to catch the ball backhanded. He skidded, and appeared to have caught the ball. Pafko held up his glove in triumph, believing the game was over with the Cubs winning 3-2.

But umpire Al Barlick, stationed at second base, signaled that Pafko had trapped the ball. Angry, Pafko charged toward the infield, continuing to hold up his glove. Diering scored. Cubs manager Charlie Grimm and the Chicago infielders screamed at Pafko to throw the ball. Cardinals third-base coach Tony Kauffman windmilled Nelson around third.

"That was the last out of the game, it should have been over," Pafko recalled. "But at that instant, I wasn't even aware he said I trapped it. By the time I realized what was going on, Nelson was between third and home. I heard Peanuts Lowery yelling, 'Andy, throw the ball.' I did, but it was too late."

Finally, as he neared second base, Pafko did cut loose a throw to the plate. But the ball hit Nelson on the left shoulder as he completed his inside-the-park job.

The Cubs argued in vain with Barlick and crewmates George Barr and Lee Ballanfant. Meanwhile, the crowd showed its displeasure by show-ering the field with cushions, garbage, fruit and vegetables. But the manna from heaven was squarely in the Cardinals' corner on this afternoon, and they emerged with the 4-3 win minutes later after the field was cleared.

Half a century later, Pafko still insists he caught the ball. But the umpire's decision stands, then and forevermore.

"I'll never forget it," he said. "I ran into Al Barlick at a hotel when I was at an old-timers' game. He still told me, 'Andy, you didn't catch the ball.'"

## Musial pitches to Baumholtz
## September 28, 1952, Sportsman's Park, St. Louis

Who says Mark McGwire and Sammy Sosa were the first Cardi-nals/Cubs duo to have fun with their race for the gold?

Betcha McGwire and Sosa never heard of the special duel Stan Musial and the Cubs' Frankie Baumholtz cooked up as Stan the Man finally outlasted Baumholtz for the 1952 National League batting title.

Cardinals starter Harvey Haddix walked the first Cubs hitter in the season finale on a Sunday afternoon in St. Louis. Suddenly, Musial came in from his post in center field to take the mound, with Haddix shifting to right field and Hal Rice moving from right to center. A pitcher in his youth, Musial—who could throw a curve and knuckler—took only a couple of warmup tosses before he was ready as the crowd of 17,422 watched intently.

Realizing the gag, the lefty-swinging Baumholtz turned around to bat right handed. He swung at a Musial "fastball" and topped the ball to Cardinals third baseman Solly Hemus. We'll never know if Hemus was distracted by the pitcher-batter spectacle. He fumbled the ball, then threw late and wide of first as Brown took third. The Cubs looked en masse toward the press box, hoping for a hit, but the play was ruled an error.

That ended Baumholtz's long-shot hopes of overtaking Musial for the batting crown. He needed a 5-for-5 day while Musial had to go hitless. Baumholtz went 1-for-4 to finish at .325. Musial went 1-for-3 to end at .336, his sixth batting title.

To complete the unusual afternoon, the Cubs won 3-0 on lefty Paul Minner's six-hitter to end the season at 77-77, their only non-losing record between 1947 and 1963.

## Cubs try to stall, get a forfeit loss instead
## July 6, 1913, West Side Park, Chicago

Modern fans have occasionally seen a team with a big lead turn a game into a farce by hurrying to complete the fifth inning before an approaching rainstorm hit.

When the Cubs hosted the Cardinals in the second game of a doubleheader on July 6, 1913, however, the home team was more interested in preventing the fifth inning.

After the Cubs easily won the opener 6-0 in two hours and six minutes, the second game started at 3:50 p.m. It was more than enough time by the standards of the day for at least five innings to be played before the agreed-upon 5 p.m. curfew so the Cubs could catch a train for New York.

But when the Cardinals jumped out to a 3-0 lead in the first inning, Cubs players resorted to all forms of stalling tactics: infielders tossed the ball back and forth much longer than needed between putouts, pitchers took forever to read catcher Jimmy Archer's signs and batters nearly crawled to the plate. Cubs pinch hitter Roger Bresnahan, who'd managed the Cardinals the year before, took eight minutes to walk in from the clubhouse.

The Cardinals added to the charade in their third and tried to speed things up when third baseman Mike Mowrey singled and ran for second in hopes of being thrown out—only to find the Cubs didn't make a play for him.

With the Cardinals winning 4-0 in their fourth, Cubs pitcher Ed Reulbach deliberately threw wild to first after fielding a bunt. The umps, who'd warned Chicago manager Johnny Evers three times already about the delays, then halted the game at 4:40 p.m. and awarded the Cardinals a 9-0 forfeit.

During the game, the Cardinals players must have felt like they were playing in St. Louis since the 10,000 or so Chicago partisans began jeering the Cubs when the stalling began. Fans even cheered home plate ump Mal Eason as he left the field.

The third-place Cubs made their 8 p.m. train to New York and improved their winning percentage but finished the season in that slot. The sixth-place Cardinals won only 20 more games the rest of the season and finished last.

The two clubs engaged in one other forfeit, and this one, too, resulted in a Cardinals victory. However, it happened on the second-last day of the 1907 season in St. Louis' League Park.

The 106-42 Cubs had already clinched the pennant—by some 18 games over the Pirates—and were looking forward to playing the Detroit Tigers in the World Series the following week. The Cardinals had long before clinched the cellar and went into the game with a 49-100 mark.

Nevertheless, the Cubs fielded their regular starting eight as they trotted out for the first game of a doubleheader that October 5. It didn't take long for the Cubs' pepper-pot second baseman, Johnny Evers, to start jawing with umpire Cy Rigler.

"Evers was probably the worst offender and was talking back to the umpire throughout the contest, though repeatedly cautioned to desist," the *St. Louis Globe-Democrat's* reporter wrote.

After Evers was thrown out trying to steal a base in the fourth inning and put up a "kick," as complaints against umpire's calls were then called, the ump tossed him.

The Cubs went into the bottom of the fourth with a 2-0 lead, but the entire team showed its displeasure when Rigler called the Cardinals leadoff man safe at first on a ground ball. First baseman-manager Frank Chance threw down his glove and was ejected. Pitcher Orval Overall protested and was also tossed. Chance ordered his players off the field. When they defied the ump's order that they get back on it within 30 seconds, he declared the Cardinals a winner by forfeit.

The Cards and Cubs then played the second game of the double-header, with Evers back at second for Chicago. St. Louis nipped old nemesis Three Finger Brown 4-3.

## Fans set the ground rules in doubleheader
## July 12, 1931, Sportsman's Park, St. Louis

Cardinals owner Sam Breadon was expecting a big crowd for a mid-July Sunday doubleheader against the Cubs.

But little did Breadon, the extra cops summoned for the occasion and especially the ballplayers expect the dubious hitting record that over-flow crowd helped produce.

In the second game, the Cardinals hit 13 doubles, the Cubs 10, most of them fly balls into the roped-off spectators in the outfield. That record 23 is still in the record books.

Going into that day's games, bad blood flowed between the two teams, stemming from a series they had recently played in Chicago.

"Rogers Hornsby and his Cubs, whose sharp spikes cut down (Jake) Flowers, (Rip) Collins and (Sparky) Adams during the series at Chicago, will meet the Redbirds in a double-header this afternoon and Manager (Gabby) Street's men will be prepared to protect themselves in all clinches," noted the *St. Louis Post-Dispatch* that morning.

This would be the second straight doubleheader for the Cubs, who the day before had beaten Pittsburgh in the first game of a twin bill then seen the second one called after 10 innings in a 5-5 tie so Chicago could catch a train for St. Louis. The fourth-place Cubs came to town six lengths behind the league-leading Cardinals, who the day before had drawn 4,500 customers while beating the Reds.

Sportsman's Park then could accommodate about 35,000 people, but Breadon told police he anticipated at least 40,000 on that sultry day. The spillover crowds in that era—at a time when large Sunday atten-dances brought in needed money—were usually roped off along the side-lines. It was a practice that had been around since the early days of the professional game but was nearing its end in 1931, said St. Louis baseball historian Bob Tiemann.

Fans started lining up to get in about 5 a.m., more than eight hours before the first pitch. It was obvious early that the crowd would spill on to the field.

But when club officials allowed the fans to come onto the field shortly before the game began, presumably to stand behind ropes that were to keep them close to the outfield walls, the spectators moved beyond the barriers.

"Like hungry bees, the overflow throng swarmed onto the playing field," wrote Martin J. Haley of the *St. Louis Globe-Democrat*. He estimated that 8,000 people were on the field. The 45,715 who paid their way in that day topped the Cardinals' old regular-season attendance record by more than 7,000.

Some fans joined the Cubs while they were having infield practice. "Hundreds dashed in front of the Cub players in a wild scramble for each baseball," the *Post-Dispatch* reported.

That put an end to pregame warmups. The fans continued to cover the field. The umpires, police, ushers and even players began trying to get the fans off the infield. They succeeded only in getting them about 70 feet behind first base, about 150 feet behind second and about 100 from third.

In foul territory, the fans were so numerous that those in the grandstand box seats had to stand to see the action on the shrunken field. Ground rules determined that balls hit into the overflow crowd in fair territory would be doubles.

The surging customers did what they could to help that process, continually jostling outfielders in hopes of getting batted balls.

When the Cardinals hit three doubles into the crowd to take the lead in the opener, Hornsby and his club protested to the umpires that Chicago should win by forfeit. Breadon personally appealed to the fans to back off. The field announcer, using his megaphone, also petitioned the mob to comply.

It did—only a bit. After the Cubs won the opener 7-5, the crowd again spilled over the ropes and invaded as much of the turf as it could. Police ranks now swelled to 80, three times what might ordinarily have been stationed at Sportsman's Park for a Sunday doubleheader. The lawmen succeeded in getting the crowd back into the outfield, but it remained only about 75 feet beyond third base.

By the end of the second game, a pop fly that dropped over the third baseman's head "was gobbled up by the insatiable mob," the *Post-Dispatch* noted.

The Cardinals won the nightcap 17-13. The Cardinals' Rip Collins and Gus Mancuso each hit three doubles. Woody English and Gabby Hartnett of the Cubs each also had a trio of two-baggers. Three players had a pair each, while five players each had one double.

Three players hit home runs in the doubleheader, and, as might be expected, there were no triples.

The *Post-Dispatch*'s sports editor, J. Roy Stockton, estimated that of the 32 doubles in the doubleheader "not more than five or six . . . would have been anything but easy outfield flies under normal conditions." He wrote that the crowd turned the game into "a farce," and a headline writer for his paper referred to it as a "burlesque."

How much that game meant for individual statistics is a matter of speculation. The Cardinals' Chick Hafey, who had two doubles in the second game, edged the Giants' Bill Terry for the batting title .3488 to .3486. Without those two ground-rule doubles, Hafey would have ended at .344.

## Dizzy fights ex-teammate, then whips Cubs
## August 10, 1936, Sportsman's Park, St. Louis

Dizzy Dean and Tex Carleton had feuded even when both were helping the Gashouse Gang win the 1934 World Series. And the animosity between the two pitchers only got worse when Carleton was traded to the hated Cubs after that season.

When Chicago came to St. Louis for a three-game set August 10-12, 1936, the bad mix between the two players boiled over.

By losing a doubleheader at home the day before, the Cardinals had dropped out of the lead and trailed the Cubs by percentage points, Chicago with a 63-41 record and the Cardinals at 64-42.

More than 31,000—including 15,398 women and 3,177 girls who got into the game for free on ladies day—settled in to watch the action on an afternoon so hot the base umpires discarded their coats. Even the paid crowd of 12,485 was astounding for a Monday in the Depression.

Many, if not most, were there to see the Ol' Diz, a man who'd not only proclaimed himself a great pitcher but shown it by winning 20 or more games in each of the three previous seasons. In 1934, the 23-year-old Dean had won 30 (and remains the last National Leaguer to do it).

Dean had set a big-league record by fanning 17 Cubs in one game in 1933. But the Chicagoans had pounded him so much since then that manager Frankie Frisch had avoided using Dean against the Cubs for much of 1934. When the rotation dictated that he pitch, the Cubs had mauled him for 23 runs in 27 2/3 innings.

As he took the mound for the August 10 match, Dizzy had an 18-8 mark. A real workhorse, he'd completed 23 of his 27 starts and relieved in 11 other games. After he'd retired the first two hitters in the Cubs' lineup, he narrowly missed hitting second baseman Billy Herman with a pitch.

"Someone on the Chicago bench yelled something at Diz which inferred the great pitcher had only nerve enough to throw 'bean' balls but didn't dare fight," *St. Louis Post-Dispatch* reporter Dent McSkimming wrote in his next day's account.

Dean figured it was Carleton and nearly ran to the Chicago dugout challenging his adversary to come out and settle the matter.

"They met—not very violently—near the first base line and went into a clinch," McSkimming wrote.

Another account said Dean and Carleton mixed it up really well. "It was reported by those close enough to the two antagonists that Carleton came out of the fray with a 'shiner' on his left eye and that Diz was cut under his left eye," wrote Martin J. Haley of the *St. Louis Globe-Democrat*.

Players from both benches surrounded the pair while the umpires, who wanted to expel both Dean and Carleton, conferred with the managers. A second-hand account of what Grimm told lead umpire George Barr was that the large crowd had come to see Dizzy pitch and that it wouldn't be right to eject him so early. Grimm, a St. Louis native, was to have told the ump he was confident his Cubs would send Dizzy to the showers in due time anyway.

Barr phoned the press box. "In order not to disappoint the large crowd, we put the question up to Manager Grimm and he consented to let Dizzy stay in the game. All the credit goes to Grimm for this move."

Jolly Cholly, as Grimm was known, may have regretted it. Dean limited the Cubs to only two hits in the first five innings as the Cardinals routed Cubs starter Lon Warneke with eight hits and took a 5-0 lead.

Dean began to wilt in the late going, giving up nine hits in the last four innings, but Frisch stuck with him all the way. The Cubs cut it to 6-3 in the eighth. But in the bottom half of that inning, light-hitting Cardinals shortstop Leo Durocher completed one of his best days in the majors as he doubled for his fourth hit in four at-bats. He then scored the Cardinals' final run in what was a 7-3 triumph.

The Cardinals moved back into first place by a game, only to fall back the next day when Carleton beat them. But on Wednesday St. Louis took the rubber game of the series.

Just as the Cardinals did in 1934 and the Cubs in 1935, the New York Giants used a September dash to outdistance all opponents and win the pennant by five games over both St. Louis and Chicago.

But back to Grimm's gesture. It was criticized by one writer who stated, "Our boy Charlie was a sucker."

McSkimming disagreed in his game account: " . . . today his

(Grimm's) club is in second place, a step lower in the team standing, but a lot higher in the estimation of those who value good sportsmanship."

## Simba's entertaining life
## May 24, 1974, Wrigley Field; September 22, 1974,
## Busch Stadium; May 27, 1978, Busch Stadium

Leave it to Cardinals catcher Ted Simmons to not only be a certified Cubs Killer, but also be at the center of strange days against his favorite opponents.

First, scoring the winning run across an unguarded home plate while being pursued by a much-faster player. Then duking it out with a player known as Mad Dog. Finally, hitting a homer off Bruce Sutter—and getting thrown out of the game while crossing home plate.

Simmons, nicknamed "Simba" for his long, flowing lion's mane-like hair that stuck out of his catcher's helmet, began his odyssey of weirdness on a Friday afternoon at Wrigley Field. He led off the ninth with a double off Cubs starter Rick Reuschel in a scoreless game. He moved to third on a sacrifice by Bake McBride and an intentional walk to Joe Torre. Then pinch hitter Tim McCarver sent a high bouncer toward the greatest Cardinals Killer, Billy Williams, then winding up his Cubs career at first base.

Williams threw to catcher Tom Lundstedt, who chased Simmons back toward third. Lundstedt then threw a bit too soon to third baseman Matt Alexander, the fastest Cub. Simmons reversed field and lumbered toward home plate.

Where was Reuschel? He had broken toward first on the plate and was near the bag as Simmons changed course. Lundstedt had moved passed Simmons near third. No one was covering home.

Alexander chased Simmons, gamely but futilely, as the baseball Clydesdale crossed home with the game's only run.

"He had too big a head start," Alexander said.

"Another five feet, and he'd got me," Simmons said.

Who should have covered home? Both managers—Whitey Lockman of the Cubs and Red Schoendienst of the Cardinals—said it was the pitcher's responsibility.

"Somebody should be there—me or Rick, I guess," Williams said. Reuschel's version: "I was almost to first. He (Williams) had a better angle to go home than I did." Lockman, his days as manager running out, was philosophical: "At least we had the best man chasing him."

Sonny Siebert made the wacky run stand up on a five hitter, also the yield of tough-luck loser Reuschel, who also fanned nine Cardinals.

Alexander had been subbing for regular third baseman Bill Madlock, who was back in the lineup on September 22 when the Cubs were trying to play spoiler against the Cardinals, locked in a death grip race for the NL East title with the Pirates.

The Mad Hungarian, Al Hrabosky, made the Mad Dog, Madlock, just plain mad with his antics in the top of the ninth in a 5-5 game. As was his crowd-pleasing but opponent-infuriating tactic, Hrabosky turned his back to the batter to psyche himself up. The Cubs planned to respond to the stalling tactic with more of the same, so Madlock left the batter's box to rub pine tar on his bat. Plate ump Shag Crawford ordered Madlock back to the box.

"He didn't hear me, so I told him again," Crawford said as Madlock stayed near the on-deck circle. Ready, Hrabosky wound and threw. Crawford signaled "strike one" to an empty batter's box.

Madlock then raced to the box with Cubs manager Jim Marshall in front of him to prevent another pitch from being delivered by standing on home plate. But Hrabosky still delivered a pitch that almost hit Marshall. Madlock then glared at Simmons. The two jawed at each other, and Simmons exploded, throwing a punch to Madlock's jaw.

The benches then emptied. Cubs first baseman Andre Thornton knocked Simmons to the ground. For his trouble, he injured his little finger on his left hand, apparently when Cardinals (and future Cub) pitcher Lynn McGlothen blind-sided him. In turn, Cubs outfielder Jim Tyrone threw a punch that knocked down McGlothen.

Marshall was then tossed from the game by Crawford when he angrily challenged the ump to throw out Simmons. Neither Simmons nor Madlock was ejected, and Madlock struck out swinging.

Everyone had trouble sorting out the mess afterward.

"It was a closet situation," Simmons said. "I was getting bumped around, and Madlock looked at me and I said to him, 'What are you looking at?'"

"I had to get at Simmons because he took a free shot at Billy (Madlock)," Thornton said.

Marshall still fumed at Crawford.

"If Crawford had the proper perspective on this, by telling Hrabosky to get on the mound instead of telling Madlock to get back in there, nothing would have happened," he said. "I told him he let the game get out of hand and that Simmons should have been chased."

Simmons got in another shot a few minutes later. His single up the middle in the bottom of the ninth tallied the winning run in the 6-5 St. Louis victory.

But baseball has a funny way of evening things up, even if it takes years. Simmons got the thumb against the Cubs in a seeming moment of triumph-a game-tying homer off top relief ace Sutter (his Cardinals tenure still four years in the future) on May 27, 1978 in front of a huge Saturday night crowd at Busch Stadium.

Leading 2-1 in the ninth, Sutter got a strike-two count on Simmons. The latter was infuriated by the call by umpire Paul Runge. So he took it out on Sutter, slugging a 400-foot homer to right and apparently collecting a prize of a cake from a local baker who had offered one of his specialties for any homer hit in the game. The punchless Cards had dropped 13 of 14 going into the game.

As Simmons crossed the plate, Simmons offered a little tip-of-the-helmet gesture to Runge. The ump gave him the thumb. Simmons had almost reached the dugout when he realized what had happened. Like an unleashed beast, he tried to get to Runge, but was held back by Bob Forsch and Keith Hernandez.

"I didn't say a word," Simmons said. "You'll have to ask Runge. He'll tell you what happened."

"I can't help it if he's going bad," Runge said. "There was no profanity."

Cubs manager Herman Franks couldn't figure out why a non-verbal, non-obscene gesture would warrant an ejection.

"I always thought as long as you didn't swear you couldn't get thrown out of a ballgame," Franks said. "It ain't so anymore. I got chased last year (1977) for throwing up my hands in the dugout."

Making matters worse for Simmons was still another Cardinals loss, this time 3-2 in 11 innings. But he won a lot more than he lost against his Chicago "cousins."

## Worrell follows orders, serves up slam
### April 22, 1987, Busch Stadium

In the good ol' days, players didn't mind taking orders from their managers.

In a slump after signing a bargain-basement free-agent contract with the Cubs in spring training, Andre Dawson took extra early batting practice on the directive of manager Gene Michael.

And when Dawson came up in a clutch situation later that Wednesday night, Cardinals reliever Todd Worrell followed Whitey Herzog's instructions to the letter. He threw a strike, just as the manager had ordered, to the Hawk.

The Cardinals led 4-0 going into the top of the seventh, but promptly bean giving up the advantage. Reliever Bill Dawley walked Ryne Sandberg with the bases loaded to give the Cubs one run. Then he threw a ball to Dawson that just missed the outside corner. Herzog had seen enough. He summoned Worrell.

"Whitey was trying to give me a day off," Worrell recalled. "We had a lead we should have been able to protect. But everybody, from our starter on, kept walking people. And if there was one thing Whitey hated it was walks."

"Whitey put his hand out and I came in. My arm was loose. When I get to the mound Whitey was standing on the high part of it and in such a way that I couldn't get on top. He's able to look me in the eye and he's not letting go of the ball. There's a moment of silence. He puts the ball in my hand and says, 'I don't give a damn what happens with this next pitch —don't walk him!' I said, 'OK.'

"I told Tony Pena, our catcher, I'm going to give him something down the chute as hard as I can.' I did."

Dawson slugged his first Cubs grand slam to give the Cubs a 5-4 lead, which held up as the final score.

"He hit a missile that just cleared the wall in left field," Worrell said. "As he's rounding the bases I'm kind of mad. I get the next three out and I'm off the mound and out of the game because they're going to pinch hit for me. I started for the runway and Whitey reaches over and pulls me back by my jersey."

"'Way to go,'" he said. "I said, 'Excuse me?' He said, 'I asked for a strike and you threw one. He could have popped up or grounded one to Ozzie for a double play and made us all look like geniuses.' He patted me on the back on my way to the showers."

Herzog's explanation after the game: "I didn't want Dawley to come up (with his pitches). If he was going to come up, I'd rather have it with Worrell."

Making the loss even crazier for the Cardinals was the fact that No. 1 St. Louis announcer Jack Buck called the Dawson grand slam-on the Cubs broadcast on WGN-TV. Buck was one of a series of guest announcers filling in for Harry Caray, who had suffered a stroke the previous February. All Buck could do was chuckle at the oddball situation as Dawson toured the bases.

Maybe Hall of Famer Bob Gibson should have zipped his lips. Prior to the game, he said on KMOX-Radio, "The Cubs just don't excite me." Maybe the team didn't, but Dawson went on to win the NL MVP award in 1987, paying tribute to the fans by slugging a farewell homer (No. 46) off Dawley in his last at-bat in the home finale at Wrigley Field in September.

## Shannon knocks out Beckert
## April 16, 1969, Busch Stadium

Why did Cubs fans speak angrily of Cardinals stalwart Mike Shannon years, even decades, after he was his hard-nosed self one cool spring night in St. Louis?

The Gashouse Gang would have been proud of Shannon for up-ending-and knocking out-Cubs second baseman Glenn Beckert in a true bang-bang play at second base.

In the seventh inning of a splendid pitching duel between Fergie Jenkins and Steve Carlton, Shannon hit a hard smash down the third-base line. A sure double, the ball hit umpire Dave Davidson and rolled to a stop a few feet away from Cubs third baseman Ron Santo. Shannon thought the ball had rolled down the line and he kept running toward second.

Santo had picked up the ball and fired to first baseman Ernie Banks, figuring Shannon would retreat to first. But Shannon continued barreling in on Beckert, who took a relay throw from Banks.

Inside of sliding, Shannon attempted to bowl over Beckert to knock the ball from his glove. Beckert was waylaid after he tagged Shannon, who then threw his helmet to the ground.

Many in the Busch Stadium crowd of 16,418 booed Shannon as he returned, head down, to the dugout. Beckert was taken to Jewish Hospital in St. Louis suffering from cuts on the lip and facial bruises. He missed the next few games.

Shannon also was shaken up. Cardinals manager Red Schoendienst immediately removed him from the game and replaced him at third base with Phil Gagliano.

"I don't know what happened," Shannon said.

Oddly enough, Gashouse Gang shortstop Leo Durocher, the Cubs manager in his 1969 incarnation, held his tongue, saying, "All I know is that we play here again tomorrow night at 8 o'clock."

The normally gracious Cubs shortstop (and future Cardinal) Don Kessinger was livid, claiming Shannon "came after" Beckert. "The ball had him beat by 10 feet, but he kept coming in and they bumped heads," he said.

The Cubs and their fans didn't have too many chances to exact revenge on Shannon. He retired the following year due to injuries. And the bad blood didn't keep Shannon confined to his hotel in Chicago at night. Nicknamed "Moonman," Shannon always enjoyed the attractions of the overnight hours during his trips to the Second City.

## Grant throws strikes at bleachers; 'Bums' toss mice at Brock
### June 28-29, 1969, Wrigley Field

The most clever players know how to win over the raucous Wrigley Field bleacher fans. They fight insults with wit.

Pitcher Roger McDowell used to hose down sun-drenched fans with a groundskeeper's hose. Other players were seen in recent years with a bucket full of dollar bills placed in the outfield. Any fan accurate enough to hit the basket with a baseball, aimed from the left-field bleachers, won the pot.

You simply can not let the bleacher creatures get under your skin; you'll only make it worse for yourself. Those players who do end up flipping the bird at the fans. But Jim "Mudcat" Grant went further—he threw strikes right at the fans.

In the supercharged atmosphere of the weekend of June 27-29, 1969 at Wrigley Field, the famed yellow-helmeted Left Field Bleacher Bums were feeling pretty heady. The Cubs were surging, 20 games over .500 in first place, while the defending NL champion Cardinals, in town for a four-game series, were reeling, not even playing break-even baseball.

The fans had their usual targets, such as longtime Cubs tormentor Lou Brock. But during this series, the fans also got on veteran pitcher Grant.

"Grant snapped," recalled '69 Bleacher Bum Ned Colletti, now assistant general manager of the San Francisco Giants, who witnessed the bombardment from a few feet away.

Mike Murphy was the official bugler of the Bleacher Bums. He'd stand atop the bleacher wall tooting "Charge!" He was not playing pretty music to Grant.

"I was standing above the 368-foot sign in left field," said Murphy, now a Chicago radio sports-talk show host. "I had my bugle in hand and I was leading cheers. It was already 90 degrees at 10 a.m. We tried to get under Mudcat's skin. But most of it was the kind of good-natured ribbing you always get: 'Go back to the American League, go back to the minor leagues.'

"Mudcat walked to the warning track, looked up at me and he was standing no more than 12 feet away from me. He had a back pocket full of baseballs. I was wearing the open-toed sandals that were popular at the time. He took the first ball and cocked his arm. I thought he was just going to fake a throw. But he fired a 90 mph fastball, and it hit the top one-inch of the wall, just below my toe. The ball ricocheted halfway back to second base. The next ball he did the same thing, hitting the wall one inch below my sandals. He had perfect aim. Not being a dense guy, I realize I'm in trouble."

Murphy couldn't escape easily. The Cubs allowed the bleachers to fill to overflowing in those years. Fans sat in the aisles. He climbed over people, zigzagging through crowd "trying to go like I'm Gale Sayers." Grant zeroed in on him, firing four more baseballs into the bleachers. One hit 11-year-old Mike Wedge in the neck. Another hit a young girl in the jaw. A third hit a kid in the arm. The fourth one missed.

Soon a gaggle of Cardinals teammates came over and pulled Grant away from the bleachers. But he was still hot hours later.

*Chicago Sun-Times* reporter Tom Fitzpatrick, who would win a Pulitzer Prize for column writing a few years later, entered the Cardinals clubhouse to ask Grant what happened after the Cardinals lost the game 3-1. Fitzpatrick would have had better luck wading into a hornet's nest.

"What the hell do you mean?" Grant asked Fitzpatrick when questioned about the incident. "Come on over here and see what they threw at me."

Grant displayed a Bleacher Bum helmet and other smaller objects. He claimed that while signing an autograph the day before, he was hit in the head with a rubber ball.

The discourse between Grant and Fitzpatrick attracted the attention of ultimate competitor Bob Gibson and his teammates.

"They got everything they deserved," Gibson said of the fans. He then fixed his fiery eyes on Fitzpatrick. "Who told you could come in here anyway and talk like this?"

Cardinals players began chanting, "Throw 'em out" in Fitzpatrick's direction.

The reporter asked Grant if he was aware he hit an 11-year-old in the neck.

"So what?" Grant replied.

Gibson was positively livid by now. "(Bleep) them all," he said. "And (bleep) you, too."

A Cardinals player chorus was chirping, "Out, out!" to Fitzpatrick, who beat a retreat, but not before he bowed to the players as he exited.

"I thought Grant would have been suspended by the league," Murphy said. "He could have killed somebody if he hit that person in the head."

Fitzpatrick came back for more the following day, June 29, and found a Bleacher Bums president Ron Grousl planning a special way to get under the Cardinals' skin. Grousl had purchased seven white mice on the morning of June 28. The rodents were to scare Brock in left field.

So in the bottom of the first inning of Game 1 of the June 29 doubleheader—Billy Williams Day at Wrigley Field, seven Bleacher Bums each heaved a mouse onto the field. Brock just laughed; Murphy said the Cubs' tormentor, along with Willie Mays and Hank Aaron, knew how to diffuse the Bums' best tactics. The problem came in the top of the second, when Cubs left fielder Willie Smith took his position. He was afraid of the mice, still running around on the grass. Smith ran back to the dugout and the game was briefly delayed while Wrigley Field groundskeepers busied themselves collecting the trespassing vermin.

That wasn't the Bleacher Bums' only experiment with wildlife in left field. Fans heard the Mets' Cleon Jones was afraid of snakes. Unable to obtain the reptiles, the Bums let loose a whole mess of frogs instead. They hopped toward Jones in left field as he kept a wary eye on them.

The Bums also threw crutches at Pete Rose while chanting "Rosey" to the macho man. Their dossiers about opposing players' private lives was extensive. Earlier in 1969, they found out the identity of Dodgers center fielder Willie Davis' Chicago girlfriend. They chanted "Ruthie" at Davis, who took umbrage by slugging two opposite-field homers into the left-field bleachers.

But the Bums' special outrage was saved for the Cardinals. Their heroes got back at Grant and Gibson in the June 29 doubleheader. Gibson lost a pitching duel to Fergie Jenkins 3-1 in the opener. Grant was racked in the 12-1 shellacking in the nightcap.

Mudcat Grant never developed the scary reputation of an Albert Belle or Rob Dibble. But for one day, he couldn't take it any more. The bleacher fans are a one of a kind—and you can get them in your pocket if you have any smarts.

## Grace vs. DiPino, one round
## June 4, 1989, Busch Stadium

Frank DiPino and Mark Grace did not like each other as Cubs teammates in 1988. They liked each other even less as foes the following season after DiPino migrated to the Cardinals.

As a rookie in '88, Grace had to take the verbal needle from lefty reliever DiPino, whose razor-sharp wit, sarcasm and cloud of smoke from his ever-present cigarette were clubhouse staples. But in 1989, DiPino graduated to shaving Grace close. The latter got mad as hell and wouldn't take it anymore. But for his sweet revenge, Grace lost three weeks' playing time.

"Frank got a wit about him that created a bandwagon effect," Grace recalled. "I was the guy he wanted to get on. He just thought I was arrogant or cocky, something about me he didn't like. My rookie year, I didn't bother anybody. I took my share of stuff from veterans. That's part of the game. But Frank's was more than good-natured needling. He was trying to be hurtful. I took it like a man."

Grace forgot all about it until the Cubs' trip into Busch Stadium the weekend of June 2-4, 1989. Cubs trainer John Fierro told him to be "steppin' lively" during this series. "He told a couple of guys on the team that he was glad he stayed in the National League," Grace said of Fierro's advance warning, which continued: 'The first chance he gets, he's going to drill you.' I said, 'That's fine, he can drill me all he wants, but I guarantee you, it will be Round One, right on the mound.' That was back in the days if you did charge the mound, you didn't get suspended for 'X' amount of days without pay. Mound charging was more prevalent then."

DiPino waited for his chance. In the fifth inning of the Sunday, June 4, game, after Cardinals starter Scott Terry had allowed five Cubs homers (of the then-Busch Stadium record of six for an opponent at the time) in the budding Cubs rout, he threw a waist-high pitch inside, moving Grace off the plate—and toward the mound.

"That was enough for me," he said. "There was a brouhaha right in the middle of the mound."

Grace got in his licks at DiPino with two lefts to the ribs and a glancing blow to the head. But the first baseman ended up getting the worst of it. Cardinals outfielder Jim Lindeman tried to pull Grace off DiPino by grabbing his arms. "The adrenaline's flowing and you feel like punching him some more," Grace said. "I wasn't ready to get off of him, he kept pulling, and he pulled my shoulder out of its socket. I got hurt trying to get pulled off. I had that thing under control (working over DiPino)."

For his trouble, Grace missed most of the rest of June and was fined $100. Cardinals third baseman Terry Pendleton left the game with an elbow injury. But not all opponents were combatants during the fight.

Mindful that Cubs manager Don Zimmer had torn cartilage in his right knee, Cardinals manager Whitey Herzog held a friendly arm around Popeye's right shoulder during the pileup of bodies.

"I told Zim, 'Don't hurt your knee,'" Herzog said.

DiPino exacted a unique form of revenge against the Cubs. Big Lee Smith had been traded away from the Cubs to the Red Sox in 1987 in a deal almost as bad as Lou Brock-for-Ernie Broglio. When Smith found his way from the Red Sox to the Cardinals in 1990, DiPino helped Smith master a forkball that made him very effective with the Cards—and enabled him to pitch until age 40 as the all-time saves leader.

## Imbiber Hack has something against milk (man)

*The Baseball Timeline*, by Burt Solomon, reported that on June 21, 1928, Cubs slugger Hack Wilson went into the stands at Wrigley Field to settle accounts with a fan who'd been heckling him.

The incident took place after Wilson, who never met any Prohibition hooch that he didn't guzzle, grounded out in the ninth during the Cubs' 4-1 loss to the Cardinals in the second game of a doubleheader. The fan was Edward Young, a milkman. Two Cub teammates, Gabby Hartnett and Joe Kelly broke it up. Wilson was fined $100 by NL president John Heydler; a Chicago judge fined Young $5.

## Cubs boot five in first
## July 2, 1977, Busch Stadium

The Cardinals kept chopping the ball down into the worn-down Busch Stadium Astroturf. The Cubs infielders kept trying to field and throw the ball. The result was a literal comedy of errors in the first inning between a near-overflow crowd of 50,320—at the time the largest night-game crowd in Busch Stadium history.

No wonder Cubs manager Herman Franks growled, "This place is a bleepin' brickyard" after the quintet of miscues, helping the Cardinals to four runs, in the Cubs' 10-3 loss.

But Franks knew the Cardinals' modus operandi of the pre-Mark McGwire, shortened dimensions Busch Stadium era.

"They're just choppin' at the ball like Matty Alou used to do," he said. "I'll say one thing. They've got that stroke down and it's a helluva stroke."

Normally sure-handed second baseman Manny Trillo committed two errors in the first, matching the fumble-fingers of Cubs starter Bill Bonham.

Lou Brock opened the first with a high hopper. Trillo nabbed the ball behind the mound, but his throw pulled first baseman Bill Buckner off the mound. Garry Templeton then grounded a single up the middle, Brock stopping at second.

Tony Scott then slashed a Bonham pitch into left field. But the Cubs' Gene Clines threw wildly toward home as Brock scored for error No. 2 as Templeton scored. Backing up the play at the plate, Bonham then threw wildly over third, trying to cut down Templeton, the ball ending up back in Clines' hands for error No. 3.

A couple of batters later, Bonham fumbled a high hopper by the slow-footed Ken Reitz for error No. 4. The final bobble came when Trillo threw wildly as he tried to complete a double play.

Trillo completed his own hat trick in the sixth when he let a double-play grounder go through his legs.

"We've got speed," Cardinals manager Vern Rapp said in an understatement, adding, "We always seemed to be a step ahead of the Cubs out there tonight."

Twenty steps ahead after the Cubs fielders threw the ball, if the truth be known.

## Poppin' 'em up and droppin' 'em
## April 12, 1965, Wrigley Field

An old baseball axiom says the ball always finds the weak spot in the defense. So on Opening Day 1965 at Wrigley Field, the target was nervous, anxious rookie shortstop Roberto Pena of the Cubs, who dropped two pop flies for errors, then bobbled a grounder for a hat trick of errors.

Pena's fumble-itis contributed to the wild contest that was called due to darkness with a 10-10 tie after 11 innings.

With two outs and the bases loaded in the top of the first, Cardinals starter Bob Gibson lofted a pop to Pena. He promptly dropped the ball and two runs scored.

Then, in the fourth, Gibson popped again to Pena. And, again, the shortstop dropped it, triggering a two-run Cardinals inning.

Pena's third error came in the top of the 10th. But he tried to atone for his bobbles with a homer into the right-field seats in the third and a two-run double in the bottom of the fourth. He added a single to make his afternoon a real three-spot—three hits, three RBI and three errors.

"I hope somebody doesn't want to kill me," Pena said after the game. He claimed he had both popups "to the last second," but the capricious Wrigley Field winds played tricks on him.

"He wasn't a good defensive player," Cubs Hall of Famer Billy Williams recalled. "But he could hit the ball hard at times."

Pena continued on for several months as the starting shortstop while his error totals mounted to 17 in 50 games while his batting average dropped to .218. He tried to burn the candle at both ends.

"He was excited about being in the majors," Williams said. "And he'd call me every night wanting to go places. I said no, I needed my rest. Pena did that for two months and ran himself to death."

Pena ran himself back down to Triple-A when another rookie, Don Kessinger, took his place at shortstop at mid-season '65. He eventually became an original San Diego Padre in 1969, a baseball vagabond whose claim to fame-or infamy-was sealed when he didn't accept gravity's gifts.

## Drinks are on "Hutch"
## Chicago, 1957

Moe Drabowsky and fellow Cub rookie pitcher Dick Drott went to a Chicago nightspot for a few drinks, knowing they were going to pitch in a doubleheader against the Cardinals the next day.

Someone from the bar kept sending drinks over to the two pitchers and they happily accepted them. As they left, Drabowsky and Drott discovered their friend was Fred Hutchinson, the Cardinals' manager.

"Hutch thought he did a job on us," said Drabowsky, who became a Cardinal on the back of his career almost 15 years later.

"But Dick and I went out and beat the Cardinals in both games the next afternoon. Hutch never sent drinks over again."

## Box-seat passion
## Wrigley Field, recently

Mark Stangl, an Anheuser-Busch employee in St. Louis, has made a few trips to Wrigley Field. While he, too, finds the rivalry between fans of the teams healthy, he sometimes has wondered about to which "game" Cubs fans are really devoted.

"One time we were sitting down in the box seats in the right field corner and some young guy with his girlfriend sitting in his lap got into a heavy embrace right in front of us," Stangl said.

"Some of the people in our group hollered out, 'Go get a hotel room,' because they were interfering with our watching the game. They ignored us. The Cubs came to bat and got a rally going but the couple continued to carry on. Finally they just got up and left."

# 17

# The Mason-Dixon Line
# of Illinois

**NEVER does the Cubs-Cardinals rivalry manifest itself** more than through the corn and soybean fields, tiny burghs, industrial cities and university towns of throughout Illinois—and not just concentrated in the central part of the state.

Here, team loyalties run generations deep. The pride for either the Cubs or Cardinals is deep and personal. The majority of the rivalry is good-natured, but it gets emotional, and heated, at times. Bets on the outcome of the teams' head-to-head are made for decades on end, with the pride of winning more important than the cash garnered.

There is no border, per se. It is like a Mason-Dixon line, cutting through individual households, zigzagging north and south helter-skelter. Cubs strongholds exist much further south than bastions of Cardinals loyalists. Radio stations deep into Chicago and St. Louis home territories carry the Cardinals and Cubs, respectively. Fans of "enemy" teams are stalwart and unbending, maintaining their loyalties even while surrounded by hordes of followers of the supposed home-market franchise.

Within the immediate St. Louis area, of course, the dislike of the Cubs is singular. There is no other arch-rival. But 300 miles north, antipathy from Cubs fans is far different. The Cardinals are disliked, to be sure, but the biggest passion in Second City is hatred of the cross-town team. White Sox fans traditionally have hated the better-publicized and more glamorous Cubs far more than the Yankees or Athletics or any other team that deprived the South Siders of pennants in the past. In response, Cubs fans abhor Sox fans and, in turn, their favorite team.

But throughout Illinois, and spilling over to much of Iowa and even parts of other states, the Cubs and Cardinals are the state baseball religions. The percentage of followers is unclear, although many residents insist loyalties often are split down the middle in their locales. The Cubs hold forth strongly north of Interstate 74, which takes a northwest turn west of Champaign-Urbana, while Cardinal red gets thicker as you go further south of the highway.

The traditional geographical alignment may have been altered somewhat with introduction of 140-plus annual Cubs telecasts, fronted by the immortal Harry Caray via WGN-TV. The Chicago independent outlet attained "superstation" status in the early 1980s, when former Cardinals broadcast pied piper Caray took over from Jack Brickhouse as No. 1 Cubs announcer until his death on February 19, 1998. Cubs fans, able to tune in on their basic cable systems, soon could be found all over the country, including in the heart of Cardinals territory. Former Cub George Altman, now living in Jefferson City, Mo., said he sees plenty of Cubs fans around town due to Caray and WGN. Similar analyses could be found all over the Midwest and even points further away.

The only actual breakdown of Illinois fans' loyalties was conducted by WCIA-TV, the CBS affiliate in Champaign, in the summer of 1977. With results also aired on sister station WMBD-TV, the CBS affiliate in Peoria, WCIA researches contacted a sample of 500 fans—100 each in Champaign, Danville, Bloomington-Normal, Peoria and Decatur. Pollsters conducted the survey from August 8 to 10, 1977. That came just as the Cubs, who had zoomed to eight games in front in the NL East with a 47-22 record on June 29, 1977, had begun a monster swan dive that would eventually end with an 81-81, fourth-place final record. The Cardinals had challenged the Cubs in June and July, but also fell back in August under the onslaught of a powerful Philadelphia Phillies club that eventually won the NL East.

WCIA found that the Cubs commanded 50 percent of the loyalties of the fans in the five cities. The Cardinals were backed by 31 percent. Favorites dropped steeply off to the Cincinnati Reds and Chicago White Sox with 4 percent each. The Sox's 4 percent figure, compiled at the time the team's "South Side Hitmen" bunch had made a first-place run at mid-summer, partially explains some of the American League club's attendance problems-the inability to tap into a regional fan base a la the Cubs and Cardinals. The Dodgers counted 3 percent as loyalists, with the Yankees, Brewers, Red Sox and Pirates each commanding 1 percent.

Of course, the numbers have changed somewhat through the past two decades, factoring in the Cubs' superstation exposure, the Cardinals' three World Series appearances in the 1980s, and the Mark McGwire-Sammy Sosa home-run race of 1998. But the survey still gives some clues as to the passions of baseball fans in the heart of the Cubs-Cardinals battleground.

Here is the percentage of breakdowns of fan loyalties in the 1977 poll, by city:

|           | Peoria | Champaign | Bloomington Normal | Decatur | Danville |
|-----------|--------|-----------|--------------------|---------|----------|
| Cubs      | 50     | 57        | 40                 | 37      | 66       |
| Cardinals | 31     | 24        | 41                 | 41      | 16       |
| Yankees   | 1      | 1         | 2                  | 1       | 1        |
| White Sox | 2      | 4         | 8                  | 1       | 5        |
| Dodgers   | 2      | 4         | 3                  | 1       | 4        |
| Reds      | 5      | 2         | 2                  | 4       | 7        |

The best two cities to focus in on the rivalry are Peoria and Decatur. The rivalry is loyal and emotional in both cities, where fan arguments spilled out of homes and taverns onto the Caterpillar assembly lines. And the best barometer of how the modern Mason-Dixon line splits families can be found in one Peoria family, which has produced one of baseball's top left-handed sluggers: Jim Thome.

Family patriarch Chuck Thome is a Cub fan. In fact, three generations of Chuck Thomes loved the Cubs—his father and one of his sons. That affection also was transferred to Jim as the family made regular trips to Wrigley Field.

"Jim's hero was Dave Kingman," Chuck Thome said. "We were at the ballpark one day. We turned around, and Jim was gone. He sneaked into the dugout to try to get Kingman's autograph. He didn't get it, but came out with two signed baseballs."

Jim Thome still was in awe of Wrigley Field when his Cleveland Indians visited for a two-game interleague series in June, 1998. He sat in the visitors' dugout 3 1/2 hours prior to the first game, gazing around the ballpark, soaking it all up from a different perspective than he had ever experienced. But Thome may not have been there to enjoy the spectacle-or play in two World Series—if not for the Cardinals fan in the family.

An older brother, Randy Thome, 40, taught Jim Thome how to bat left-handed. "I knew most of the parks in the majors were shorter to right field and there weren't a lot of great left-handed hitters," Randy Thome said. A left-hander himself, he figures that such a status explains why he's the family's Cardinals fan. Or maybe there's a rebel bloodline in the Thomes. Chuck Thome's brother, Art, was a Cardinals fan. Randy's and Jim's mother, Joyce Thome, said she tried to play it down the middle, but was "kind of a Cubs fan."

So how does a Cardinals fan grow up among a gaggle of Cubs followers? Chuck Thome doesn't understand. "I don't know where he went wrong," said pops.

"You gotta understand," Randy Thome said, "I wasn't a follower. I couldn't just go with what everyone else was doing." When the Cardinals won the World Series in 1967 and followed up with an NL pennant in '68, Randy's loyalty was clinched for life.

Surprisingly, family baseball talk wasn't too raucous. The Cubs' often-losing ways was a fail-safe assurance for family harmony. "We used to rub it in whenever we could-but it wasn't too often," Chuck Thome said. "Randy pretty much had the hammer on us."

Oddly enough, Randy Thome liked the family outings to Wrigley Field. "I enjoyed going to Wrigley Field," he said. "I liked going there better than Busch Stadium."

He had one sturdy shoulder on which to cry about being a majority of one as a Cardinal fan in a family. Fellow Peorian Mike Dunne grew up as a St. Louis rooter among father Dick, mother Sandy, and brother Tom, all Cubs fans. The difference was the Dunnes had to root for their contra-son in the Cardinals organization. Right-handed pitcher Dunne was St. Louis' No. 1 draft choice in 1984, but never got to take the mound for the Cardinals. April Fools was true; on April 1, 1987, he was traded along with center fielder Andy Van Slyke and catcher Mike LaValliere to the Pirates for catcher Tony Pena. He pitched a few seasons in Pittsburgh before moving on with his life.

"The family rooted for me," Mike Dunne said. "Actually, the Cubs were one of the teams scouting him. They were at all my games. I was originally in discussions with three teams, and the Cardinals were not one of them." The Cubs instead took left-handed college pitcher Drew Hall in the first round. Dunne did not have a chance to be taken on Round Two in '84, and the Cubs picked some skinny high-school kid from Las Vegas named Greg Maddux, anyway.

Mike Dunne, who now conducts pitching lessons for kids in Peoria, can't figure out exactly why he became a Cardinals fan. "I collected baseball cards, and I couldn't get enough of Bob Gibson," he said. "I always read box scores, and I couldn't wait to see what Gibson or Ted Sizemore did."

But, like any youthful Cardinals fan in Peoria, Dunne had a rivalry with Cubs followers. His top antagonist was a kid named Craig Hislop.

Although many claim Peoria is split down the middle between Cubs and Cardinals fans, both Randy Thome and Mike Dunne believe the Cubs have the advantage in the area, backing up the 1977 WCIA poll.

"I would have thought Peoria is 60-40 in favor of the Cubs," Thome said. "I'm around more Cubs fans than Cardinals fans." Said Dunne: "The Cubs Caravan usually draws more people coming through town." Backing up their notion is Cubs fan Trish Epley, wife of Cardinals fan Darrin Epley, a former minor league teammate of Jim Thome: "I think the Cubs fans have the advantage here. Growing up, the Cubs games were always on WGN, while the Cardinals were not on TV. That's why I became a Cubs fan."

Some interest in the Cardinals was built when the local Class A Midwest franchise, owned by longtime Harry Caray chum Pete Vonachen, switched its affiliation to the Cardinals in 1993. Vonachen previously had linked up with the Cubs, who sent such future stars like Mark Grace through town. But old loyalties, dating back to the days when Jack Brickhouse broadcast for WMBD-Radio, are hard to break.

All along the Illinois River valley, the Cubs-Cardinals rivalry rages. In one instance, a Cubs fan married a Cardinals lover who ended up pitching for both teams.

Amy Clark, wife of Texas Rangers pitcher Mark Clark, grew up in the tiny town of Kilbourne, with 450 residents. Amy attended both grade school and high school with Mark, who lived in nearby Bath, Ill. She got her Cubs fan's allegiance largely from her grandmother, Frances Markley, a resident of Havana, Ill., another river town.

"Mark's family were big Cardinals fans, and they'd looked at me funny when I'd show up at his house wearing a Cubs T-shirt," Amy Clark said. "There was a lot of teasing between fans of both teams when I went to school."

Mark Clark got his wish, starting his career with the Cardinals in the early 1990s. He moved on to the Indians and Mets before being traded to the Cubs in 1997. The Clarks now live in Springfield in the off-season.

They escape a lot of barbs by not living in Decatur. The birthplace of the Chicago Bears always has been an active battleground for the Cubs-Cardinals rivalry, even though geographically the agri-business center is closer to St. Louis: a two-hour drive compared to more than three hours to Chicago (more when the zigzag city route to Wrigley Field is factored in).

"A number of bars and radio stations will have annual bus trips to Busch Stadium for a Cubs-Cardinals game," said Mark Tupper, executive sports editor of the *Decatur Herald*. "Half the people on the bus are Cubs fans; the other half Cardinals fans. I've heard of fist fights on the way back to Decatur where those people had all those Budweisers after sitting in that sweat bowl (Busch Stadium) for hours. One time they had to stop the bus to restore order. They're going at it, throwing fried chicken at each other."

On other occasions in local bars and restaurants, Tupper said he witnessed fathers and sons, possessing opposite loyalties, being separated after almost coming to blows watching a Chicago-St. Louis game on TV.

"In this town, there are probably thousands of wagers made at the start of each season," Tupper said. "They bet for 30 years on end, maybe a $1 a bet or beers on the Cubs-Cardinals season series. The winner gets the right to be top dog all winter. Those winning bets are worth gold to them."

The partisans make their opinions known loud and clear, whether in print or via broadcast media.

"It doesn't matter which team you cover more," said Tupper. "One guy writes me all the time. He feels we hate the Cubs and are shills for the Cardinals. Another person writes in all the time to say we're out to get the Cardinals, and can prove it with statistics to show that we're favoring the Cubs. You're never going to please everybody."

Tupper's background as a Cubs fan who grew up in Evanston, Illinois, also draws barbs from both outside and within the *Herald* newsroom.

"When the Cubs started out 0-14 in 1997, Cardinals fans were leaving the clippings of the losses on my desk," he said. "They'd be laughing and said maybe we should put the results in the comics section. If the Cubs get off to any kind of cold start, the same cartoons and jokes that have been around since 1908 get circulated."

Chuckling about the heated rivalry is Bob Fallstrom. He's above the fray. As Tupper's predecessor as executive sports editor, from 1964 to 1986, White Sox fan Fallstrom enjoyed tossing out bait to the rabid fans.

"If one of those teams was doing badly, I'd make fun of it in my column," said Fallstrom, who just celebrated his 50th anniversary at the Herald . "I'd get hate mail. I probably led the league in that. These people are too stubborn. They change wives, cars and jobs, but not the affiliation to their favorite teams."

Over at WSOY-Radio, the city's top news-talk station, program director Jeff Daly, a native St. Louisan and Cardinals fan, also notes the fans' split. But the Cubs fans tend to be more vociferous in their calls to the station's shows.

The fans' split also is prevalent in the colleges/insurance headquarters-twin cities of Bloomington and Normal, 45 miles north of Decatur. Although the cities are physically closer to Chicago than St. Louis, the longtime Cardinals radio outlet in the area is WJBC-Radio. The station is a ratings powerhouse in central Illinois and has swayed many fans toward the Cardinals.

"I think it's 55 to 45, even 60 to 40 in favor of the Cardinals here because we've been the Cardinals affiliate for so long," said former WJBC sports director Craig Bertsche.

But WGN's Cubs telecasts, even in the pre-superstation days, balanced out the fans' loyalties, said Bloomington native Jay Blunk, now the Cubs' director of advertising. Bloomington-Normal was one of the first central Illinois areas to get cable TV, which picked up WGN via a relay system from the Chicago area.

Blunk, who grew up a Cubs fan, remembers the rivalry being played out in kids' baseball games. "You'd be Ron Santo, Billy Williams or Ernie Banks, and the other kids would be Lou Brock or Bob Gibson," he said.

How partisan was Blunk? In fourth grade, attending Field School in town, he stole a Cardinals hat off the head of a classmate. Blunk took the cap home, where he and a friend burned it in the back yard. His parents made him buy a new hat and go over to the Cardinals fan's house to apologize.

Blunk's father, Dave, also a Cubs fan, worked at his Uncle Carl's Blunk's Barber Shop in Normal. "My great-uncle was a Cardinals fan who hated the Cubs," he said. "They worked next to each other with sharp instruments. There was Cardinals stuff all over the shop, but my dad was a young guy, working for his uncle, and had to be humble."

One day, Jack Brickhouse, of all people, walked into the barber shop. He was in town to speak at Illinois State University. The merry man of Wrigley Field needed a haircut, but Uncle Carl was not going to do the trimming.

"Carl had someone in his chair," Jay Blunk said. "He said, 'Mr. Brickhouse, nice to meet you. But this guy (pointing at Dave Blunk) is the Cubs fan, and he's the guy who's going to have to cut your hair. Jack remembered that story when he was on the Cubs Caravan a few years back going to Bloomington-Normal. He called out to my dad in the crowd, and said he had given him a hell of a haircut 30 years before."

One other family story concerns Blunk's birth on May 2, 1963. Dave Blunk was listening to the Cubs-Cardinals night game out of St. Louis. Suddenly, Mom said it was time to go to the hospital. Dave Blunk never found out the score that night. He needn't have bothered. Recently, Jay Blunk looked up the game. Of course, the Cubs lost.

Meanwhile, splits of fans' loyalties also were reported in such Illinois cities as Danville and Quincy, although the former municipality was rated as a big pro-Cubs town in the WCIA poll.

General manager Mike Hulvey of Danville's WDAN-Radio reported that he switched his station's baseball affiliation from the Cubs to the Cardinals two years ago when he learned that numerous local fans would sit in their cars at night to pull in Cardinals flagship station KMOX-Radio. Hulvey figured that Cubs fans easily could get Cubs flagship WGN-Radio during the daytime, so he wanted to go with the audience that was being underserved in the market.

Quincy, the next market up the Mississippi River from St. Louis, would figure to be a pro-Cardinals town. But Tim Kinscherf, sports director of WTAD-Radio, rates the allegiances as only slightly tilting toward the Cardinals.

"Cubs fans are a vocal minority," Kinscherf said. "If they feel they don't get the treatment they deserve, they'll let you know."

Cardinals fans are the same way much further north.

Joe Morrissey, retired sports editor of the *Register-Mail* in Galesburg, Illinois, a city about equidistant from both Chicago and St. Louis and divided in its loyalties (with a shade toward the Cubs), has always been impressed with how civil fans in both the big cities are toward each other.

"They've got a different attitude than the fans up here (Galesburg). Cubs and Cardinals fans are on two different sides of the street in Galesburg."

For many years, Morrissey bet a good friend a beer on each game between the Cubs and Cardinals. "Most times I edged him out," Morrissey said. "Remember 1978 (when the Cubs won the first 12 from the Cardinals and won the season series 15-3)? That year I really wiped up."

Another 40-some miles further up the road from Galesburg is the Quad Cities, made up of Rock Island, Moline and East Moline in Illinois and Davenport, Iowa, across the Mississippi. More Cubs-Cardinals debates rage here.

"This is a large Cubs market, about 60-40 in favor of the Cubs, but I was surprised at the number of Cardinals fans in the area," said Travis Fox, operations manager of all-sports KJOC-Radio and a native of nearby Burlington, Iowa. "We'd get a lot of Cardinals fans coming out in my hometown, when the Cardinals Caravan would come through town with guys like Todd Zeile and Tom Pagnozzi."

Cubs-Cardinals debates rage on Fox's afternoon talk show with callers named "Cardinal Mike," "Birdman," "Cubbie Glen" and "Ryno."

The Mason-Dixon line then zigzags back east through northern Illinois as Chicago itself starts to draw closer.

In Sterling, 40 miles east of the Quad Cities, Lisa Taylor has been a staunch Cubs fan for the better part of 35 years. But her father, Joe Adami, is a Cardinals fan. "Ernie Banks, Ron Santo were big and one of the TV stations out of the Quad Cities (WQAD-TV) carried the Cubs on weekends and some road night games when I was younger," said Taylor, assistant program director of WSDR-Radio in Sterling.

Taylor engages in friendly office debates with Joe Martin, a station salesman and Cardinals fan. She and her fellow Cubs fans had nothing but pride in 1998. "We all knew Sammy (Sosa) was a better all-around player (than Mark McGwire)," she said.

Taylor estimated that about 30 percent of baseball fans in the area back the Cardinals.

"There's more Cardinals fans than White Sox fans, and that's somewhat surprising because we're closer to Chicago," she said. "I don't care anyway. I'm more of a Sox hater. I'd never root for them in the World Series. But if the Cardinals were in the World Series, I would cheer for them. They're in the same division as the Cubs."

Cubs fans also abound in supposedly strong Cardinals areas. The Cubs were carried for many years on WINU-Radio in Highland, Ill., only 40 miles east of St. Louis. Station executives had said Harry Caray's presence and the heavy schedule of daytime baseball made the games appealing to listeners even in the Cardinals' backyard. At the same time, WCIL-Radio in Carbondale was a longtime Cubs network affiliate in a market where thousands of Chicago-area students attended Southern Illinois University.

These stations satisfy the needs of fans like lifelong Cubs fan Jim McCarthy, born in Evanston, Illinois, but now living in St. Louis since he married local woman while in graduate school there in the late 1950s. McCarthy first witnessed the split among Illinois fans while attending Bradley and Eastern Illinois universities.

"I'd say, 'You're from Illinois. The Cubs are our team.' And they'd say, 'No, we're Cardinals fans.'"

But McCarthy always found the rivalry between fans constituting of "good-natured kidding."

If McCarthy has to take some ribbing as a Cubs fan in the capital of Redbird passions, then folks like James Hage have to deal with a sea of Cubbie blue in their homes deep into "enemy" territory. A dentist in Plano, Ill., just 55 miles southwest of Chicago, Hage, 65, is a rare breed in the Cubs-Cardinals rivalry—a convert. He began life as a Cubs fan, like most folks in surrounding Grundy, Kendall and DeKalb counties. Father Randolph Hage rooted for the Wrigleys.

"I was a Cubs fan in 1945," Hage said. "Then things kind of deteriorated with the team. Call it hero worship—I liked Stan Musial. He was in his prime then. I kind of swung over."

Hage found other Cardinals rooters in the area. He converted wife, Kay, to the St. Louis faith. He raised daughters Debbie, Laura and Jenny to regard red as the politically correct color. He took the whole bunch down to Busch Stadium to see Stan Musial's statue dedicated on August 4, 1968. The Hages endured a Cardinals defeat to the Cubs that day.

"I go through a fair amount of ribbing," he said. But being a dentist, precision timing is of the essence. By departing the Cubs' fold when he did, he has not had to endure five-sixths of his life in the baseball wilderness, enjoying six Cardinals World Series appearances in that time.

Growing up 70 miles east, at the other outskirts of the Chicago metropolitan area, was another Cardinals fan, John Schoon. A retired teacher, Schoon grew up in Gary, Indiana, before eventually settling in St. Louis.

"I think my dad became one because he was a big Rogers Hornsby fan and he didn't like the way the Cubs had treated him in 1932," Schoon, now an usher at Busch Stadium, said about the Cubs firing Hornsby two-thirds of the way through that pennant-winning year.

"Half the family liked the Cubs. There was a lot of stuff that went back and forth between us."

Schoon remembers the many times he went to Wrigley Field to see his beloved Cardinals.

"The first time I saw the Cardinals it was in Wrigley Field in 1941. We sat a few rows behind the dugout. Vern Olson (Cubs pitcher) beat 'em 6-2."

"My bitterest moment was going to a game in 1952 on the day before I was inducted into the Army. The Cubs beat 'em and they (Cardinals) played just terrible. (Hank) Sauer hit the ball all over the place. The next day, August 12, Stu Miller (of the Cardinals) shut them out on one hit."

As an usher at Busch Stadium, he's had a few eye-opening experiences at Cardinals-Cubs games. "I had just started there, I guess it was

'87, and I'll never forget the first time I heard the sound of the crowd. I was downstairs and couldn't see the field and I heard this resounding outburst. I thought something good had happened (the Cardinals scoring). But when I looked up I saw the enemy had scored. I was dismayed."

As an usher, Schoon stays away from controversy. Yet he remembers once getting close enough to the field to razz Cubs coach Billy Williams. "It was the year they added some red to their uniform (red bill on the cap). I saw Billy Williams and I said, 'How do you like that red?' He said, 'I don't like it.'"

Hage and Schoon were brave growing up the way they did. But the majority of Cubs and Cardinals fans stay true to their geographical birthrights. They stick with their favorites. They always end up with an interesting summer, win or lose, throughout the Prairie State.

# APPENDICES

## CUBS-CARDINALS BY NUMBERS, NAMES

### Cubs players' lifetime records vs. the Cardinals (through 1998 season)

|  | AB | H | HR | RBI | AVG. |
|---|---|---|---|---|---|
| Lance Johnson, CF | 95 | 30 | 2 | 11 | .316 |
| Mickey Morandini, 2B | 271 | 70 | 0 | 23 | .258 |
| Sammy Sosa, RF | 286 | 73 | 17 | 48 | .255 |
| Mark Grace, 1B | 528 | 168 | 10 | 83 | .318 |
| Henry Rodriguez, LF | 144 | 37 | 10 | 29 | .257 |
| Benito Santiago, C | 318 | 85 | 8 | 32 | .267 |
| Gary Gaetti, 3B | 7 | 4 | 1 | 2 | .571 |
| Jose Hernandez, SS | 119 | 31 | 8 | 19 | .261 |
| Jeff Blauser, SS | 336 | 64 | 4 | 20 | .190 |
| Glenallen Hill, LF | 163 | 49 | 7 | 29 | .301 |
| Manny Alexander, SS-2B | 38 | 12 | 0 | 1 | .316 |

| Pitchers | G | IP | W- L | ERA | SV |
|---|---|---|---|---|---|
| Kerry Wood | 1 | 7 | 1-0 | 1.29 | 0 |
| Kevin Tapani | 3 | 18 | 1-0 | 3.00 | 0 |
| Steve Trachsel | 18 | 108 | 8-6 | 4.00 | 0 |
| Jon Lieber | 15 | 45 1/3 | 4-1 | 4.37 | 2 |
| Terry Mulholland | 32 | 156 | 7-9 | 4.62 | 0 |
| Rod Beck | 29 | 33 2/3 | 4-2 | 2.14 | 14 |
| Matt Karchner | 8 | 9 | 1-0 | 3.00 | 2 |
| Terry Adams | 18 | 18 | 1-1 | 8.50 | 0 |
| Felix Heredia | 13 | 10 | 0-0 | 3.60 | 0 |

## Cardinals players lifetime records vs. the Cubs (through 1998 season)

| Player | AB | H | HR | RBI | Avg. |
|---|---|---|---|---|---|
| Edgar Renteria, SS | 119 | 31 | 1 | 6 | .261 |
| Mark McGwire, 1B | 49 | 15 | 11 | 18 | .306 |
| Ray Lankford, CF | 412 | 112 | 19 | 70 | .272 |
| J.D. Drew, RF | 2 | 0 | 0 | 0 | .000 |
| Eric Davis, LF | 284 | 76 | 14 | 53 | .268 |
| Fernando Tatis, 3B | 31 | 10 | 0 | 3 | .323 |
| Eli Marrero, C | 44 | 14 | 3 | 5 | .318 |
| Willie McGee, OF | 656 | 202 | 9 | 91 | .308 |
| David Howard, IF | 10 | 5 | 0 | 0 | .500 |
| Luis Ordaz, IF | 30 | 8 | 0 | 2 | .267 |

| Pitchers | G | IP | W-L | ERA | SV |
|---|---|---|---|---|---|
| Matt Morris | 4 | 29 | 2-1 | 4.34 | 0 |
| Kent Mercker | 20 | 63 | 4-7 | 3.57 | 2 |
| Darren Oliver | 2 | 12 1/3 | 2-0 | 0.73 | 0 |
| Donovan Osborne | 9 | 58 1/3 | 2-4 | 4.01 | 0 |
| Alan Benes | 5 | 24 1/3 | 3-1 | 7.40 | 0 |
| Juan Acevedo | 8 | 14 2/3 | 1-1 | 1.84 | 2 |
| Kent Bottenfield | 9 | 28 2/3 | 2-1 | 4.39 | 0 |
| Manny Aybar | 1 | 6 | 0-0 | 1.50 | 0 |
| Lance Painter | 15 | 22 | 1-0 | 3.69 | 0 |
| Ricky Bottalico | 13 | 14 2/3 | 0-0 | 1.84 | 5 |
| Scott Radinsky | 12 | 10 2/3 | 0-0 | 0.84 | 1 |

## 19th Century Chicago vs. St. Louis season series

### National Association
1875    Chicago 5, St. Louis Brown Stockings 5
1875    Chicago 4, St. Louis Red Stockings 0

### National League
1876    St. Louis 6, Chicago 4
1877    Chicago 8, St. Louis 4
1885    Chicago 14, St. Louis 2
1886    Chicago 13, St. Louis 4
1892    Chicago 7, St. Louis 5
1893    St. Louis 9, Chicago 3
1894    St. Louis 6, Chicago 6
1895    Chicago 10, St. Louis 2
1896    Chicago 9, St. Louis 3
1897    Chicago 8, St. Louis 4
1898    Chicago 10, St. Louis 4
1899    Chicago 8, St. Louis 6

World's Series (Chicago White Stockings of the National League vs. St. Louis Browns of the American Association)
1885    Chicago 3, St. Louis 3
1886    St. Louis 4, Chicago 2

## 20th Century Chicago vs. St. Louis season series:

| | | | | |
|---|---|---|---|---|
| 1900 | St. Louis 11, Chicago 9 | | 1913 | Chicago 16, St. Louis 6 |
| 1901 | St. Louis 10, Chicago 10 | | 1914 | St. Louis 12, Chicago 10 |
| 1902 | Chicago 12, St. Louis 5 | | 1915 | Chicago 12, St. Louis 10 |
| 1903 | Chicago 16, St. Louis 4 | | 1916 | Chicago 14, St. Louis 8 |
| 1904 | Chicago 15, St. Louis 7 | | 1917 | St. Louis 12, Chicago 10 |
| 1905 | Chicago 17, St. Louis 5 | | 1918 | Chicago 15, St. Louis 3 |
| 1906 | Chicago 15, St. Louis 6 | | 1919 | Chicago 13, St. Louis 7 |
| 1907 | Chicago 16, St. Louis 6 | | 1920 | St. Louis 12, Chicago 10 |
| 1908 | Chicago 19, St. Louis 3 | | 1921 | St. Louis 14, Chicago 8 |
| 1909 | Chicago 15, St. Louis 7 | | 1922 | Chicago 13, St. Louis 9 |
| 1910 | Chicago 15, St. Louis 7 | | 1923 | Chicago 12, St. Louis 10 |
| 1911 | Chicago 16, St. Louis 6 | | 1924 | Chicago 15, St. Louis 7 |
| 1912 | Chicago 15, St. Louis 7 | | 1925 | St. Louis 14, Chicago 8 |

| | | | |
|---|---|---|---|
| 1926 | Chicago 11, St. Louis 11 | 1963 | St. Louis 11, Chicago 7 |
| 1927 | St. Louis 12, Chicago 9 | 1964 | St. Louis 12, Chicago 6 |
| 1928 | Chicago 11, St. Louis 11 | 1965 | Chicago 10, St. Louis 8 |
| 1929 | Chicago 15, St. Louis 5 | 1966 | St. Louis 14, Chicago 4 |
| 1930 | Chicago 11, St. Louis 11 | 1967 | St. Louis 11, Chicago 6 |
| 1931 | St. Louis 14, Chicago 8 | 1968 | Chicago 9, St. Louis 9 |
| 1932 | Chicago 12, St. Louis 10 | 1969 | Chicago 9, St. Louis 9 |
| 1933 | Chicago 11, St. Louis 11 | 1970 | St. Louis 11, Chicago 7 |
| 1934 | Chicago 12, St. Louis 10 | 1971 | Chicago 9, St. Louis 9 |
| 1935 | St. Louis 14, Chicago 8 | 1972 | Chicago 10, St. Louis 8 |
| 1936 | St. Louis 13, Chicago 9 | 1973 | Chicago 9, St. Louis 9 |
| 1937 | Chicago 17, St. Louis 5 | 1974 | St. Louis 13, Chicago 5 |
| 1938 | Chicago 13, St. Louis 9 | 1975 | Chicago 11, St. Louis 7 |
| 1939 | St. Louis 12, Chicago 10 | 1976 | Chicago 12, St. Louis 6 |
| 1940 | St. Louis 14, Chicago 8 | 1977 | St. Louis 11, Chicago 7 |
| 1941 | St. Louis 12, Chicago 10 | 1978 | Chicago 15, St. Louis 3 |
| 1942 | St. Louis 16, Chicago 6 | 1979 | St. Louis 10, Chicago 8 |
| 1943 | St. Louis 13, Chicago 9 | 1980 | Chicago 9, St. Louis 9 |
| 1944 | St. Louis 16, Chicago 6 | 1981 | Chicago 5, St. Louis 4 |
| 1945 | St. Louis 16, Chicago 6 | 1982 | St. Louis 12, Chicago 6 |
| 1946 | St. Louis 14, Chicago 8 | 1983 | Chicago 8, St. Louis 8 |
| 1947 | St. Louis 12, Chicago 10 | 1984 | Chicago 13, St. Louis 5 |
| 1948 | Chicago 11, St. Louis 11 | 1985 | St. Louis 14, Chicago 4 |
| 1949 | St. Louis 14, Chicago 8 | 1986 | Chicago 10, St. Louis 7 |
| 1950 | St. Louis 12, Chicago 10 | 1987 | St. Louis 12, Chicago 6 |
| 1951 | St. Louis 13, Chicago 9 | 1988 | St. Louis 11, Chicago 7 |
| 1952 | Chicago 11, St. Louis 11 | 1989 | Chicago 11, St. Louis 7 |
| 1953 | Chicago 11, St. Louis 11 | 1990 | St. Louis 10, Chicago 8 |
| 1954 | Chicago 14, St. Louis 8 | 1991 | Chicago 10, St. Louis 8 |
| 1955 | Chicago 14, St. Louis 8 | 1992 | Chicago 11, St. Louis 7 |
| 1956 | St. Louis 13, Chicago 9 | 1993 | Chicago 8, St. Louis 5 |
| 1957 | Chicago 12, St. Louis 10 | 1994 | Chicago 5, St. Louis 5 |
| 1958 | St. Louis 15, Chicago 7 | 1995 | Chicago 9, St. Louis 4 |
| 1959 | St. Louis 12, Chicago 10 | 1996 | St. Louis 8, Chicago 5 |
| 1960 | St. Louis 14, Chicago 8 | 1997 | St. Louis 8, Chicago 4 |
| 1961 | St. Louis 15, Chicago 7 | 1998 | St. Louis 7, Cubs 4 |
| 1962 | St. Louis 11, Chicago 7 | | |

# Measuring the Cubs' and Cardinals' accomplishments

## Cardinals

*National League pennants:* 1926, 1928, 1930, 1931, 1934, 1942, 1943, 1944, 1946, 1964, 1967, 1968, 1982, 1985, 1987

*Divisional titles:* 1996 (Central Division)

*Wild card:* none

*World Series championships:* 1926, 1931, 1934, 1942, 1944, 1946, 1964, 1967, 1982

## Cubs

*Pennants:* 1906, 1907, 1908, 1910, 1918, 1929, 1932, 1935, 1938, 1945

*Divisional titles:* 1984, 1989 (Eastern Division)

*Wild card:* 1998 (Central Division)

*World Series championships:* 1907, 1908

*Times the Cardinals have finished higher in the standings than the Cubs:* 58

*Times the Cubs have finished higher in the standings than the Cardinals:* 38

*Times the teams have tied in the standings:* 4 (both halves of the 1981 split season counted, hence 100 total for 99 years)

*Highest place the two teams have ended tied:* second, 1936

*Lowest place the two teams have ended tied:* fifth, 1900, 1920, 1958.

*Times each has finished last:* Cubs 12, Cardinals 7.

*First-second finishes:* 3

1930 — Cardinals first, Cubs second, 2 games behind

1935 — Cubs first, Cardinals second, 4 games behind

1945 — Cubs first, Cardinals second, 3 games behind

*Times one team finished first and the other last:* 4

St. Louis finished last three times when Chicago finished first—1907, 1908 and 1918 (all eighth in the old eight-team NL).

Chicago finished last once when St. Louis finished first—1987 (sixth in the six-team Eastern Division).

*Seasons when one won the pennant and the other finished five or fewer games behind:* 1. St. Louis won the 1928 pennant and the third-place Cubs were four games behind.

*Seasons in which neither won the pennant but finished within five games of first place:* none.

*Seasons in which neither won the pennant but finished between five and 10 games from first place:* 4 (1927, Cardinals second, 1 1/2 games behind; Cubs fourth, 8 1/2 games behind; 1933, Cubs third, 6 games behind; Cardinals fifth, 9 1/2 games behind; 1936, tied for second, five games behind; and 1973, Cardinals second, 1 1/2 games behind; Cubs fifth, 5 games behind).

# They played for both teams

## A list of players who performed for both the Cubs and Cardinals

*Players who played for both teams (other than those listed below for playing for both in one season):*

**Player, position, era**

Sparky Adams, inf, '20s-'30s
Ethan Allen, of, '30s
George Altman, of, '60s
Shad Barry,inf, '00s
Lester Bell, 3b, '20-'30s
Sheriff Blake, p, '20-'30s
Bobby Bonds, of, '80s
Kent Bottenfield, p, '90s
Bob Bowman, p, '30-'40s
Roger Bresnahan, c, '00-10s
Herman Bronkie, 3b, '10s
Mordecai Brown, p, '00s
Byron Browne, of, '60s
Ray Burris, p, '70s
Ellis Burton, of, '50-'60s
Guy Bush, p, '30s
Chris Cannizzaro, c, '60-70s
Doug Capilla, p, '70s
Jose Cardenal, of, '70s
Tex Carleton, p, '30s
Cliff Chambers, p, '40-'50s

Mark Clark, p, '90s
Rip Collins, 1b, '30s
Jimmy Cooney, ss, '20s
Walker Cooper, c, '40-'50s
Jim Cosman, p, '60s
Hector Cruz, of ,'70s
Jim Davis, p, '50s
Dizzy Dean, p, '30s
Ivan DeJesus, ss, '70-'80s
Bobby Del Greco, of, '50s
Frank Demaree, of, '30-'40s
Paul Derringer, p, '30s-40s
Pickles Dillhoefer, of, '10s
Frank DiPino, p, '80s
Taylor Douthit, of, '20-'30s
Dave Dowling, p, '60s
Moe Drabowsky, p, '50-70s
Leon Durham, ss, '80-90s
Rawley Eastwick, p, '70s-80s
Dennis Eckersley, p, '80-90s
Jim Ellis, p, '60s
George Frazier,p, '70-'80s

Joe Garagiola, c, '40-'50s
Mike Garman, p, '70-'80s
Dave Giusti, p, '70s
Burleigh Grimes, p, '20-'30s
Charlie Grimm, 1b, '10s-20s
Ray Harrell, p, '30s
Vic Harris, of, '70s
Chuck Hartenstein, p, '60s
Harvey Hendrick, of, '30s
George Hennessey, p, '30-'40s
Roy Henshaw, p, '30s
Jim Hickman, 1b-of, '60-'70s
Rogers Hornsby, inf, '20-'30s
Terry Hughes, of-3b, '70s
Bob Humphries, p, '60s
Herb Hunter, 3b-of, '10-'20s
Danny Jackson, p, '90s
Larry Jackson, p, '50s-'60s
Elmer Jacobs, p, '20s
Hal Jeffcoat, p, '50s
Lance Johnson, of, '80s-'90s
Sam Jones, p, '50s
Vic Keen, p, '20s
John Kelleher, inf, '10s-'20s
Mick Kelleher, inf, '70s
Don Kessinger, ss, '60-'70s
Paul Kilgus, p, '80s-'90s
Darold Knowles, p, '70s
Les Lancaster, p, '80s-'90s
Hobie Landrith, c, '50s
Roy Leslie, 1b, '10s
Gene Lillard, ss-p, '30s-'40s
Dick Littlefield, p, '50s
Grover Lowdermilk, p, '00s-'10s
Peanuts Lowrey, of, '40s-'50s
Lee Magee, of-inf, '10s
Gus Mancuso, c, '20-'30s
Les Mann, of, '10s-'20s
Rabbit Maranville, ss, '20s
Morrie Martin, p, '50s

Stu Martin, inf, '30s-'40s
Gene Mauch, 2b-ss, '40s-'50s
Jackie May, p, '20s-'30s
Ike McAuley, ss, '10s-'20s
Lindy McDaniel p, '50s-'60s
Lynn McGlothen, p, '70s
Larry McLean, c, '00s
Sam Mejias, of, '70s
Steve Mesner, ss-3b, '30s-'40s
Ed Mickelson, 1b, '50s
Fritz Mollwitz, 1b, '10s
Donnie Moore, p, '70s-'80s
Bobby Morgan, inf, '50s
Mike Morgan, p, '90s
Jamie Moyer, p, '90s
Jerry Mumphrey, of, '70s-'80s
Ron Northey, of, '40s-'50s
Gene Oliver, c-of, '50s-'60s
Jack O'Neil, c, '00s
Mickey Owen, c, '30-'50s
Gene Packard, p, '10s
George Pearce, p, '10s
Mike Perez, p, '90s
Tom Poholsky, p, '50s
Howie Pollet, p, '40-'50s
Mike Proly, p, '70s-'80s
Dave Rader, c, '70s
Ken Raffensberger, p, '30s-'40s
Ken Reitz, 3b, '70s-'80s
Del Rice, c, '40-'50s
Hal Rice, of, '40s-'50s
Ken Rudolph, c '70s
Jack Russell, p, '30s
Ed Sauer, of, '40s
Hank Sauer, of, '50s
Carl Sawatski, c, '50-'60s
Jimmie Schaffer, c, '60s
Bob Scheffing, c ,'40s-'50s
Johnny Schulte, c, '20s
Buddy Schultz, p, '70s

Joe Schultz Sr., of , '10s-'20s
Clyde Shoun, p, '30s
Ted Sizemore, inf, '70s
Bobby Gene Smith, of, '50s-60s
Charley Smith, 3b, '60s
Lee Smith, p, '80s-'90s
Eddie Solomon, p, '70s
Lary Sorensen, p, '80s
Chris Speier, ss, '80s
Pete Standridge, p, '10s
Eddie Stanky, ss, '40s-'50s
Ray Starr, p, '30s-'40s
Rick Sutcliffe, p, '80s-'90s
Bruce Sutter, p, '70s-80s
Steve Swisher, c, '70s
Bud Teachout, p, '30s
Bob Tewksbury, p, '80s-90s
Bobby Tiefenauer, p, '60s
Moe Thacker, c, '50-'60s
Fred Toney, p, '10-'20s
Coker Triplett, of, '30-'40s
Mike Tyson, ss-2b, '70s-80s
Emil Verban, 2b, '40s
Ben Wade, p, '40-'50s
Harry Walker, of, '40s
Ty Waller, of, '80s
Lon Warneke, p, '30s
Carl Warwick, of, '60s
Pete Whisenant, of, '50s
Jerry White, of, '70s-'80s
Hoyt Wilhelm, p, '50-'70s
Mel Wright, p, '50s-'60s

## Players who have appeared on both the Cardinals and Cubs the same season:

**Player, Position, Year**

Ted Abernathy, p, 1970
Grover Alexander, p, 1926
Fred Beebe, p, 1906
Steve Bilko, 1b, 1954
Lou Brock, of, 1964
Ernie Broglio, p, 1964
Jim Brosnan, p, 1958
Leo Burke, inf, 1963
Lew Burdette, p, 1964
Pet Childs, 2b, 1901
Doug Clemens, of, 1964
Jeff Cross, inf, 1948
Clarence Currie, p, 1903
Alvin Dark, ss, 1958
Max Flack, of, 1922
Howard Freigau, ss, 1925
Gary Gaetti, 3b, 1998
Phil Gagliano, inf, 1970
Mike Gonzalez, c, 1925
Hank Gornicki, p, 1941
Alex Grammas, ss, 1962
Cliff Heathcote, of, 1922
Irv Higginbotham, p, 1909
Glen Hobbie, p, 1964
Tony Kaufmann, p, 1927
Charlie King, of, 1959
Steve Lake, c, 1986
Don Landrum, of, 1962
Doc Marshall, c, 1908
Walt Moryn, of, 1960
Pete Noonan, c, 1906
Irv Noren, of, 1959
Bob O'Farrell, c, 1925
Ted Savage, of, 1967

Barney Schultz, p, 1963
Bobby Shantz, p, 1964
Curt Simmons, p, 1966
Jack Spring, p, 1964
Jack Taylor, p, 1906
Paul Toth, p, 1962
Bob Wicker, p-of, 1903
Otto Williams, ss, 1903
Todd Zeile, 3b, 1995

## Managers who have led both the Cubs and Cardinals

Roger Bresnahan, Cubs 1915, Cardinals 1909-12

Rogers Hornsby, Cubs 1930-32 (fired before Cubs won pennant in 1932), Cardinals 1925-26 (pennant in 1926)

Frankie Frisch, Cubs 1949-51, Cardinals 1933-38 (pennant in 1934)

Stan Hack, Cubs 1954-56, Cardinals 1958

Current (1999) Cubs manager Jim Riggleman was a Cardinals coach in the 1980s. Current (1999) Cardinals manager Tony LaRussa played one game for the Cubs in 1973.

# ABOUT THE AUTHORS

This is George Castle's third book. During 1998, he co-authored *I Remember Harry Caray*, a compilation of memories and stories about the great broadcaster. Castle also wrote *Sammy Sosa: Clearing the Vines*, the first full-scale biography of the Cubs slugger.

A native of Chicago's far North Side, Castle spent much of his youth in Wrigley Field's right-field bleachers. In addition to his books, he hosts Diamond Gems, a nationally syndicated baseball radio talk show. Castle covers the Cubs and major league baseball for *The Times* of Northwest Indiana, a daily newspaper based in Munster. He also writes for the Lerner Newspapers chain; *Chicago Sports Profiles* magazine; the publications departments of the Chicago Cubs, New York Yankees and Chicago Bulls, and a variety of other Chicago-area and national publications.

Jim Rygelski makes his book debut here. He spent his youth on St. Louis' North Side and nearby Dellwood. Rygelski frequented the cheap seats of his city's local ballpark, in this case the old and new Busch stadiums.

Rygelski is a copy editor for the North County Journal, one of the main editions of the St. Louis-area Suburban Journals chain. He also served as a reporter for the now-defunct *St. Louis Globe Democrat* and the Galesburg (Ill.) *Register-Mail*. In addition, Rygelski worked in the public information office of Knox College in Galesburg and taught high school in the St. Louis area.

# More Cardinals and Cubs Titles

The Associated Press (AP) presents:

## Home Run: The Year the Records Fell

*This book* chronicles the record-setting home run chase and features every home run by Mark McGwire and Sammy Sosa. Some highlights include features on Ruth and Maris, McGwire's son Matt, Sosa's 20 home run month in June, statistics and the All-Star home-run contest plus much more.

1998 • 144 pp • 8 1/2 x 11 hardcover • $24.95

*The Sporting News presents*

## Mark McGwire: Mac Attack!

*by Rob Rains*

*Mac Attack!* is a retrospective of Mark's life from growing up as a kid in California to crushing the single season home run record with 70 home runs in 1998.

1998 • 108 pp • 5 1/2 x 7 paperback • $5.95

*The Sporting News presents*

## Mark McGwire: Slugger!

*by Rob Rains*

*Slugger!* is a biography geared toward children between 6-11, it describes how Mark overcame poor eyesight and various injuries to become one of baseball's most revered hitters. This inspirational book encourages children to overcome life's difficult experiences and to "never give up on following..." their dreams.

1998 • 47 pp • 10 x 8 3/4 hardcover • $15.95

*Updated Best-Seller*

## Jack Buck: "That's A Winner!"

*Jack Buck with Rob Rains and Bob Broeg*

Updated from the original best-seller, this book includes Jack's perspective on the incredible record-breaking 1998 baseball season, his working relationship with Mark McGwire, and the state of the game.

1999 • 240 pp • 6 x 9 paperback • $14.95

## I Remember Harry Caray

*by George Castle and Rich Wolfe*

*I Remember Harry Caray* is a firsthand account of what the broadcasting legend was like from broadcasters Vin Scully, Jack Buck, Paul Harvey and Chick Hearn; players Stan Musial, Sammy Sosa, and Mark Grace; newspaper reporters Irv Cupcinet and Jerome Holtzman; and others including Dutchie Caray, and Chip Caray.

1998 • 225 pp • 6 x 9 paperback • $12.95

## Sammy Sosa: Clearing the Vines

*by George Castle*

*Clearing the Vines* is a biography that takes sports fans from the Dominican streets where Sosa grew up, to his days in Wrigley Field where he has developed into a national hero.

1998 • 223 pp • 6 x 9 paperback • $14.95

## Sammy Sosa: Slammin' Sammy

*by George Castle*

*Slammin' Sammy* details the life of Sosa, from his days as a young boy shining shoes on the Dominican streets in order to help provide food for his family, to his current status as one of baseball's true superstars.

1999 • 96 pp • 5 1/2 x 7 paperback • $4.95

## Mark Grace: Winning with Grace

*by Barry Rozner*

*Winning with Grace* talks about how Mark developed his love of baseball, and his experiences with the Cubs, like winning the division championship in 1989, and his relationship with home run star Sosa.

1999 • 96 pp • 5 1/2 x 7 paperback • $4.95

**Visit your local bookstore or order by calling 877/424-2665**